"A BANG-[...] THE
READER F[...] .. IF
YOU LIKE[...]
LIKE *PLAY*[...]

—[...]*r-Star*

"The former prosecutor uncorks an
excellent thriller the first time out."
—*Houston Post*

"The author knows the seamy side of the
nation's capital all too well and uses that
knowledge in this complex story of murder, drug
dealings, money laundering, double-crosses."
—*Los Angeles Times*

"VIVID, GRITTY FICTION . . . the cast is
as diverse as the city . . . the dialogue
crackles . . . the man can write . . . a good
yarn and then some." —*Washington Times*

"A VIVID, STRONG, BRISK
THRILLER . . . STYLISHLY GRITTY
AND THOUGHT-PROVOKING."
—*Publishers Weekly*

For more rave reviews, please turn page . . .

PLAYING
THE
DOZENS

William D. Pease

A SIGNET BOOK

SIGNET
Published by the Penguin Group
Penguin Books USA Inc., 375 Hudson Street,
New York, New York 10014, U.S.A.
Penguin Books Ltd, 27 Wrights Lane,
London W8 5TZ, England
Penguin Books Australia Ltd, Ringwood,
Victoria, Australia
Penguin Books Canada Ltd, 10 Alcorn Avenue,
Toronto, Ontario, Canada M4V 3B2
Penguin Books (N.Z.) Ltd, 182–190 Wairau Road,
Auckland 10, New Zealand

Penguin Books Ltd, Registered Offices:
Harmondsworth, Middlesex, England

Published by Signet, an imprint of New American Library,
a division of Penguin Books USA Inc. Originally published in a Viking
edition.

First Signet Printing, February, 1992
10 9 8 7 6 5 4 3 2 1

PUBLISHER'S NOTE
This is a work of fiction. Names, characters, places, and incidents either are
the product of the author's imagination or are used fictitiously, and any
resemblance to actual persons, living or dead, events, or locales is entirely
coincidental.

To Anne, who bore the brunt

Acknowledgments

I offer my gratitude and appreciation to those friends who in their own way offered help and encouragement when it was needed most: to Bill Hardy, Barry Leibowitz, Alan Kellock, Elsa Walsh, and Patricia Griffith;

And with special affection to Mary Lou Soller, whose insistent optimism carried me through the dark days, and to Bob Higdon, without whose prodding support and good counsel this work would still be nothing more than an odd assortment of random sketches;

And most especially to Kathy Robbins, whose wisdom, patience, dedication, and friendship have meant so much.

Finally, I wish to acknowledge the lessons learned from those police officers and federal agents too numerous to list here who gave so much and received so little and from those few people on the other side who can never be acknowledged publicly.

Author's Note

Having spent so many years as a federal prosecutor in Washington, D.C., I suppose it inevitable that there will be those expecting a roman à clef. That is not the story. This is a work of fiction. The characters and events described herein are a product of my imagination and nothing more. Any resemblance to actual events or to any person, living or dead, is purely coincidental.

"Man, like it weren't about nothin'. Like it don't make no difference what it's about. The man was playing the dozens with me. You know what I'm sayin'? It's like the man was disrespectin' me, so like I had no choice but to pop a cap on him. And that's that. Like that's the way it is on the street."—Adonis Smith,
aka "The Peeper"

≫ ≪

"These people terrify me,
but I am one of them."

—George Smiley in John Le Carré's
The Honorable Schoolboy

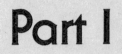

Part I

One

It was an empty afternoon. The few customers sat scattered in a thin breath of alcohol and cigarette smoke, their talk barely mixing with the sounds of the television perched above one end of the bar where the Maryland–North Carolina football game was late in the fourth quarter. Both waitresses sat huddled in a corner booth, delaying the start of a long night shift over an early dinner, while their boss delivered a second Carta Blanca to a table near the front window. Jorge set the bottle in front of a young man in starched blue jeans and a white button-down shirt. "Can I get you folks anything else?" he asked.

The young man, only a step out of boyhood, looked to his companion, sitting stiff and erect, as if otherwise something might rub off on her Vineyard pinks and greens. Her nose crinkled and her fingers impatiently tapped the stem of her still-full margarita glass. The young man shrugged, "No, I guess not."

Jorge glanced up and through the window to the outside. A half moon of reversed letters, CARILLO'S, framed his view of the only life on the street, a few locals leaning in the doorway of a bankrupt hardware store and a man bent into the engine compartment of a Black Rose cab. The sun had all but gone and the only things moving were the few leaves dropped from a tree on some other street being rolled along by a late October breeze. Only the naïve or more dedicated eclectics among Washington's boulevardiers ventured here, east of Sixteenth on the sometimes uneasy border between the poorer quarters of blacks and Hispanics and the transition neighborhoods where estate sales and tax foreclosures drew real estate speculators like sharks to blood.

From across the room a group of soccer players, soiled and sweated from their game, raised a muffled cheer and two empty glass pitchers, signaling for a refill. Jorge retrieved the pitchers and returned to the bar. Holding the side of one against the tap as it filled, he looked over to the only customer seated at the bar and asked, "Need another?" The man nodded and without a word turned his attention back to the television.

The man looked no different now from when he had first sat down and ordered a Colt .45. It had been nearly two hours and he had spent it alone, almost motionless except for the lifting of his glass or the lighting of another cigarette. His dark-blue windbreaker remained zipped just above his belly, his gaze ranged no farther than the television, and his conversation confined itself to an occasional call for another beer. Jorge slid a frosted bottle in front of him and lifted two one-dollar bills off the dwindling pile of change from the original twenty. He then returned to the tap, refilled the second pitcher, and carried both to the soccer players' table.

Turning back toward the bar, Jorge again stopped at the front window and looked out as a Metropolitan Police scout car pulled to the curb. Wiping his hands on his apron, he moved to the kitchen door and leaned in. "Harry, watch the bar for a few minutes, will ya? I'm gonna get some air."

The few minutes passed, then a few more, and Jorge returned, followed by a police officer with whom he stood for a moment by the front door. Jorge cocked his head toward the man seated alone at the end of the bar. The officer nodded and started down the line of empty bar stools, approaching the man's back. Tall, with the bearing of a weight lifter in pose, the officer passed one hand over his close-cropped hair like a young man smoothing himself for a date. The other hand fingered but did not unsnap the leather strap laying over the hammer of his revolver. "Hey, bro" was all anyone heard before the solitary man twisted to his right and froze at the sight of the officer.

For an instant neither man moved and Jorge could not hear if any words were passed. The officer flipped his head slightly as if inviting the man to follow him outside. The man turned slowly and stepped from the stool as his hands reached down to hitch up his pants. Suddenly, in a gesture almost friendly, like the offer of a hand, the man raised a large, dark pistol to the officer's face. There was a bright flash and a sharp, concussive boom. The officer's head snapped back from the force of the bullet's neat entry between the bridge of his nose and left eye and its explosive exit through the back of his skull. The body dropped to the floor like a discarded rag doll. There was a short, gurgling groan and a single, violent twitch of his right leg and the officer was dead.

There were no shouts, no cries, no other sound except the distant cheer and excited commentary of the television. No one moved. Transfixed on the crumpled heap lying in a slowly expanding pool of blood, neither Jorge nor his customers reacted to the gunman's hesitant backing toward the door, trembling, his hand fused with the gun now dangling at his side, his stare fixed on his kill. The gunman then turned and bolted out the door as shouts erupted from the street. All eyes but Jorge's turned toward the sounds and no one saw him sweep the gunman's few dollars from the bar.

Two

At the western edge of the city, at its highest elevation, where the shops and restaurants and theaters were confined to a single boulevard bordered by quiet streets of quiet homes, a small frame house stood on a patch of yard whose autumn-colored oaks and maple were kept alive by the bright amber streetlights. A block away, the traffic passed in waves and the Saturday-night voices traveling to and from the neighborhood pubs were as distant as the sound of children at the far end of a beach. Through a window just above the porch, the chill of the night crept in against the close warmth of the bedroom. If it touched them, they did not know it. Inside this room, inside themselves, the city was somewhere else and, for the moment, forgotten. The telephone's first ring brought it home.

Katy jerked at the sound and Michael Holden lifted to feel the night air slip between them. His eyes flipped toward the phone and remained fixed until the third ring when he reached over with a groan and yanked the receiver off its hook. Katy took a deep breath and shook her head at his choice.

"Mike? 'Sthat you?" a voice called as Holden rolled back against the headboard, unconsciously draping the curled cord across Katy's throat.

"Oh, sorry," he whispered, as she tossed the cord

aside and sat up on the edge of the bed, slowly freeing a strand of auburn hair held by perspiration to the side of her face.

"Mike?"

"Yeah, hello, who's this?"

"Mike, this is Jimmy Legget. Look, I hope I haven't caught you at a bad time, but . . ."

The voice faded into random noise as Michael reached over to massage the back of Katy's neck with the tips of his fingers. She did not respond except for a brief shiver. "I'm sorry, who's this?"

"Jimmy Legget. You know, from Homicide. Listen, I'm sorry to be calling you at home or wherever, but I've got an unusual problem on my hands here. Actually, *we've* got a problem and I need you to meet me at headquarters. You know, tonight? Like right away?" Detective Legget paused for a response but none came. "You still there?"

"Yeah, Jimmy, I'm listening," Michael said, watching Katy lift her hair in her fingers and fluff it with a quick and impatient toss of her head. "I'm not happy, but I'm listening."

"Look, I wouldn't be calling if it weren't an emergency. The problem is that—"

"Hold it a second," Michael interrupted, his voice hinting at anger. "How'd you get this number? Who gave you this number?" Michael Holden had reason to be angry aside from watching Katy rise and walk toward the bathroom, picking her clothes from the floor as she went. Fifteen years as an Assistant United States Attorney had infected him with an intolerance for the late-night calls from city cops and federal agents who routinely prefaced their intrusions with the descriptives "emergency" or "unusual" for situations that, to him at least, rarely were. To avoid such annoyances, he had long ago silenced the bell on the kitchen phone attached to the answering machine he seldom checked and that carried the number required to be listed in the U.S. Attorney's files as the one where he could be reached in an emergency. The number for the phone by his bed was unlisted. He had given that number to only two cops, and Detective James W. Legget, assigned to the Metropolitan Police Homicide Branch for less than two years, was not one of them.

"Look, Mr. Holden," Legget said, reassuming the formality that had been dropped a year before when Holden had prosecuted the detective's first murder case, "I understand that this is your private number and I'm sorry, but . . . So, okay, like Eddie Nickles gave me your number and said it'd be all right, you know, because of the circumstances."

There was a long pause before Michael asked, very slowly, "Where's Eddie?"

The detective's voice abandoned its calm. "Man, like Eddie doesn't matter right now and I've already wasted a lot of time just trying to track you down. It's that important. Hell, I was going to send a squad car around to your house but nobody seems to know where the fuck you live. And I'm not callin' on no jive-ass warrant, man."

"Just tell me where Eddie is."

"He's over at Chaney's."

"Is he drunk?"

"He's had a few but he's still sitting up."

Michael hesitated and then asked, "Okay, now what's got you so worked up you're talking that street shit?"

A few seconds passed before Detective Legget spoke, his tone softening. "Look, a cop was shot and killed late this afternoon. Now we've got the shooter in custody but the man won't say anything, won't even give up his name, except to say that he wants to see you. Hasn't even asked for a lawyer. Just you. By name, man."

Michael sat up and drew his knees closer to his chest. "What?" came out in a whisper. Katy, now draped in the white dress shirt Michael had tossed aside less than an hour before, returned to the bedroom and stood staring at him from the darkened doorway at the opposite end of the room. He gave no sign that he saw her. "What happened?"

"You mean the shooting? It's not all that clear. A Three-D uniform just walked up to this guy in a bar up off Sixteenth and, from what the witnesses say, hardly a word passed between them. The bartender claimed there was some dispute over a bar tab or something. But none of the customers saw any argument. No tussle, nothing. The officer just walked up and this guy pulled an automatic— strange weapon, too, some Israeli make no one's ever seen around here. . . . Anyway, he just pulled it outta his waist and shot him in the face. We haven't got a clue about a motive."

"Jesus," Michael murmured. "Who was he? The officer, I mean."

"His name's Arteaza, Carl Arteaza. Did you know him?"

"No . . . I don't think so. I'm sorry but I don't understand why you're calling me. I'm not on the duty list."

"Mike, I just got finished sayin' the man's asking for you by name. You're the only one he'll talk to."

"*Me*? Why?"

"Look, all I know is that he said he wanted to talk to you and to tell you that he came recommended by Nate. No last name. Just Nate."

There was a long silence as Michael sucked in a breath. He released it slowly and looked up to see Katy still standing in the doorway. He acknowledged her with the silent plea that she be patient and the silent lie that this interruption would soon be over. She watched him without expression.

"I take it the name rings a bell," Detective Legget started before Michael cut him off.

"Exactly what did he say? The shooter."

"Man, it's a long story. Why don't you just—"

"Jimmy, just give me the short version. All right?"

"Look, the man hasn't really said shit, you know? I mean Pritsker and I worked on him for an hour or more and he never said a word. I mean nothing. He just sat there staring at us. Then the captain showed up."

"The captain? You mean Ursay?"

"Yeah, Ursay. He showed up with some guy from IAD."

"IAD? What's Internal Affairs' interest in this?"

"Hell, I don't know. There's a lotta strange shit going on. Anyway, I was in the interrogation room when Ursay showed up with this guy from IAD who just sat down and took over. Like he started with this bullshit about how he's from Internal Affairs and he wanted this guy to understand that he was there to make sure his rights were protected. And then he said something about how if the man wanted, he'd tell the Homicide people to leave the room and he'd talk to him alone. I couldn't fuckin' believe it. I mean, Ursay's standing there and never says a word."

"Who is he, the guy from IAD?"

"I've never seen him before." Jimmy hesitated a moment. "In fact, now that I think about it, I never did catch a name. Ursay never introduced us. He just showed up with him and took over the interview—if you could call it that."

"What happened then?"

"Well, as soon as the shooter hears 'Internal Affairs,' he looks up at me and says, 'I'll talk to him alone.' You know, pointing to me and like I'm looking around to see who the fuck he's talking about. Anyway, so Ursay and IAD huddle for a minute and then leave. I mean they're pissed but they leave. So like I start with my rap. But Mike, I didn't get two words out before this guy looks up at the air vent and says, 'Tell them to turn off the tape machine.' "

Several years before, the department had installed a videotape recorder behind the air vent in one of the interrogation rooms to record the questioning of suspects surreptitiously. Despite the detectives' repeated failure to remember that they, too, were being recorded and thus called upon to modify some of their more imaginative and effective interrogation techniques, a number of taped confessions had survived defense motions to suppress, been introduced at trial and given wide publicity by the press. Still, it was rare that a suspect even would know of the existence of the tape recorder, much less where it was placed.

Michael's frown was almost audible as Katy moved to the end of the bed, where she sat, legs crossed in front of her, a pillow cradled to her stomach. "Should I go?" she whispered. Michael shook his head but his eyes drifted away as Detective Legget went on.

"So I stepped out and told the captain, and Ursay looks at the IAD man like he's asking him what to do, and the IAD man just shrugs and says 'Okay.' Can you believe it? I mean, Ursay's asking this jerk what to do?"

"And?"

"And so I go back in the room and tell him that the tape's turned off. And before I could say anything else he just gives me this little speech like he was ordering a fuckin' hamburger, you know? He said that he wouldn't answer any questions but asked me to just listen. That's when he said he wanted to talk to you. He said that he'd talk, lay it all out, but only if he talks to you directly. He said that I'd be making a big mistake if I didn't get a hold of you right away and to tell you that he was sent by Nate."

"That's it? That's all he said?"

"Well, not exactly. I know this is gonna sound weird, but he also said that I'd be making an even bigger mistake if I told anyone, including my officials—and that's his word—if I told my officials that he had asked for you." Detective Legget paused but Michael offered no response. "I know. It's weird. I mean, I just looked at him and said, 'How the fuck you think you're gonna get to see the DA without anybody knowing about it? I mean, it's not like you're gonna make bond or someone's gonna invite you home for dinner, y'know?' "

"What'd he say?"

"He just said something like he wasn't worried about who knew what once he talked to you, but that I'd be making a big mistake to let anyone know about it beforehand. I assume you know what he's talking about. Right?"

"Not a clue, Jimmy. Did he give you his name?"

"No, he wouldn't say."

"He wasn't carrying any ID on him?"

"Yeah, plenty of it, but all phony. Bunch of drivers' licenses. Uh . . . four, I think. Yeah, two D.C., one Maryland, and one Virginia. All different names and different addresses. The D.C. addresses are apartments listed to the same names on the licenses. Same for Maryland. We haven't heard back from Virginia yet. Ran his prints through the computer but came up with zero. The FBI's got people on overtime but nothing so far."

"What're the names on the permits?"

"Uh . . . wait a minute, I've got 'em here somewhere."

Michael could hear Jimmy flipping through the pages of his notebook. "Where are you, by the way? You're not in the squad room, are you?" he asked a bit nervously.

"Nah, I'm down in Morals. They're all out watching dirty movies and drinking in topless joints. Mike, what's going on here? I mean, I've kinda got my neck stuck out here. Like I haven't said anything to anyone about you yet, except to Eddie, of course, but . . . you know." Detective Legget paused but again Michael said nothing. "Shit, Mike, there's sure as hell more going on here than some guy going off the deep end and killing a cop over a bar tab. And I can't run this little game on the captain much longer. I mean Ursay's an idiot and all that, but he's getting restless and I wasted a lot of time just trying to find you. By the way, you live in a restaurant or something? That's some bullshit on your answering machine."

It was Katy's voice on the recorded message: "Hello. Thank you for calling Holden's. We're busy right now but if you'd like to make a reservation, just leave your name and telephone number and we'll call you back at our earliest convenience."

"Nah, it just keeps the flies away."

"What?"

"Nothing. You got those names?"

"Yeah, here they are," Detective Legget said, "John Willie Brown, James Wilburt Benton, Joseph W. Bryant, and, ah . . . shit, what's the other? Oh, yeah, Jervis W. Banyon. Think his real initials might be J.W.B?" Legget laughed.

"Probably not," Michael mumbled. "Nothing rings a bell, Jimmy. I don't know who this guy is."

"Well, he sure as hell knows you," Legget said, his voice rising, "and we're not dealing with some bullshit purse snatching here."

"I know, I know," Michael said softly as his eyes fixed on Katy and the fingers of one hand massaged his forehead. "You're certain he said Nate?"

"No question!" the detective answered.

Again there was silence before Michael said, "Jimmy, go back and ask him who Nate is. And when you do, ask him what Nate does for a living."

"Are you serious?"

"Just ask him, Jimmy, and call me back." Michael hung up the phone and settled back without a word.

Katy leaned forward. "What is it? Are you all right?"

Michael nodded briefly. "Yeah, it's just . . . A policeman was murdered this afternoon."

"God, that's awful. Someone you know?"

"No. It's just that the man who shot him is asking to see me."

Katy's brow furrowed. "Why you?"

He averted his eyes. "Old business, apparently. He told the detective to mention a name to me, a name from an investigation a coupla years ago. Except no one should know that name except me . . . or Eddie Nickles." Katy did not move, her expression filled with the question she did not need to ask. Michael nodded. "Yeah, *that* case."

"Nate's reappeared?"

Michael was startled. "You know about him? I told you?"

She answered quietly, "You said a lot of things you probably don't remember, or don't want to remember."

"Look, I'm sorry," he started.

Katy shook her head with a smile that made no attempt to conceal the effort it took. She reached over and brushed back a lock of hair from his forehead as if she were preparing a child for his first day of school. "I think I'd better go," she said.

"No, stay. There's no reason—"

"No," she stopped him, "you're going to be busy. I'd better go. We'll talk later."

Katy stood up, slipped out of Michael's shirt and laid it on the bed. He watched her walk from the room and listened to the sounds of her leaving— the splash of water in the sink, her hands rummaging through her purse, the quiet brushing of her hair, the light jangle of clothes pulled from their hanger and the rustle of her dressing. When she returned to the bedroom it was with the movement of someone late for an appointment. Her kiss was a gesture, and she said, "Call me tomorrow . . . or whenever."

"Kate, listen—"

"No, it's okay. I understand," she said and turned to leave.

He wondered, sitting motionless on the bed listening to the thud of the front door pulled shut, the wooden footsteps across the porch turning to a light click on the slate walk, the rattle of the fence gate, and, finally, the wheezing rumble of Katy's twenty-year-old Porsche starting and quickly fading into the distance. *She understands,* he told himself.

Conceding the inevitable, Michael crawled out of bed and went to the bathroom where he splashed cold water on his face and erased the taste of his frustration with mouthwash. He dressed slowly in a pair of blue jeans and the shirt that still held a hint of Katy's perfume. Settling in a chair by the bedroom window, he waited for Detective Legget's call, alternatively looking out to the street and inward to the scraps of his Saturday night: the tousled bedclothes; the small television still rolling without sound a movie they had ignored; the remains of Chinese carry-out on plates set midmeal on the floor and forgotten. Babe, an aged, mixed-breed retriever, slinked into the room, following her nose to the now stale rice and General Tsao's chicken. Her body quivered slightly, trying to hold her point while her eyes pleaded with him. "Help yourself," he smiled, and she did.

It took twenty minutes for the call to come, and when it did, Michael hesitated, his thoughts crowded with the intersecting histories of Nate and Katy, of him and Eddie Nickles, histories whose memories seeped acid in his stomach. On the fifth ring, he pulled the phone from its hook and put it to his ear without a word.

"Mike?"

"What's the story, Jimmy?"

"Christ, I thought you had bolted on me."

"Just tell me what's going on."

"Well, I asked the man what you told me and he says that this guy Nate used to be in the recording business but his best stuff never made the charts. Quote, unquote." Detective Legget waited for an explanation but none was offered.

"Listen, Jimmy, if you can, keep the jackals away from him until I get there. It shouldn't take me more than a half hour or forty-five minutes."

"Do I say anything to the captain about you? I mean, it's gonna look awful strange your just showing up out of the blue."

"I know," Michael said, pacing in short, slow steps, his hands in his pockets, the phone cradled between his ear and shoulder. "Give me a minute to think." He knew there was no choice. "Yeah, go ahead and tell the captain that I'm on my way, and if this guy doesn't like it, fuck him."

"Okay," the detective said. After a brief pause, he asked, "Are you gonna let me in on what's going on?"

"I don't know what's going on, Jimmy. I have no idea who this guy is or why he's asking for me. But maybe he's got something to say we'd want to hear. Until we figure out who he is and why he's talking like a B movie, let's just run with it and see what happens. All right?"

"Yeah, sure . . . I guess," Legget said, sounding disappointed and more than a little insulted that the prosecutor was holding out on him.

"I'll be there as soon as I can, but I need to talk to Eddie first."

"Eddie? I don't understand."

"I'll explain it all later. But right now I'd appreciate it if you didn't say anything about Eddie until I'm sure he's in shape to deal with this. Okay?"

"Yeah, sure," Legget repeated, his voice even more sullen.

Michael hung up and began to rummage through the old matchbooks, bills, and letters that stuffed the drawer of the nightstand where he kept a small address book. Sitting on the edge of the bed, he flipped through the worn pages of scribbled names and phone numbers listed in no particular order. Under the neatly inked entry for his ex-wife was the penciled phone number for Chaney's Tavern, one of Washington's seedier bars, located just a few blocks from police headquarters.

Long one of the favorite haunts of the old-line

CID detectives, in recent months Chaney's had become home for Homicide Detective J. Edward Nickles. Only six months away from retirement, Eddie Nickles was spending most of his off-duty hours and a disturbing percentage of his on-duty time holding court in the rear booth, drinking bar Scotch and grousing about the new generation of detectives who bought suits that fit, wore gold jewelry, and took night courses in psychology and community relations. Eddie was just doing time. His friends were fewer, the department having decided that the Homicide Squad needed new blood, particularly new blood that brought with them an appreciation for form and lines of authority. It was not one of Eddie's strengths. But he had survived the recent purges of experienced men on the strength of his reputation, although there were few people left who could pinpoint the basis of that reputation. Michael Holden was one of the few, and although they rarely socialized beyond an occasional drink after work, he and Eddie were close, even fraternal. For Michael, Eddie's indiscretion in giving out his unlisted number was more than a disappointment.

As he dialed the number for Chaney's Tavern, Michael vacillated between anger and forgiveness, the latter spawned by the knowledge that he was going to need Eddie. Whatever his failings, Detective Nickles still had an uncanny ability to sift the few morsels of truth from the feast of lies routinely fed every investigator. He also had the most extensive network of reliable snitches in the city. Nate had been one of Eddie's best.

The wall phone rang repeatedly before an impatient voice answered, "Chaney's."

"Let me speak to Eddie Nickles."

"I dunno no Eddie Nickles. You got the wrong

number." Dirty Red, the owner-bartender, never violated the confidences of his customers, unless, of course, he saw some personal advantage in doing so.

"Listen, Red," Michael said calmly. "Eddie's there, in the back booth, drunk, and this isn't his ex-wife, IAD or Captain Ursay."

"Who is it, then?"

"Just tell him it's his fucking mother, all right?"

"Yeah, sure," Dirty Red said and let the receiver drop and bounce against the wall. Michael jerked the phone from his ear but could still hear Dirty Red shout across the room, "Hey, Eddie, there's some guy on the phone that says he's yer fuckin' mutha." Michael heard the chiding hoots and laughter as it took some time for Eddie to reach the phone.

"Hello?" the detective said in his best effort to sound sober.

"Eddie, I'm going to assume that it was only because you're drunk that you gave Jimmy Legget my number instead of calling me yourself. But if you're not too drunk to remember my number, you're not too drunk to meet me in front of headquarters in a half hour."

"Mike, I'm sorry, really, I—"

"Not now. Just meet me in a half hour. All right?"

"What's going on?"

"*Jesus Christ!*" Michael almost shouted. "You mean you never even bothered to ask Jimmy what the fuck he was trying to call me about before you gave him my number? Goddamn it!"

"Hold it, son. Just hold it," Eddie interrupted, his own voice rising. "I don't know what the fuck's going on. Shit, it doesn't matter. I'll be there. Where'd you say you were?"

"Listen, Eddie, it's got something to do with Nate."

"*Nate?*"

"A cop was killed tonight. I assume you heard about it. Anyway, the guy who shot him wants to talk to us," Michael lied. "He's using Nate as his intro."

"Nate's *alive?*"

"Hell, I don't know. He just told Jimmy to get ahold of us and to mention Nate."

"What the fuck? Okay, listen, I'm sorry. I'll meet you in a half hour. Where'd you say again?"

"In front of headquarters. Are you listening? I need you to be there."

"Yeah, yeah, I got it."

Michael hung up the phone. For just a moment he had the strange sense that he might be sick. Six miles away, in the rancid aroma of smoke, stale booze, and the scented men's room ammonia that clouded the interior of Chaney's Tavern, so did Eddie Nickles.

Three

It was after eleven P.M. when Michael Holden and Detective Nickles stepped off the elevator on the third floor of police headquarters and turned toward the Homicide office. Their sidewalk meeting had been brief and the conversation one way as Eddie took in the scant information Michael had gathered from Detective Legget and gave back no more than a few grunts of curiosity. "Well, whaddaya think?" Michael had asked to break a long silence and Eddie just shrugged. "No sense thinking anything. We'll know soon enough."

He was right, but still Michael was irritated by the enforced cool. It was wearing like a rash. They had spent too much time in the same trench for him to accept Eddie's indifference. It wasn't his style. It wasn't their style. Over the years, they had developed an almost parasitic reliance on each other's skills and the mutual gamesmanship it often took to translate the realities of the street into the liturgies of the courtroom. It was a game of manipulation, of aggressive control, a game they thought they had mastered until two years ago when they had been outmaneuvered by those they had not even known were players. They had been burned, badly and together, and on the front pages of the local papers and in the lead stories of the television news. But when it had come time to salve their wounds, they had done so alone. And although they spoke often, they had not worked a case together since, and, but for an occasional and mostly obscure reference, they never talked about it.

Now they walked in silence and not quite together down the dimly lit hallway toward Homicide. Michael looked back at Eddie, shuffling a few steps behind, his slouch diminishing his five-foot, eleven-inch frame, his huge hands stuffed in the distended pockets of his unpressed pants, his jaw muscles working with the effort of grinding down the last of a full pack of breath mints.

"You all right?"

Eddie looked up without lifting his head. "Don't worry about me, Counselor. The question is whether you're ready for the bullshit that's about to be dumped on us."

"You do what you gotta do," Michael tried.

Eddie rolled his eyes. "Your mother been sending you clippings from the *Reader's Digest* again?" and Michael laughed.

They turned the corner and saw a covey of reporters flocked around the doorway to the Homicide office. Michael was suddenly impatient with Eddie's unhurried pace and self-conscious as the reporters turned silent at the sight of the two men approaching.

"Gentlemen," he addressed the group, maintaining his stride to emphasize his disinterest in conversation either on or off the record.

"Hey, Mike,"—Sid Rollins waved with his notepad—"you here on the policeman's killing?"

When Michael deadpanned a "no comment," one of the other reporters could not resist. "Hell, if they've called you two in, they must be interrogating Hizzonner back there."

"Cute, Harry," Michael answered the reporters' laughter, and he quickened his pace through the door, leaving Eddie behind and muttering obscenities to himself.

As he entered the office, Michael nodded to several detectives gathered around the coffeepot exchanging war stories. Nearby, two more detectives sat at desks pecking out the typed statements of the last two eyewitnesses to Officer Arteaza's murder: the young man and his girlfriend from Martha's Vineyard who was trying to erase with a handkerchief the crusted reminders of her earlier nausea while emphasizing that she had never wanted to go to a Mexican bar in the first place.

By himself, at the far end of the squad room, Detective Legget sat at a small desk talking quietly on the phone. A tall and uncommonly handsome black man, Jimmy Legget did not look the part. It was the end of a long shift and still his soft, clean-shaven features gave little sign of stress. His blue suit held its press and the collar of his shirt was crisp and clean and held close by a perfectly knotted tie of twilled silk—a display ad for *Esquire* posted in the midst of government gray. When he saw the prosecutor, Jimmy dropped the phone back into its cradle and jumped up. "Jesus, I'm glad you finally got here," he said. "Listen, don't say anything, but I just heard that the captain kept the video rolling while I talked to this guy, so they know about him asking for you 'n' Nate."

Michael nodded. "All right, we'll handle it. Do they know how you got ahold of me?"

"The captain never asked. But he did say that he wanted to see you as soon as you got here. He's back in his office."

Eddie Nickles approached the two men.

Jimmy asked quietly, "Y'all gonna let me know what's going on here?"

Michael turned to Detective Nickles. "I gotta see the captain. Why don't you fill Jimmy in while I talk to Ursay."

"C'mere, son," Eddie said, leading Detective Legget to an empty corner of the squad room while Michael walked down a short hallway to the captain's office.

The two men had little use for each other. Captain Roger Ursay, recently transferred to Homicide from the Special Operations Division as part of the chief's continuing effort to fill the command ranks with men who had passed the test of political loyalty, had quickly distinguished himself as having even less interest in actual cases than he had knowledge of how they were to be investigated. Holden, on more than one occasion, had refused to approve arrest warrants the captain had ordered his detectives to present. His refusal to sign the warrants would have been comment enough, but Michael had openly questioned the captain's competence to certain Homicide detectives who both repeated and embellished on the senior prosecutor's comments.

Michael did not bother to knock at the captain's open door but walked in to greet him and another detective whom he had never seen before. "You wanted to see me, Captain?"

Ursay looked startled and obviously tired, the slight shake in his hand exaggerated by the movement of the coffee cup held to his lips. His once brown hair, now a thin, dishwater gray, lay flat along his head, greased from the habit of running sweated palms along his skull when faced with difficult decisions. For a brief moment he stared at the prosecutor as if trying to recall the face, then said, "Hey, Mike, come on in. I'm told we can't get on with this party until you arrive." He then nodded toward his companion. "Mike, you know Ernie Tarble, don't ya? Ernie, this is Mike Holden you've heard so much about." The two men nodded and mumbled how-ya-doings at each other.

"What's the story?" Michael asked.

"You tell me. Jimmy Legget says this guy won't say anything unless you're there. He shot a Third District man, Carl Arteaza. Did you know him?"

"No, I didn't. I'm sorry."

"Yeah, a real tragedy. His wife's seven months pregnant with their first kid. A first-rate officer. Real tragedy."

Michael shook his head and asked, "What's the man's name? The shooter."

"We're still working on that. He's got a bunch of aliases but won't give up his name. You know what it takes to ID a John Doe on prints."

Michael knew but he doubted that the captain did. "Why me? Did he say?"

"He says he knows a friend of yours called Nate. . . ." Detective Tarble shot a look at Captain Ursay, who reacted visibly to his apparent blunder. "Anyway, this guy . . . uh . . . tells Jimmy he's ready to give it up . . . uh . . . if he can, y'know, talk to you. So we've been holding him up here until we could get ahold of you. By the way," he tried to joke, "even your boss, Joslin, couldn't come up with a better number for you than some restaurant answering machine or something. How'd Jimmy find you?"

"I guess he must have learned something in detective school," Michael grinned. "Well, let's get this over with. I'd like to get out of here before morning. Where is he? In the video room?"

Tarble and Ursay looked at each other. "Yeah,"

said the captain. "I'll take you down there and introduce you."

"That's okay, Captain, I know where it is and Jimmy can do the honors. Oh, by the way, I ran into Eddie Nickles and asked him to come along. Any problem?" Captain Ursay looked to Detective Tarble for an answer as Tarble just stared at Michael and shrugged slightly. "You new to Homicide, Detective?" Michael asked. "I don't remember seeing you around here."

"No," Tarble said carefully, "I was just in the neighborhood."

Michael only nodded and returned to the squad room where Eddie and Jimmy were talking quietly by themselves. "Who's Ernie Tarble?" he asked both of them.

"Tarble?" Eddie growled. "Short black guy? Early forties? Dresses like a fuckin' downtown lawyer? 'Sthat the Internal Affairs guy you were talking about, Jimmy?"

"Who is he?" Michael asked again.

Eddie's eyes narrowed to a squint as he turned from Jimmy. "You remember those intelligence reports on the poker games and those vans filled with young boys and high-priced hookers from Philly and New York? You remember how those reports somehow got to city hall, how the other side was figuring out everything you were doing? That's Ernie Tarble!"

Michael stared at Eddie for a moment. "How come I never knew anything about him?"

"Because, friend, by the time I tracked it all down, you'd lost interest. Remember?"

Michael paused, expressionless. "Well who the fuck is he? How come I've never heard of him?"

"He showed up out of nowhere in the old Intelligence unit. Stays to himself, mostly. Word is he's the chief's man. Some say he's the mayor's man. I don't know who he belongs to. But I can tell you the sonofabitch's no friend of ours."

"What else should I know . . . ?" Michael started. "Never mind, we can talk later." He turned to Detective Legget. "Jimmy, listen."

"I know, man," Jimmy said. "I don't want to know. And I never heard of any of this. Right?"

Detective Nickles nodded approvingly at the young detective in the tailored suit and gold ID bracelet.

"Come on, let's get this dog and pony show over with," Michael said.

"Am I supposed to wait out here?" Legget asked, as if he were expecting to be disappointed.

Eddie grinned. "Hell, no, we gotta have someone to dump on if we blow it."

"By the way," Michael asked Detective Legget, "what's this guy been acting like? From what you were saying on the phone, he sounded too calm to be real."

"He was trying to be in the beginning," Legget said, "but he's scared. Real scared. Keeps asking about whether you're coming and who I've told about you 'n' all. He's been having real trouble sitting still for the last hour or so. He's still trying to hold his cool, but he's scared. No doubt."

Michael and Eddie shrugged at each other. Jimmy Legget wondered if he, too, should have shrugged as the three men walked back to the interview room with the video recorder hidden behind the air vent.

≫ ≪

The interview room was short and narrow. Its walls, once a pale shade of green, now suffered a gray paste of sweat and cigarette smoke. All along its perimeter, like trophies, were the scuffs and gouges of past interrogations and a wainscot of grease stains from heads set back in fear and arrogance, contrition and defiance. The only furnishings were a single table, two straight-backed wooden chairs, and a man seated in the corner fidgeting with the manacle that chained his wrist to a steel eye bolted to the wall. Eddie Nickles entered first and moved quickly to the edge of the table where he picked up a tin ashtray and sat in its place, looking down on the prisoner. No amenities were exchanged. Michael Holden entered next, scraped the second chair across the unwaxed linoleum to within a few feet of the prisoner, and sat down. Jimmy Legget closed the door and stood leaning against it.

"I understand you wanted to see me," Michael said, leaning forward and resting his forearms on his knees. The man did not speak but acknowledged the statement with a short nod. Even seated, his height and bulk were apparent. His thick arms and shoulders hunched forward, straining at the seams of a light blue polyester shirt. The knot of a thin black tie was pulled down a bit but still held his open collar close to a stump of a neck barely distinguishable from a coal-black face with deepset eyes. Traces of perspiration edged the man's cheeks and he did not move. He had the appearance of someone holding his breath, trying to keep the nausea under control.

Michael sat back, slipping off his rumpled tweed jacket and draping it over the back of his chair where it hung more loosely than it had on him, his once athletic leanness now a bit puffed and softened by the neglect of middle age. His dark brown eyes never moved from the prisoner, questioning but not revealing. "All right," Michael said, "let's get the introductions over with. What's your name?"

Again the man said nothing but turned toward Detective Nickles, holding up the burning butt of his cigarette and silently asking for the ashtray Eddie had moved out of his reach. Eddie made no move to accommodate him and the man lowered his hand to the table, holding the remains of the cigarette upright by the filter.

Michael allowed a smile and a brief shake of his head. "Look, friend, let's make this real simple. A few hours ago you shot and killed a policeman and nobody here owes you a fucking thing. Now, if you want to play games, you get yourself a good lawyer and play with him. We'll just book you as a John Doe, toss you in the cellblock, and go back to enjoying our Saturday night. Understand?"

The man tried a stare but could not maintain it. His eyes drifted toward a vacant corner of the room and he mumbled a name.

"Say again?" Eddie barked. "I couldn't hear ya."

The man leaned back and announced, "Wheatley, Adrian Wheatley."

"You got a middle name?" Eddie asked as Jimmy Legget reached for his gold-filled pen and patted his pockets looking for something to write on.

The man shook his head as Jimmy murmured, "Shit," and left the room calling over his shoulder, "I'll be right back."

Eddie did not wait. "Date of birth?"

"Three, fifteen, fifty-two."

"Place?"

"What?"

"Where were you born?"

"Oh . . . uh . . . St. Kitts, West Indies."

"How long you been in the States?"

The man's cheeks puffed in thought. "I dunno, since maybe I was six or five. I don't remember, 'zackly."

"You got a Social Security number?"

"Yeah, uh . . . oh-four-six . . . uh . . . two-eight, oh-two-six-one."

"PDID?"

"You mean like a police number?"

"Yeah, like a police ID number. You got an arrest record?"

"Nothin' adult, man. I got a coupla juvenile cases. Y'know, boostin' outta Woodies and a bunch of us stoled a car once. Never did no time, though. Y'know, got probation both times."

"Figures," Eddie shrugged.

Jimmy Legget returned to the room as Michael stood up suddenly and turned to the air vent. "Did you get all that, Captain? That ought to be enough for you to finish off the ID. We're going to move down to another room where we can get a little more comfortable." Adrian Wheatley's eyes widened as they followed Michael's address to the air vent and then turned to Jimmy Legget, who looked as startled as the prisoner.

"How 'bout the big room in the back?" Eddie asked as he unlocked the cuff on Wheatley's right wrist and stood him up. Michael nodded and followed the two men out of the room. Jimmy was close on their heels and started to speak when he saw Captain Ursay and Detective Tarble marching across the squad room.

"Here comes the captain," Jimmy mumbled. Michael nodded but did not turn.

"What's the problem, Mike?" Ursay demanded, watching Eddie walk the prisoner down the hall.

"No problem," Michael answered.

"Look, this is still Homicide's case and I don't appreciate your—"

Michael raised his hand to cut him off. "Captain, I'm not going to argue with you. You're right, it's Homicide's case. This wasn't my idea, remember? You were the one who called me in—interrupting a perfectly pleasant evening, I might add—because you weren't getting anywhere. I don't know any more about this than what you just heard on your monitor. Never seen or heard of him before. But if I'm going to talk to him, I'm going to do it my way. Now, if you and Detective Tarble want to take over, that's fine. You write your reports and I'll write mine. No arguments."

"Mike, there's no reason we can't cooperate on this."

"I thought we *were* cooperating, Captain. He's your prisoner. Do what you want. But like I said, if I'm going to talk to him, it's going to be in another room without your recording everything on the video." Michael then slowed his speech for emphasis. "Just like you promised the man in the first place." Ursay hesitated and then looked at Tarble. Michael turned on the Internal Affairs detective, his eyes narrowing. "Is there some reason I should know about that IAD has an interest in this case?" Tarble drew back, looking uneasy.

"Let's just get on with it," the captain said abruptly. "Jimmy, I want all your reports finished before you check off tonight."

"Yes, sir," Jimmy said. He waited for Ursay and Tarble to retreat before blurting out, "Man, you trying to get me busted down to school crossings?"

"It's just between him and me," Michael answered, and motioned for the detective to follow him down to the large office with four empty desks and as many swivel chairs. The two men picked out their chairs and sat down while Eddie sat on the desk to which Wheatley was now handcuffed, talking to him quietly.

Michael started the questioning, again without the warm-up of explanations or advice or shallow attempts to put the man at ease. "I presume that you know who we are."

"Uh-huh, yeah. You're DA Holden and he's Officer Nickles."

"*Detective!*" Eddie emphasized.

"Yeah, right, Detective. And him I just knows from tonight, you know," Wheatley said, motioning to Jimmy.

"Why did you ask for me?" Michael asked. "I've never seen or heard of you before."

"Well, like that's what I wanna talk about, you know? Like that's part of what I know that I wanna make a deal."

"Jesus, man," Eddie said in a voice as mean as his bloodshot eyes, "what'd I just get finished tellin' ya? The man's already said he's not gonna play games with you. You shoot a policeman in the face in front of a roomful of witnesses and then turn around and walk into his partner waiting outside with the gun in your hand and you 'like wanna make a deal'? Shit, son, you gotta do better'n that. You wanna dance with us you gotta start singing the right song. You know what I'm sayin'?"

Wheatley looked at all three men in silence. His free hand squeezed the arm of his chair and his cuffed hand steadied itself by straining against the short chain. No one said anything for what seemed in the tense silence twenty minutes. It was closer to twenty seconds.

"Look," Eddie said finally, "you know how deep your shit is and for whatever reason you decided to pick up sides with Mr. Holden. And Jimmy, Detective Legget here, stuck his neck out to keep that pack of wolves away from you. Now you got to tell us why we're here and whether it's worth our time to do anything more'n just walking you down to the cellblock and heading out for a drink. Understand?"

Wheatley rocked forward a bit and looked directly at Michael. "Ya got a smoke?"

Eddie handed him a crumpled, unfiltered Camel, which the man inspected as if he had never seen one before. Eddie held the match while Wheatley took a long pull and then released the smoke with resignation.

"Man," he started in a quiet voice, "I know I ain't walkin' 'way from killing the police. But like I gots more'n you guys to worry 'bout. And like I gots to know that if I talk, I ain't just burnin' myself over nothin'. Y'know, like I'll take the fall and do my time, but like I needs to know I ain't gonna die on top of it."

"We haven't had the death penalty here for years," Eddie noted regretfully.

"Nah, man, I'm not talkin' 'bout no 'lectric chair. I'm talkin' 'bout being done in jail."

Michael stepped in. "Why don't we get to the point? Why are we here? What do you want from us?"

Wheatley's nod was reflexive, his resolve seemingly pricked by confusion. He took some time before answering, drawing with a fingertip imaginary figures on the desktop, not looking at his interrogators. "The man y'all called Nate? Like we was real close. Y'know, we spent lotsa time together. And we'd talk, him and me. You know, he'd tell me things." He lifted his eyes to Eddie, then glanced at Michael and shrugged, "Like, what y'all were doing."

"Doing? What do you mean by that? What do you think we were doing?"

"You know, when y'all were investigatin' the mayor 'n' all. Back then."

"Who's Nate?" Michael asked.

Wheatley frowned and then said, "Yeah, okay, I unnerstand. His name's Roland. Roland Havens. But y'all called him Nate. Y'know, it was the snitch name you gave 'im."

Jimmy began to scribble in his notebook but stopped when Michael looked over and slowly shook his head. Wheatley watched the signal and seemed to relax just a bit.

"Tell me about this Nate or Roland or whatever his name is," Michael continued.

Wheatley looked confused, as if he had just answered the question, and his free hand motioned back and forth between the prosecutor and Detective Nickles. "Like the man was your snitch, am I right? I mean, the man was your agent or whatever and wearin' a wire to listen in on the mayor. Am I right?"

Neither man said anything. Neither man had to. Wheatley had his answer. Roland Havens: Snitch 1M16–82C on Eddie's indecipherable list; codenamed "Nate" for the purposes of all telephone calls, messages, meetings, even private conversations, for any communication that might be overheard or intercepted; at one time the mayor's private chauffeur, turned snitch by Eddie Nickles—how, Michael never asked and Eddie never explained; and who for almost six months had worn a body recorder and reported on the mayor's unofficial movements and meetings; missing and presumed dead for more than two and a half years. Only Jimmy Legget was left wondering as Wheatley began to fill the uneasy silence with a rambling description of his relationship with Roland Havens, his "play brother," the man whose father and Wheatley's mother had spent years "you know, together" in one of those relationships definable only by the parties involved and, often, not even by them.

"So like I's sayin', we'd talk, y'know, but Roland never unnerstood who I was workin' for, really."

"Who do you work for?" Michael asked.

"Milton Higgs." Wheatley waited for a response. He got one as Michael and Eddie looked quickly at each other. "Yeah, man," Wheatley said, "you know all about Milton Higgs. Am I right?"

"What's Higgs got to do with Nate?" Eddie asked.

"Ah, man, c'mon," Wheatley chuckled before Michael cut him off.

"Just answer the question."

The half grin disappeared. "Yeah, okay. Like Roland's workin' for you guys and lettin' you know what's happenin' with the mayor. Am I right? And he's wearin' that wire 'n' all and trying to pick up on all that shit when the mayor'd meet in his car and Roland be driving 'em around. Am I right?"

The room went silent. Jimmy began a slight but quick rocking of his chair, his eyes darting back and forth among the three men.

"Yeah," Wheatley went on, "well, like Roland got scared, y'know? Like, man, he's just a kid. I mean he weren't no kid really, but y'know, he acted like it sometimes. Shit, the man thought he was somebody. Hot style, y'know? Driving the mayor around and doing all that shit for him and makin' deliveries and all those politicians callin' him by name. And then you guys got him wired up and after while he just got scared. Couldn't handle it. And so like he's thinking like he's turnin' on his own people. And everybody's talkin' 'bout how the only reason you were after the mayor 'cause he's black. Man, all that street shit. They dunno all the shit's goin' on and even if they did . . . don't matter. And all that time"—he shook his head with a smile—"all that time you're chasin' after the mayor, you never figger'd that it was Higgs makin' the deals. Am I right? I mean, shit, the mayor never gave out no contracts without it being Higgs givin' the okay. For real."

"What happened to Nate?" Michael asked.

Wheatley's finger erased the invisible doodles on the desktop and he spoke without looking up. "I gave him up."

"What happened to him?"

"You know . . . they killed him when they couldn't use him no more."

Michael leaned forward. "What do you mean, when *they* couldn't use him anymore?"

Wheatley winced and he reached for the pack of Camels Eddie had left on the corner of the desk. His speech was punctuated by his single-handed effort of shaking loose a cigarette and placing it in his mouth and waiting for a light. His eyes could not stay fixed on the cigarette or the match Eddie held, but swept back and forth between Eddie and the prosecutor, furtively, searching for their reaction. "Like I say, the man was scared and he's listenin' to all that talk and, y'know, we got to talkin' 'bout stuff. So like he tells me he's looking for a way out and I give 'im one. I thought I'd help him, y'know?"

"And help yourself, maybe?" Michael said coldly.

Wheatley went on as if he had not heard. "So's me and Roland worked up this plan. Like he'd tell his people y'all were trying to get him to testify or somethin' and maybe he could help 'em out. But after while things got outta hand. Y'know, it got to where he's tryin' to run a game on both sides and gettin' really fucked up. I mean really fucked up in the head. Shit, you guys musta knowed he was goin' bad."

"Why didn't he just tell us he wanted out?"

"I dunno, man. Maybe he figgered he couldn' get out."

"Maybe you told him he couldn't get out. Maybe your people told him he couldn't get out."

"Yeah, mebbe."

Jimmy Legget sat in his chair, rocking faster, while his pen tapped nervously on the blank page of his notebook.

"Who killed Roland, Mr. Wheatley?"

"I dunno. Square business, man, I dunno."

"Did you kill him, Mr. Wheatley?"

"No!" he erupted. "I didn' kill him. We was tight. I dunno who did it. Y'don't ask questions like that. You just know it's done. You don't ask who done it."

"How come his body never showed up?"

Wheatley looked exasperated. "Man, you just testin' me or you really dunno?"

"Doesn't matter which. Just answer the question."

"Higgs runs a whole buncha funeral homes, am I right? And they ain't stupid 'nuff to let y'all find a body. Shit, they just burn it up and the police got nothin' but a missing person. No murder, man. Same's that guy today. You'll never find him. The man's already spread over half the city. No body, no murder."

Eddie's brow furrowed and he asked the question he saw in Michael's confused expression. "What the fuck're you talking about?"

Wheatley's head drooped, his stare focused on the glowing ash of the cigarette creeping toward his fingertips. "The guy I killed this morning. Not the police, the man in the alley, you know . . . this morning. Square business, I never killed nobody before, never even . . . never even beat nobody. It just all happened, you know? Like alla sudden you kill somebody, and it's just like . . . I dunno."

"Jesus Christ," Michael murmured and slowly turned his head toward Jimmy Legget. "He's been advised, right?" Jimmy nodded. "Did he sign the forty-seven?" Jimmy shook his head and Michael turned back to the prisoner, unconcerned with the man's failure to sign the card acknowledging that he had been advised of and understood his constitutional rights. "This . . . uh . . . killing in the alley, and the officer—they both got something to do with Higgs?"

Wheatley shook slightly, whether from fear or the release of confession wasn't clear. The cigarette, which had burned out against his fingers, dropped to the floor and his speech became animated. "Ever'thing, man, ever'thing gots to do with Higgs. No lie. Like I figger I'm a dead man behind the fact of what happened, y'know, me shootin' that police 'n' all. Like I figger it was Higgs that sent the man there in the first place. They told me to be in that bar and wait and not do nothin' till they took care of things. And I'm sittin' there and sittin' and nothin' happens and nobody's comin' and I'm figgerin', shit, mebbe someone saw what went down in the alley and Higgs and his people thinkin' there's no way to cover it and they got to do somethin' fast, you know, to cover before they's too many questions asked. And I know they got plenty a rollers'd do a job for 'em. Like take me out and say I bucked on 'em or drew down on 'em or somethin' and I'd be dead and nobody'd be askin' no questions, y'know? And when that *po*-lice came up on me, I just . . . I just . . . I dunno, just panicked.

I dunno if the cop's workin' for Higgs or not." His voice lifted with his head, angry and cocked toward Jimmy Legget. "And, man, I'm tellin' ya, *you* dunno if that man's workin' for Higgs!"

Jimmy frowned and looked to Detective Nickles and Michael Holden for support, but neither man took his eyes off Wheatley. Eddie picked up the crumpled pack of cigarettes and shook one loose as an offering.

Wheatley ignored it as he spoke directly to Michael. "For real, man. I go to D.C. Jail and I'm dead 'cause there's no way Higgs figgers he can leave me be. He can tell me all he wants that he'll take care of things, but there's no way he's gonna take the chance of me layin' chilly. The man don' take chances like that. You know what I'm sayin'? Like all the chasin' you been doin', y'all ain't caught shit. Am I right? The man jus' don' take no chances."

Eddie continued to hold out the offer of a cigarette and spoke softly. "By the way, Mr. Wheatley, what do they call you?"

Wheatley took the change of direction without notice. "My people call me Sly," he answered, staring at the Camel.

Eddie chuckled. "You don't mind if we stick with Mr. Wheatley, do ya?"

"Whatever, man," the irony completely lost on him. "You got any filters?"

Michael nodded. "We'll get you some." Then, to the two detectives: "Let's talk."

As he followed them out the door, Michael glanced back at Adrian Wheatley. Alone and tethered to a gray, steel desk, he looked less a double murderer than a dog left out in the rain. Michael closed the door and looked at his watch. Twelve thirty-five A.M.

The three men stood for a few moments until

Eddie broke the silence. "We've got no choice, Mike. We've gotta go for it," he said with some urgency and a glint of excitement.

"I know, I know," Michael sighed and glanced at Detective Legget, then back to Eddie Nickles.

Eddie nodded that he understood Holden's silent question of whether Jimmy Legget was to be included. "It's already on the table, man."

Michael turned to Detective Legget. "Jimmy, we don't have the time now to go over a lot of history, but you're going to have to make a decision here." Jimmy said nothing. "But before we go any further, I've got to ask you if we can keep this conversation just between the three of us." Jimmy nodded his agreement. "The bottom line is that if you stay in with us for the rest of the questioning, there may be a lot of things that come up that you just can't put in your reports. That's asking a lot of you, I know."

Jimmy was looking at the floor but raised his head to ask, "Are you guys still working on the mayor? I thought that case was dead years ago."

"It was," Michael answered, "but who knows, this guy just may resurrect it. That's why we've got to bend the rules a little."

Jimmy turned toward Eddie. "And you think Tarble's a leak?"

"Tarble for sure," Eddie said, "and others we don't even know about. What Mike's sayin' is that if you're uncomfortable, now's the time to step out. We can explain things later, when we got time, but the point is, if we're right, this man is probably gonna be talkin' about shit that could make a lot of very important people very nervous. And if any of it ends up going beyond that room, we might as well not bother talkin' to him at all. Y'understand what I'm saying?"

"I understand he's talking about the mayor and I know Milton Higgs pulls a lot of weight around town, backroom politics and rumors that he's dirty, but how're you planning to handle the reports? I mean what are the rules here? Holding back in the report's one thing, but shit . . . is that all?"

"That's all." Eddie nodded. "No more'n you'd do to protect the identity of a snitch, except here the snitch is known. We're just protecting his information. We've just got to know up front that it's not gonna end up in the wrong hands. The report's simple. The man confessed to killing the officer but kept trying for a deal by only hinting at the reasons. You know, saying he could deliver Mr. Big without ever giving up the specifics. Same old bullshit. Right?" Michael nodded slowly, but with a slight frown. "We can work all that out later," Eddie said.

Jimmy tugged uncomfortably at one earlobe, while his eyes traveled back and forth between the two men.

"Jimmy, if you're not sure, don't step in it," Michael said. "No questions asked. It'd take us five minutes to come up with a dozen legitimate reasons for you to be working on something else while we talk to the man. But if you come back in with us, it's gotta be our way. All right?"

Jimmy shrugged. "I understand. I probably should know better, but I'll stick it out. What about taking notes?"

"Take all the notes you want," Michael said, "just as long as no one but us ever sees them, at least for now. Agreed?" Jimmy nodded. Michael reached in his pocket for some money and asked the young detective, "How 'bout finding the man a coupla packs of Kools. I gotta make a phone call." And then to Eddie: "Let's waltz him for a while. Why don't you use the phone in there to call around for some place to hold him outside D.C.? At least let him know we're trying."

Eddie nodded and Jimmy headed for the door.

Eddie started to turn away but Michael stopped him with a grab at his sleeve. "You're sure we can trust him?"

"Like I said before, we got no choice. He'll be okay. I mean, the man showed the right instincts in calling you without runnin' his mouth to the captain. Besides, the more we suck him in, the more we've got him under control. Right?" The two men just stared at each other for a moment until Eddie answered his own question—"Right!"—and walked back to the room where Adrian Wheatley waited.

Michael strolled into the squad room and picked out a phone on an empty desk and started dialing. A detective called out from the other end, "Any luck?"

Michael smiled. "We're still dancing but he hasn't kissed us yet." The detective laughed and went back to his magazine while Michael listened to his home phone ring twice before he hung up, the signal to Katy that it was him calling. He dialed the number a second time before remembering that she had left. He called her apartment house.

"I'm sorry, Miss Reynolds is out for the evening," the front-desk receptionist reported. He set the receiver down slowly, a sudden, hollow feeling coming over him. Where was she? He sat down, threw his feet on the desk, and tried to think of other numbers to call. Glancing at his watch, he gave up the idea and just stared out the window.

It was almost one o'clock when Jimmy returned with two packs of filtered menthols and Michael followed him to the back room. Eddie was ending a telephone conversation and nodding success to

Wheatley. "Yeah, right. 'Preciate it, Sam." He hung up and turned to Michael. "Loudon County says they'll take him, but not till morning. My man's gotta check with the sheriff. Anne Arundel's full and Fairfax is still holding those Jamaicans for us." He then turned back to Wheatley, who was lightly scratching the wrist Eddie had freed from its manacle. "The best we can do is to hold you here till morning and then take you out to Virginia." Wheatley accepted the verdict without comment and leaned back in his chair as if the achievement of his first objective had given him the license to relax. Eddie gently revoked that license. "How long we can keep you there, I don't know. We only got so many chits, understand?"

The process began with positioning. Eddie rolled one of the swivel chairs up close to Wheatley and sat down. Michael moved toward one end of the room, behind his subject. He paced slowly, asking each question in the same low, even voice, emphasizing nothing. For a time Wheatley would try to twist his chair around to face Michael, only to be stopped by Eddie, who pulled him back with a question of his own. Wheatley learned quickly and soon gave no more effort to the direction of his answers than a simple cock of his head. Jimmy sat at a desk in the middle of the room, quietly jotting notes on his pad, rarely asking anything more than for a question or answer he had not heard to be repeated—a habit ended by Michael's scowl at the third such interruption. Wheatley's stiffness began to evaporate as they purposely avoided the subject of murder. They let him ramble through the history of his employment with Higgs Funeral Homes: from maintenance man at the Fourteenth Street home and main office, to driving the limousines filled with mourners and hearses filled with the dead. Ultimately, he had reached the pinnacle, personal chauffeur to Milton Higgs, a reward for his loyalty so firmly established by the betrayal of Roland Havens. He was well paid, receiving a base salary of five hundred dollars a week, which often was doubled by the cash bonuses he received for special jobs.

"Special jobs?"

"Yeah, y'know, like makin' pickups and deliveries and stuff like that." Wheatley's feet began to shuffle.

"What were you picking up, and where?"

"Man, I don't 'member all the places."

Michael walked over and sat down in front of him, pointing a finger toward his heart. "Don't fuck with us, Sly. We can walk out right now, big smiles on our faces and patting each other on the back, and just tell the man to take you down to the cellblock. And you're on your own. Understand?"

Wheatley drew back and stared for a moment before nodding his confirmation that they both knew what happened in jail to men who made DAs and cops smile and pat one another on the back. The choice was easy. "The Air Force base in Delaware. Mostly from there, man. I mean it weren't that often, but mostly from there."

Eddie nodded his approval, recalling his snitches' tales of drugs being shipped into the city in cadavers, and of the reputed use of the largest military morgue in the country as a point of entry for shipments coming in from overseas, a holdover of the system developed during the Vietnam War. But Eddie's informants had never been specific enough to justify a warrant, and he had grown so distrustful of the people in his own department that he would not share the information with enough people to run a proper surveillance. It was Nate who three years before had let Detective Nickles know that every police intelligence report submitted on his and Michael Holden's investigation had been transmitted directly to the mayor.

Jimmy sat up and asked, "What are we talking about here? Coke? Heroin? What?"

"Tell 'im, Sly," Eddie said.

"Herron, mostly. I mean like they don't deal no coke. Too many crazies fightin' over that. I mean they gets it for themselves and to use with people, y'know. But like dealing loads, it's herron. But listen, man, I never knew what I was pickin' up. For real. I mean, like I knew but I never saw nothin' y'know? Man, I just drove the wagon and never asked nobody nothin'."

"And the white house down by the bay? Did you pick up from there, too?" Michael asked.

"Yeah, sometimes. Man, y'all know 'bout that place, too, huh?" Wheatley shook his head with a confused smile. "Like, if y'all knows about this shit, how come you ain't never busted the man?"

"Life's a mystery," Michael said as Eddie stood up and took Michael's place, pacing the rear of the room and pressing another subject.

For the next two hours the process continued: pressing and pulling back, feeding Wheatley informational questions to let him know that they knew; ignoring his questions about the extent of their knowledge; letting him talk, then cutting him off; switching back and forth between subjects, repeating questions answered fifteen minutes or a half hour or an hour before.

"Man, why you askin' 'bout stuff I already tole you?"

"Because, friend," Michael answered, "we both know you're not telling everything."

They caught him in little lies and forgave him. They caught him in little lies and threw them back at him—quietly, persistently, insisting on better answers, letting the threat of their dissatisfaction hang in the air, but always, always questioning. Never a raised voice, never a silence. Jimmy soon picked up on the rhythm, filling any gap created by the sidelong glances Michael and Eddie occasionally gave each other with questions of his own and suppressing a grin whenever Michael would come over and whisper talk of football or vacations or whatever occurred to him while Wheatley strained to answer Eddie's questions while watching the huddled conferences for some hint of how well he was doing.

Whenever Wheatley resisted or relaxed, they would introduce the subject of the murders but would not let him talk of them.

"All this leads up to the killings today, right?"

"Yeah, you know, like what happened was that—"

"Wait a minute, let's finish talking about these payoffs. You're telling us you'd deliver envelopes to the same cops in each district every month but you never knew what was in them?"

"Man, I know it was money, but I weren't about to look inside the package, and, yeah, it was the same people. I mean, a coupla 'em changed ever' once t'while, but mostly the same ones I told you."

On and on, wearing him down, bracing him up, softening him, worrying him, until he started apologizing for his mistakes and lapses of memory. He began answering everything, volunteering anything, even knowledge he did not possess, trying to give them what they wanted. They caught him, several times, and their anger confused him. He was trying too hard. They knew they were closing in on that point where even he would no longer be able to distinguish between truth and fiction. It set off alarms.

"Is it just me, or do you get the feeling there's something he's holding back, something that's got nothing to do with the murders?" Jimmy asked in one of his huddles with Michael.

"Yeah, he is. I just can't figure out what it is. It's almost like he's dying to talk about the murders to avoid something else. He's got me beat, though. I haven't got a clue, unless it's got something to do with those phony drivers' licenses. That's as close as I can get. But that doesn't make sense. I mean he's just killed two people and he's nervous about some bullshit trick pad operation?" Michael looked around at Wheatley, aka John Willie Brown, James Wilburt Benton, Joseph W. Bryant, and Jervis W. Banyon, the man used by Milton Higgs to rent apartments in those and other names for the use of special friends, some of whose activities were secretly videotaped, some of whose were not.

They had been at it nonstop for more than two hours and Wheatley's fatigue was showing. His body seemed to be folding in on itself. His forearms rested on his knees, and as he leaned lower, they looked incapable of supporting his weight.

"He looks whipped. I guess we better get to the killings before we lose him."

Wheatley drew new energy from their introducing the subject of murder and the progressively detailed questions about the events leading up to the killing in the alley and the death of Officer Carl Arteaza.

On Friday evening, Milton Higgs had hosted a dinner party at his home in Crestwood, a neighborhood of large and expensive homes in which many of the city's more prominent and accomplished black professionals resided. Whether

Wheatley's spotty knowledge of names and details was feigned they could not tell, but of those things he did tell, he professed absolute certainty. The mayor had attended, without his wife. And "that big-titted bitch from the New Horizons," he said, referring to political activist and real estate developer Ora Fisher. "Yeah, that's her, and some congersman's aide from Detroit and some white dude from Miami. I think he's a lawyer or something. And they's all there to see the gov'ner."

"Governor? What governor? Who are you talking about?" Michael asked.

"I don't really know the dude, y'know. Like I don't think he's no gov'ner for real. It's just like ever'body calls him that. I mean like I mebbe seen the man three, four times. Like pickin' him up to the airport, y'know, and drivin' him 'round with Higgs. Like mebbe he's been here three, four times in all the time I been drivin' for the man."

Michael frowned. "And you never heard a name?"

"Nah, man, like nobody calls his name. Like it's always 'gov'ner' or somethin'. Like nobody calls his right name."

"Not even Higgs?"

"Nah, not really. 'Cept once or twice I heard him say his name, like it was Ish or somethin', but I dunno no name. It's like nobody's s'posed to call his name. Just if you hear someone say somethin' 'bout him or he's comin' or somethin'? They say 'The gov'ner's coming' and you know like this guy's a heavy dude. That's all."

"What's he look like?"

"Who?"

"The governor! The heavy dude, the one Higgs calls Ish."

"I dunno. Like he's Porta Ric'n, y'know? Like he's

not white and he's not black. Good-lookin' dude. Like Cochise, y'know. Looks like a fuckin' Indian. I figger he's Porta Ric'n."

Michael turned to Eddie, who shrugged his ignorance, and they both turned to Jimmy, who did the same. "This is just a dinner party?" Michael continued.

"Well, yeah, but it's really a meetin'. I mean like they's sittin' down for dinner before the real meetin', but yeah, it's a party."

Michael shook his head with exasperation. "Sly, is it a meeting, or is it a party? What's going on there?"

"Look, man"—Wheatley smiled with the effort of explaining the obvious—"like it's no cabaret. You know what I'm sayin'? It's all these high-rollin' dudes there for this sit-down dinner. And after dinner they all go down to Higgs's library where the man holds his meetin's."

"Are you there at the dinner or for the meeting?"

"No, no way. I'm there in the house 'n' all, but like I don't set horses with these folk. I'm there for security, y'know? Me 'n' a coupla dudes outside. Nah, man, I don't participate with 'em. Anyway, after the meetin' ever'body leaves 'cept the gov'ner. He stays in the house with Higgs and ever'body else leaves."

"What time did the party break up?"

"Weren't too late. Like mebbe three, two o'clock." Wheatley hesitated to allow for the next question, but the three men were silent. "Anyway, like this morning I'm in the kitchen waiting for the gov'ner and Higgs to finish breakfast and—"

"Did you stay at the house all night?"

"Nah, man." He shook his head and sighed deeply, exasperated with the interruptions, the senseless repetition of unimportant details. How

many times would he have to tell them? "I tole you,
I'm just there for security and to drive the gov'ner
wherever. Y'know, to the airport, mebbe, but I
don't stay with them at night. Anyway, I'm waitin'
for 'em to finish breakfast and the gov'ner, he
comes into the kitchen and, like, you know how it
is, like he's sayin' all this stuff to me an 'Lizbeth—"

"Who's Elizabeth?" Jimmy Legget asked. All
three men turned toward Jimmy as Wheatley acknowledged him with a look that surprised them.
Impatience or real anger?

"Man, you don't need to be askin' no questions
'bout 'Lizbeth. She ain't got no part of this. Nice
lady. Real nice. Special lady, y'know? She ain't inta
their shit."

"Special to who?" Michael asked.

"Whatjou mean?"

"I mean, who is she special to?"

"You know, man, she's just a special lady."

"To you?"

Wheatley looked even more annoyed, resentful,
and his voice threatened that there was a point
beyond which he would not be pushed. "Man, 'Lizbeth don't have nothin' to do with this. You unnerstand?"

Michael looked over to the far corner where
Eddie signaled his agreement that they should let
the subject pass for the moment. "Go on," Eddie
said to Wheatley's back.

"Anyway, me 'n' 'Lizbeth are in the kitchen and
the gov'ner's sayin' this stuff 'bout how nice ever'-
thing is and how he 'preciates how we take care of
him and being real nice and just talkin'. And then
he looks out the window. You know, out the back
to the alley and he sees this guy and, man, he turns
white as you," Wheatley said, nodding at Michael.

"Write that down," Michael said to the two detectives. "The Puerto Rican turned white as a Welshman." Jimmy Legget snickered along with Eddie. Even Wheatley grinned, warming to his story.

"Yeah, man, like the man was *white!* . . . But he don't say nothin', least ways not to me or 'Lizbeth, and he just leaves. I mean like outta there. And he's in the other room talkin' with Higgs for a minute and then Higgs comes inta the kitchen with this other dude Roscoe."

"Roscoe?" Michael asked.

"Yeah, Roscoe. Roscoe Barbosa."

Eddie actually stood up straight and moved quickly to Wheatley's side and leaned in close.

"You talkin' about the man they call Double Dip? That Roscoe Barbosa?"

"Yeah, man. You know the Dip, huh?"

"Uh-huh," Eddie confirmed.

Wheatley reflected, "Yeah, Roscoe. Mean dude, Roscoe. Crazy mean."

"Wait a minute, Sly," Eddie pressed, "the Dip's an independent. What's he doing with Higgs?"

Wheatley just shook his head slowly. "Man, you think the 'dependents grow the shit? You wanna score weight in this town, you deal with Higgs or his people."

Michael asked, "Was Barbosa at this meeting you were talking about? The one last night?" He looked at his watch. Three-twenty-five A.M. "Friday night?"

"No, he's just there for breakfast with Higgs and the gov'ner."

"Why?"

Wheatley was slow to answer. Finally he shrugged. "I dunno. Mebbe, I guess mebbe they's gettin' ready to bring in another load."

"Is that what the Friday-night meeting was about?"

"I dunno, man. For real, I don't. But if I was guessin', I'd say no."

"Why would you guess not?"

"I dunno, 'cause like those people like the mayor 'n' all? I never knowed them to be 'round or even talkin' with the people dealin' the dope. 'Cept Higgs, of course."

Eddie Nickles and Michael Holden looked at each other, and then to Jimmy Legget as if he might have some clue. His look was as blank as theirs. "Let's get back to the alley," Michael said.

Wheatley took in a deep breath. "Okay, Higgs is lookin' out the window and I'm lookin' and Roscoe's lookin' and there's this white dude like standin' next to the garage, like 'cross to the alley. And he don't belong there, y'know?" His pace began to quicken. "Like we knows who's in that house and this dude don't belong. And he says like don't let that man go and—"

Michael: "Who says?"

"What?"

"Who's saying not to let the man go?"

"Man," Wheatley snapped, "Higgs is sayin'."

Eddie: "Where's the gov'ner while all this is going on?"

Wheatley's voice came just short of a shout. "Shit! I dunno where he's at." He stopped himself by gripping the arms of the chair, bringing himself down, and restarting in a slow singsong. "Like I never . . . seen him . . . after he's outta . . . the kitchen . . . okay?" He paused to see if *now* they would let him go on.

"Go on," Michael ordered.

"Anyway, Roscoe goes 'round the front so's to

cut the man off if he goes that way, and I go out the back. But I don't get halfway 'cross to the gate before this dude sees me and makes a move like he's splittin'. Not fast at first, but like he seen me and he's outta there, y'know? So I starts to run, and this dude, he splits for real. And man, I dunno what the fuck's goin' on and, like, y'know, I'm not even thinkin' and I'm lookin' down the alley and I don't see no Roscoe and this muthafucka's runnin' hard and I'm not even thinkin' and like I dunno," he stopped and with a light shrug, muttered, "I just popped a cap, mebbe two." Now soft, almost to himself: "Like I shot the man." His brow suddenly furrowed, quizzical, speaking in a slow-motion replay. "And he went down . . . on his face. He kinda slid on his face and when I came up on him . . . it was all kinda scraped off. His face. I never saw nothin' like it. I didn't think about it. . . . I dunno, shoulda let the man run, shoulda been Roscoe that did it. . . . Stupid." There was a long, silent pause. "I swear I never shot nobody before. Never even seen a dead man before, 'cept in a casket. His face . . . like it was all torn off. You know, from slidin'." The perspiration was now thick on his face and neck and his body began a quick, chilling shake.

"What happened then?" Eddie asked flatly.

Again Wheatley grasped the arms of his chair, more for support than control, and took several gulps of the warm, stale air. His head and eyes rolled back and he spoke to the ceiling. "It was crazy. I don' remember 'zackly, 'cept I was lookin' at the man's face and Roscoe grabs me and he pushes me down the alley. Like not back to the house but down the alley, and he's yellin' at me to do somethin' but I don't know what he's sayin'. And he gets me to the end of the alley where there's that old house where nobody lives and the yard's all fulla bushes so's you can't see? You know?" They didn't know, but didn't ask. "And he pushes me inta the yard and he's got me on the ground and he's talkin' as mean as I ever heard."

Wheatley rocked back and forth and he brought his eyes down to a spot on the wall where he fixed them. He detached himself from his interrogators, talking to himself, wondering if any of it made sense, and his breathing had trouble keeping pace.

"And Roscoe, he wants my piece and I'm sayin' 'No, man' and he pulls this automatic and puts it in my face and I start listenin'. The man takes my gun and gives me his and he's wipin' it an' all and I dunno why he's doin' that shit and he gives me his gun and says that I gotta take off and get lost for a while. Like I gotta go somewhere, but not to my place, and not to see nobody or nothin'. And he's thinkin', I can tell, and he says for me to be in this bar where I was at, where the officer was at. And he's yellin' that I gotta be there by three or somethin'. But I don't know the place. Like I know the place he's talkin' 'bout, but I dunno nobody there. Never been there before. And I'm sayin' like 'Who do I see?' Like I never been there and I'm askin' like who do I see."

"What time is all this happening?" Eddie asked.

Wheatley blinked, coming out of his dream. "What? I dunno, it's early, like mebbe one or twelve o'clock, and I just took off and rode the bus for as long as I could. Just rode the bus till it was time to be in that bar."

"Did Roscoe ever tell you who to see in the bar?"

"Never did. He's sayin' not to see nobody, and like I don't unnerstand, y'know? Like he's sayin' I'm not to see nobody but I'm s'posed to be in the bar at three or somethin' and wait there and not move. He said they'd take care of things but like they hadda do some things first, but like they'd come for me. He kept sayin', 'Man, don't let nobody take you outta there till we come get you.' That's what he said . . . but nobody came. And I sat and sat and nobody came until . . . y'know, the *po*-lice. And I like panicked." He slumped forward and mumbled more than spoke, his head down, his attention inward. "No time to think or figger it. Stupid. Just never thought nothin' like this would come of it. Just never thought nothin'," he finished.

Michael and the two detectives huddled at Jimmy's desk while Wheatley several times drew the palms of his hands down his face, wiping the perspiration—and perhaps tears; they did not look—from his cheeks and onto the thighs of his dark cotton pants. "He's had it for tonight," Michael said.

Eddie looked startled. "What? You're not stopping now, are you?"

Michael bristled. "Let's take this outside."

Eddie apologized quietly to the prisoner for again having to cuff him to the desk while the three men left the room. From the hallway they could hear Wheatley rattling the chain of his manacle in an awkward effort to strike a match to his cigarette.

"Well?" Eddie asked finally to break the silence.

"Look," Michael answered, "this is obviously going to take days. We're not about to get everything from him tonight, right?"

"Yeah. So? The man's on a roll. We can't cut it off now. Not yet."

"What do you think, Jimmy?"

Detective Legget looked surprised to be asked and hesitated before responding. "I don't know enough background to say whether he's telling the truth or not. But it sure sounds like it to me. And he sounds like he figures we're his only chance. I mean, whether or not he's right about Higgs or whoever trying to snuff him to keep him quiet, he believes it and that's all that matters. I think this guy'll do whatever we want, except maybe talk about this lady 'Lizbeth, whoever she is. Whether he'll change his mind overnight, who knows?"

"He won't," Michael said.

Eddie looked curiously at the prosecutor, not sure how to read Michael's reluctance to go on. "Look, Mike, I'm not saying you're wrong, but so what? The man's talkin' now, so why not get as much outta him as we can?"

"Because it's almost four in the morning and I'm beat. Wheatley's beat. The man's in there mumbling, for Christ's sake. You guys can talk to him all night if you want, but I'd like to wait until we clear our heads a little, when we can take it slow and easy—"

"Mike," Eddie interrupted, "all I'm sayin' is the more we get outta him tonight, the more we'll get later. You know that. I'm not tellin' you anything." Eddie stopped, his expression hardening with the effort of holding back. "Look, can we talk? Jimmy, would you mind—"

"You don't have to go anywhere," Michael snapped at Detective Legget. "Listen, Eddie, I'm not gonna argue with you. I'm just saying that as far as I'm concerned, we've got enough for tonight. The man has given up Higgs. He's given up a murder we knew nothing about and he knew we knew nothing about. All he wants is to stay alive and he figures that we're the only ones who'll help him do that. Shit, he's not gonna change his mind, and, frankly, I don't feel like staying here all night getting details we'll be better able to get tomorrow or Monday or whenever. Why not take our time and do it right?"

"Because we're doing it right, now. But you're

the boss, man. It's a mistake, but you're the boss."

"Fuck you, Eddie," Michael shot back. "I'm not the boss here. It's still Homicide's case, and if you want to spend all night with him, go ahead. I'm not stopping you. I'm just telling you what I'm gonna do."

"You guys go ahead and fight it out," Jimmy said impatiently, trying to avoid the center of a controversy he did not understand. "I'm gonna get the man a soda." Without waiting for an answer Jimmy turned and left. When he returned, Michael and Eddie were standing by the coffee urn talking quietly. Jimmy passed them and took Wheatley his soda and returned to the then silent pair.

It was an uneasy, uncertain air in which the three men discussed the parameters of what should and should not be included in the reports. Anxious to end the discussion, Jimmy agreed to the limits, accepting the justification of a history he had yet to understand.

Michael began a suggestion about any further questioning of Adrian Wheatley when Eddie cut him off. "Don't worry, Mike, we'll handle it from here."

Michael hesitated and then said, "I'll go tell him I'm leaving." The two detectives turned toward the coffeepot as Michael returned to the room alone. He tapped Wheatley's shoulder. The man's eyes looked up, but his head barely lifted from the crook of his arm resting on the desk. "I'm leaving you in the hands of the detectives," Michael said. "When they're finished, they'll take you downstairs and put you in a private cell. In the morning they'll drive you out to Virginia. We'll get you a lawyer on Monday and work things out with him. All right?"

Wheatley cocked his head in a close approximation of a nod and said, "I didn't say nothin' before, but you better know that Higgs is got someone in your office. I don't know who it is, but it's for sure he's got someone."

Michael wondered if the flush of his face showed or if the hesitant attempt at calm sounded false. "Yeah, I figured. We'll be talking . . . soon."

He informed the detectives of Wheatley's comment in a flat tone of acceptance and then walked slowly out of the squad room and down the hall toward the elevator, suddenly hungry for a drink.

By five o'clock in the morning, complete confusion had overtaken Adrian Wheatley, and Detective Nickles knew that he had squeezed all he could from this first session. Wheatley was quiet and barely responded to Eddie's attempts at light chatter as he was taken down to the basement of police headquarters and placed in a cell at the far end of the block, away from other prisoners, away from everybody. Jimmy remained in the squad room and debated with several detectives working the midnight tour the wisdom of going home and getting some sleep before writing the reports the captain had ordered finished before he left. "Fuck it," he finally decided, and idly drank two cups of coffee while waiting for Eddie's return. They still had to pay a brief visit to Wheatley's apartment, and Eddie suggested that afterward maybe they could have a drink at his place.

At six forty-five A.M., Adrian Wheatley was found hanging from the crossbar of the door to his cell, his shirt coiled tightly around his throat, his arms hanging free, his knees almost touching the floor.

Four

Katy resisted the urge to look back at Michael's still-dark bedroom window and she took her time opening the car's sunroof before slowly starting down the long hill toward Reno Road. Her thoughts wandered aimlessly as the car seemed to pick its own direction, following Reno's hills and curves until it stopped at the corner of Massachusetts Avenue and the entrance to the vice president's compound, where the guards stood bored. Resting her head on the back of the seat, she stared up at the haze of reflected light and for a moment thought of turning right toward the carnival of bars and bistros along Georgetown's M Street midway. An impatient horn behind her interrupted the thought and she turned left, accelerating down the hill toward her Foggy Bottom apartment.

Her apartment house was, like most of its residents, old and resistant to change. Even the telephones were of a different era, having no dials or buttons, but were wired directly to a switchboard in the lobby where a receptionist placed the calls and took the messages. Katy had taken some comfort in that during those first months alone after the house had been sold and the furniture divided according to the terms of her carefully negotiated divorce. The divorce, like her marriage, had been a civil affair, she and her ex having passed through the rituals with efficiency and decorum, and they had wished each other well. And for that, she could not forgive him. He could have cared enough to have put up a fight, to have been angry.

But that was almost six years ago and mostly forgotten, except on nights like this when she walked alone down the darkened hallway from the rear entrance to the lobby.

Martha, the night receptionist, sat behind the ancient switchboard, whose worn plugs awaited calls that rarely came this late at night. Martha preferred the night shift, when she could escape the frustrated pleadings of her husband and occasionally slip down the hall to Henry the maintenance man's free apartment. As Katy approached the desk, Martha was howling, undoubtedly at one of Henry's dirty jokes.

"Hi, guys," Katy chirped, handing her car keys to Henry, who let her park next to the building's service dock in exchange for an occasional bottle of good sipping whiskey.

"Hey, Miss Kate," Henry said. Martha could not stop laughing and waved a hello with the hand that was not trying to stifle her raunchy guffaws.

"You gonna let me in on the joke?" Katy asked, beginning to laugh herself.

"Oh, Lord!" Martha cackled and laughed even louder.

Henry snickered a bit and said, "I'd best let Martha tell you that one later."

"Any messages?" Katy asked, and Martha reported that her mother had called earlier in the day. Katy nodded and said, "Listen, if anyone calls tonight, I'm not here. All right?"

Martha's smile faded and she lifted a bottle of E&J brandy from behind the desk. "You want a little sip to lift your spirits?" she asked.

Katy smiled and shook her head. "No, thanks, not tonight. We'll talk later." She turned quickly toward the elevator.

Inside her eighth-floor apartment, Katy leaned against the door and stared at the several small rooms stuffed with the furnishings of her past. "Shit!" she murmured, and tossed her purse on the unmade bed she had left two days before.

From the tiny kitchen she retrieved a chilled bottle of Mosel and then moved to an alcove the management called a sun room where she turned on the stereo. She searched the drawer of a cherry end table for a pack of stale Marlboros and lit her third cigarette of the year. Settling back on a small couch, she stared out across the rooftops of the city. The Washington Monument, brightly lit and ribbed with the shadows of floodlit flags barely a half mile away, dominated the view, but all she could see was the vision of Michael's face and its change of expression in the midst of the phone call from that side of his life about which he rarely spoke. Once more she heard his voice as he had directed whoever it was to call him back. She had seen that expression and heard that voice before. She understood him but she wondered about herself.

She had met him four years ago at a party to which they had been separately invited by friends determined to end the self-imposed solitude that had followed each of their failed marriages and the first awkward rounds of reactive dating. He had respected her caution and even her moods and she found that with him she laughed easily and whenever she pleased. Without design or even much thought she soon found her priorities—as seemed his—settled on their time together. Neither her job as the art director of a small advertising agency nor his as a federal prosecutor had commanded as much attention as did their finding a new weekend retreat or following the fortunes of the Baltimore Orioles. They had fallen easily into the comfort of needing only each other.

But that was before the phone calls started, the late-night calls on Michael's unlisted phone filled with hushed conversations that he never cut short and that kept him from sleep long after he had hung up. His work quickly consumed him and left her alone.

In the beginning he had shared bits and pieces about the investigation he was conducting. He'd ask her questions, testing his theories much as she might ask him what struck his attention in a magazine layout. She knew that it had started as a routine case of petty graft by petty officials. City inspectors were demanding payoffs from electrical contractors before issuing permits and approvals. Billy Colquit, a tall, gangling FBI agent whose South Carolina drawl was as thick as it was smooth, had convinced one such contractor, Lester Poteer, to wear a wire and record a series of payoffs. It had been the second or third investigation Michael and Billy had worked together, and he was only the second "cop" to whom Michael had revealed his private number.

The investigation seemed routine, Michael had said, perhaps better than most. The payoffs had led to some higher officials in the city government and plans were being made to videotape a meeting between one of the mayor's department heads, Poteer, and an undercover agent brought in from Buffalo. That meeting never took place.

It was nearly eleven o'clock one clear night in May when Michael's bedside phone rang as he and Katy had sat on his front porch, laughing at Babe burying a tennis ball she had grown tired of chasing. Michael moved quickly to answer the phone, but when he did not return, Katy went upstairs and sat on the bed. Two more phone calls were made and two were received. The conversations were cryptic and Michael seemed too preoccupied to offer her any more than that a Homicide detective, Eddie Nickles, and Billy Colquit were coming to meet with him. They returned to the porch and, in silence, waited.

Eddie Nickles arrived first, shortly after midnight. It was the first time Katy had met him. Dark and thick, he spoke in short grunts and she could see nothing gentle in him. Billy Colquit arrived a few minutes later. He greeted her formally, not like the soft Southern boy with whom she and Michael had spent the day sailing the Chesapeake two weekends before. He seemed almost angry at her being there and she retreated to the kitchen to make coffee while the three men talked quietly in the living room.

When she returned with the coffee she heard Michael ask Detective Nickles, "Is this for real, or just street talk?"

"It's serious. You're in a snake pit, my man," the detective said, "and they're all poison." He turned to Katy. " 'Preciate the coffee, ma'am, but I gotta go. You boys'd better watch your back," he said to the two men and, without more, left.

Billy Colquit went to use the phone in the kitchen and Katy could hear his voice rising. "Man, it doesn't matter what the hell you want, we're on our way over there. You tie that dawg up, ya hear, or Ah'll shoot the bastard."

Within minutes the two men were gone, and Michael did not return for hours. When he did, she was awake and Michael sat on the edge of the bed sipping a small tumbler of Wild Turkey and offered her a shorthand explanation. Lester Poteer had been made, the undercover operation blown.

Eddie Nickles, who had had no knowledge of the investigation before that day, had learned that Poteer was working with the Bureau and specifically with Michael Holden. What had them confused was the improbable source of the detective's information, a snitch who dealt only with the narcotics trade, with people who generally could care less about what was going on with the white collars. The snitch had been swept up in a routine raid on a stash house and had contacted Detective Nickles to negotiate his freedom with the information that there was a contract out on Poteer and the reasons for it. That spelled trouble for which they were not prepared, much less could explain. They had met with Poteer and he was as naïvely recalcitrant as they had feared he might be. He refused to leave town for a few weeks to let things quiet down. "No way, man," he had insisted. "I don't want no witness protection from no FBI and I don't want no agents following me 'round." D.C. had been his home since birth and no one was going to scare him off. He had a gun and an attack-trained shepherd and "Just let the muthafuckas try somethin'."

Two weeks later, Lester Poteer was electrocuted on the job. He had been careless, the inspectors said, and the death was ruled an accident.

In the weeks that followed, Michael withdrew from any talk about his work, deflecting Katy's questions with little more than "Everything's fine." It felt paternal, not unlike a smug "Don't you worry your pretty little head about it." But she could feel the tenseness increasing as the late-night calls became more frequent. Michael slept less, sometimes pacing for an hour or more after a call. He started to take a drink or two to help him sleep, but the sleep that came was fitful and filled with the angry mumblings of dreams he would not share.

He worked more and saw her less. As the months wore on, he became more sullen and withdrawn, often too exhausted to do more than watch her eat as he picked at his food and drank a third and fourth bourbon mixed with less and less water. Sometimes they made love, but more often he just fell asleep in her arms until the booze wore off and he would awake abruptly, startled by some secret thought.

He apologized, of course, again and again, and made plans for weekends together away from the city. But the plans too often were canceled at the last minute for reasons he would not explain beyond "Something came up." Soon he stopped making plans altogether and she would not see him for days. He often failed to return her phone calls until late at night, sometimes at his house, where she had fixed a dinner he would not eat, sometimes at her apartment, where she sat alone wondering why she was waiting.

She began to press him to talk about the investigation, hoping that if she understood it she would understand him. But what little he shared with her was disjointed, a series of rambling vignettes he seemed unwilling or unable to put in any clear context. Tales of corruption in the awarding of city contracts incongruously linked with narcotics shipped in cadavers; of bribes passing hands in high-stakes poker games at posh hotels where a key department head could easily take a ten-thousand-dollar pot with no more than a pair of deuces; of a private club somewhere on the banks of the South River known simply as "the white house," where deals were consummated over drugs set out on silver trays like hors d'oeuvres; of controlling interests in corporations changing hands after a videotaped evening with high-priced hookers and fresh young teenagers imported to service those marked for extortion.

"If you know about some of these people who have lost their businesses like that," she once asked, "why can't you get them to testify?"

"Losing control of your business in a poker game is one thing," he had answered, "but getting on the witness stand and admitting that you traded away your business and probably your family and friends for a few lines of cocaine or a blow job from a fifteen-year-old is quite another."

At one point, Michael's spirits soared. He never said anything beyond a single reference to a mole. He never volunteered a name or what the mole was doing, but often during too many phone calls she had heard the name "Nate." But Michael's high was short-lived. Soon articles began appearing in both the local newspapers; articles that focused on specific allegations before the grand jury and referred always to "sources close to the investigation." With every article Michael's anger grew more intense and more internal and Katy was never sure whether that anger was focused on the "bosses" Michael was investigating or on those for whom he worked. They all sounded the same to her.

Security in the U.S. Attorney's office was at best lax, Michael had said, particularly when it came to reporters' access to the executive suite. U.S. Attorney Thomas E. Joslin was proud of his "open administration" and of his warm relationship with the press. Soon, both dailies were running articles and editorials that suggested that the U.S. Attorney's office was purposefully leaking information damaging to the mayor for political reasons. If the prosecutors had evidence against the mayor or other city officials, an indictment should be returned and a trial commenced quickly. Put up or shut up, the press argued.

Michael stopped talking of his work and soon he and Katy stopped talking at all. The last question she asked of him, Michael turned on her with meanness. "It's none of your goddamned business! But if you've got to know, Nate's disappeared and we don't know if he's dead or alive. Do you feel better now?"

It had been nearly a year and she had tried to be patient. But it was clear that she had become secondary to an obsession that he would neither explain nor let go. And she left.

Three months later Katy read the front-page reports of a press conference called by the U.S. Attorney. Tom Joslin announced that the mayor had never been a target of any investigation and that while he was legally prevented from discussing the specifics of any matter before the grand jury, he felt that the irresponsible conduct of some people in leaking information and encouraging rumors had forced him to clear the record. Michael Holden, named as the prosecutor in charge of the investigation, was quoted as having "no comment." Case closed.

Despite Michael's sporadic efforts at reconciliation during the first few months after their separation, Katy considered the break permanent and acted accordingly. She did not see him for nearly two years, not until one hot April afternoon at a Georgetown restaurant. She had started to turn away but decided not to. They spoke for a few minutes, exchanging "How have you beens" and "Are you still working fors," a halting and uneasy effort to bridge the chasm between ex-lovers trying to be just friends. They reassured each other that they looked well and, there seeming to be nothing more to say, she explained that her friends were waiting.

"Kate," he said, "I've missed you."

"Me too," she said after a pause, then quickly walked away.

Over the next two months, she was alternately flattered and angered by Michael's obviously planned chance meetings on street corners near her office, in galleries that had once bored him, and by his enrolling in a photography course she taught at the Corcoran.

"Stop it!" she yelled finally in exasperation. "I'm not going to be your friend."

"I don't want to be just your friend," he pleaded.

She did not give in easily or completely. But in spite of herself, she wanted to believe that time and circumstances had changed him, had dispelled the ghosts.

Now, as the night crept toward morning, she sat alone in an apartment that began to close in on her. She felt restless, unable to keep still, and so, with the bottle of wine, the pack of cigarettes, and a comforter taken from the bed, she left the apartment and climbed the single flight of stairs to the roof where a canvas chaise sat gathering the soot of the city. She dropped her provisions on the chaise and let the cool north wind cleanse her of the temptation of doing something stupid like calling Michael's house to see if he was still there.

Looking eastward down F Street, she slowly swept the floodlit panorama of Foggy Bottom, from the White House and Executive Office Building just four blocks away to the south and west past the monument grounds and the somber memorials to

Jefferson and Lincoln. Her city enjoyed a certain simplicity, a visual neatness; so many buildings almost uniform in design and dimension, clean and only occasionally imaginative, set along tree-lined streets traveling from park to park.

She scanned the sky looking for the moon as she lit another cigarette and raised the bottle to her lips. But the wine held sway and her eyes would not focus, the effort only heightening her dizziness. Settling into the chaise, she pulled the comforter around her to ward off the chill. She took the last swallow of wine as her thoughts dissolved in a jumble of memories, and she fell into a sleep of dreams she would not remember.

She had no idea what time it was when she finally awoke with a crushing headache and a bladder so painfully full she was afraid to get up. But the rooftop no longer seemed friendly and she felt nervous in the midst of its shadows. Stumbling to her feet, she crept down the stairs to her apartment, which seemed no more inviting than the roof. She remained just long enough to relieve herself and to drink a glass of milk before returning to the lobby, where she grabbed her car keys from behind the desk and left. All along her route back to Tenleytown and Michael's always about-to-be-restored house, she admonished herself. "This is stupid, Kate. Really stupid."

It was not quite five A.M. when she pulled up in her car and stopped next to the fence gate beside Michael's house. He sat leaning against a roof post on the front porch, a half-bottle of St. Pauli Girl in one hand, an empty by his side. Katy walked up silently and sat on the stair below him, leaning into the protective nest between his legs, her head on his chest.

"Hey, Babe," she whispered to the old dog, whose

snow-white muzzle rested on Michael's thigh. Her fingers scratched slowly behind the dog's ear, almost in time with the tail thumping rhythmically on the wooden floor of the porch.

Michael started, "Don't you think it's time we—"

But she quickly stopped him. "Not tonight, okay? I just want to sleep." And after a pause: "There's no moon."

Five

"*What?*"

"He's dead, Counselor. Hung himself in his cell, or so they say."

Michael leaned back and let the kitchen wall support him while his thoughts caught up. He looked to his wrist for the time, but his watch still lay on the bedside table next to the phone on which Detective Nickles had called a few minutes before. He had caught it on the first ring and whispered to Eddie that he'd call him back, hoping Katy had not been awakened. She had been, but had curled quietly back under the covers.

"I don't believe it," he said finally.

"What, that he hung himself?"

"Yeah, I don't believe it."

"I don't either. At least I don't think so. You never know. I mean, the man did have a bad day yesterday. I mean, a real bad day. It's not like he wouldn't've had a reason."

Michael deflated with a long sigh and asked flatly, "What happened?"

"They found him a coupla hours ago. They say he used his shirt tied to one of the crossbars in the cell. I haven't seen the body yet, but apparently there was no sign of a struggle. No bruises, abrasions, no broken bones or nails, nothing."

"It doesn't make any sense, Eddie."

"No sense worrying about it until after the post."

"Is it possible? Suicide, I mean?"

"Possible, but I think they got to him."

"No one heard anything? No injuries? Whaddaya think? Dope? Stun gun, maybe?" Michael asked, referring to the electric device sometimes used by U.S. marshals and the police to immobilize an unruly prisoner instantly without showing any lasting sign of its use.

"I don't know. By the time I heard about it and got down to the cellblock, the body was on the way to the morgue. IAD had already seized the logs and put the men on duty on ice. No one's sayin' shit, 'pending a full investigation.' Know what I mean?"

"Who's doing the autopsy? Do we know?"

"Yeah. We got lucky. Doc Crowell. I already called him. Told him every official in D.C.'d want this thing to come out suicide but that we had reason to think otherwise. Didn't tell him anything about what Wheatley said, just that he had bellied up. We reached an understanding, so to speak, the doc and me. I'm gonna head over there as soon as I hang up. Take a look for myself."

"Good. How'd you hear about it, by the way? I mean, Jesus, what happened after I left?" He stopped and then added, "Look, about last night . . ."

"Forget it. Nothin' happened. He came up with a few new names but nothin' to make me think he was ready to check out. I mean, the man wasn't exactly chipper, but I seen worse. No, he was ready to do his part. If anything, I think he figgered he'd been had and wanted the chance to talk. By the way, he did say one thing you oughta think about. He really couldn't explain it, y'know, since he was just picking up bits and pieces, but he said that all that shit that was showing up in the press a coupla years ago, y'know, the 'sources close to the investigation' crap?"

"Yeah. What about it?"

"Well, he claimed most of it was coming from Higgs's people. Like they wanted it leaked. It doesn't sound right but that's what he said."

Michael didn't say anything for a moment, the knot of nerves beginning to dissolve in a flood of questions and hypotheses. "Unless . . ." he offered, but then fell silent.

"Unless what? Why would Higgs want that stuff on the street? Why bury the mayor if he's his man?"

"Well, maybe Higgs or whoever is running the show is more of a gambler than we thought. Maybe they understood just how much those leaks to the press disrupted everything we were doing. Remember how nervous witnesses would get? I mean, every time something hit the papers, sources would scatter. Nobody wanted to testify in the grand jury, tell us they'd meet us and never show up, laugh in our face whenever we'd talk about secrecy or confidentiality. And at the same time the press was putting an awful lot of pressure on Joslin. Y'know, the 'put up or shut up' argument. Maybe Higgs figured he could put more pressure on our sources—and Joslin—than they could handle. And it worked. We never had a chance."

"I don't know, man, that's some serious hardball."

"Maybe, but look what happened. We looked like fools, the mayor came out the victim, and if we ever tried to resurrect anything, how much credibility would we have?"

"Yeah, well, maybe," Eddie said, as if that subject had been exhausted.

Michael went on. "Anyway, what's next? What about Wheatley's apartment? Think you oughta go through it? I can come down if you need a warrant."

"Already covered, Counselor. Jimmy and I went over there right after I put Wheatley in the block but someone had already tossed the joint. Professional job, too. I mean the place was clean. Looked like they even went through the icebox. Nothing left but dirty underwear and a boom box."

"Who else knows you went through his apartment?"

"Get serious," Eddie laughed. "Everyone thinks Jimmy and I just went out for a drink or two after we finished. Jimmy went back to the office to start the reports when he heard about Wheatley and called me. That's about it."

"And Jimmy?"

"Well, the man's not happy, but he's on board. I kinda like the kid. He's gonna take a little hand-holding, but he'll be okay. He doesn't buy suicide, either. More angry than anything else. Feels like someone pissed on him personally. Know what I mean?"

"Yeah, I know. What about his partner?"

"Damjek's been out sick for a coupla weeks. Something about a bad back he got going through a door. He's gonna be off for a while, and Jimmy's been working alone. It'll work out."

"You think Ursay'll let Jimmy team with you?"

"It'll work out. Don't worry about it. Anyway, after I get back from the morgue, Jimmy 'n' I are gonna get some crime-scene people and go up to the alley behind Higgs's place. See if they mighta left something behind. Maybe canvass the houses around there, including Higgs's. Any problem?"

Michael thought a moment. "No, no problem, I guess. You think you ought to talk to Higgs this early?"

"Why the fuck not? It's not like it's any secret we

spent the night talking to Wheatley. I mean I'm not about to fill him in on what Wheatley said, but we oughta hear what the man's got to say. Another thing—I think we oughta try 'n' find this 'Lizbeth lady. See what the story is. Any problem with my signing your name to a Jane Doe subpoena if we find her?"

"No. Go ahead."

"Maybe afterward, I'll work the sewers for a while."

"Working the sewers" was Detective Nickles's standard descriptive of dealing with the street life who collected bits of information to sell for a fix or a favor, sometimes just for the pleasure of dropping a dime.

"Need anything from me?"

"Nah," Eddie said, "you just do what lawyers do best—lay in bed thinking up all the things us cops shoulda done out here on the street."

"How 'bout breakfast in the morning?" Michael suggested. "You 'n' Jimmy and me."

"Yeah, sure," Eddie agreed. "Meet us at Chaney's around seven."

"Jesus, man," Michael groaned. "How can you stand that place first thing in the morning?" Michael's revulsion at the thought of having breakfast in a fog of stale smoke and booze was made even more acute by the comparative freshness of the morning air being warmed by a bright and rising sun.

"Look, I'm tellin' ya," Eddie said, "they serve a good breakfast, cheap. Just meet us there, and if you puke when you walk in we'll go somewhere else."

Michael was not going to argue. "Can't resist an offer like that." He hesitated and then said, "Hell of a way to make a living, eh?"

"Yeah, it sucks, but only six months to go and I'm history," Eddie boasted, and hung up.

> ≫ ≪

Michael sat by the bedroom window, his long legs stretched toward the sill where he propped his feet, his thick, nearly black hair tousled like a bramble on the hard ground of an expression almost winter pale in the early light. He held a cup of coffee close to his lips, but he did not drink, did not move, except for his eyes, which seemed to twitch in thought.

Katy saw him sit up a bit, a hint that he sensed her watching him from the bed. "It's starting all over again, isn't it?" she said without moving.

Michael looked over and smiled as if he had not heard. "Mornin'. You want some coffee?"

Katy shook her head slowly without raising it from the pillow. "That wasn't my question."

"No, I guess it wasn't." Michael looked away as he took a sip of coffee. "The man from last night, the one who shot the officer, they found him in his cell a coupla hours ago. Dead. They say he hung himself."

"Hanged," Katy corrected, then quickly apologized. "I'm sorry, I didn't mean that. Are you all right?" She sat up, wrapping her arms around her knees, and softly brushed her cheek on the edge of the woolen blanket, her dark green eyes fixed on his lack of expression.

He looked at her and nodded. "I'm fine. It's a job, you know, like anyone else's."

"Not quite," she said quietly. After a moment she asked, "What's it mean?"

"I don't know, I really don't."

"Jesus, Michael, what's going on? What's this all about?"

He raised the coffee cup but, again, did not drink, holding it in both hands as he spoke. "It's strange, I was just sitting here thinking that I was actually relieved he was dead. As if it was one less problem I'd have to deal with. The man kills a cop, then kills himself. Case closed. Sounds sick, doesn't it?"

"I don't know. Not really. I don't pretend to understand what it's like for you. You don't ever want to talk about it and I guess I'm like everyone else who'll read about it in the paper. You think what a shame and then go on to the comics. After a while it doesn't mean anything. It's a body count, a statistic, it's impersonal. Maybe you just want to be like everyone else on the outside." She stopped and watched him as he continued to look away. When he said nothing she added, "There was a time when I wanted to understand. Two years ago I wanted to, but I'm not sure I do anymore. The last time I tried, it just turned ugly. Maybe that's what it's all about, it's just ugly. There's nothing more to it than that." Michael turned toward her and she said, "I suddenly feel like I shouldn't have come back here."

He put the coffee cup on the sill and moved to the bed. "Kate, what happened to us two years ago is not going to happen again. But I still have a job to do."

"No one's suggesting that you not do your job. But there's a difference between doing your job and letting it become an obsession." She could see Michael's back stiffen.

"It was never an obsession," he said very slowly, "it was my job. Maybe I let it get out of hand and maybe a few priorities got screwed up along the way, but it was never anything more than my job. It still is."

"It is starting over again, isn't it? You don't believe it was suicide."

"No, I don't."

She let out a long sigh as she reached over and put her arms around him, laying her head on his shoulder, looking away. She started rocking them slowly and her words came almost in a whisper. "God, what's gonna happen to us? I came back here last night because . . . I don't know, I guess I had to. I tried to tell myself not to—to stay away because I saw that same look in your eye. It was that awful look you used to get when everything about you turned so mean. I don't know how else to describe it except mean. Scary, maybe." She looked up and kissed him. "You know I love you. I wish I didn't sometimes, but I do. But it's not enough. You have to understand that. You have to understand that I just won't go through that again. I can't."

He shook his head. "It won't happen, Kate. It won't touch us. I promise."

She took his face in her hands. "Don't! Don't promise anything. You don't know what's going to happen. You can't tell me . . ."

His fingers moved to her lips to stop her. "I promise," he said.

She gave up with a weak smile. "Come back to bed," she said, and he did. As they settled back she watched his expression and asked, "You okay?"

He only smiled and pulled her closer. In the quiet he listened to her breathing slow to a light, snuffling snore and felt the faint brush of her eyelash against his chest as deep sleep overtook her.

Where's the moon? she asked in her dreams as Michael stared out into the bright morning, unable to sleep.

Six

Jimmy Legget's head throbbed and the bright sun hurt his eyes as he squinted at his watch. It was Sunday afternoon and he had not slept for thirty-three hours. Eddie Nickles had offered a few hours' sleep on the couch in his apartment only a few minutes from police headquarters but Jimmy had declined. Certain that sleep was less important than a shower and a change into clothes not reeking of his marathon shift, Jimmy had driven fifteen miles to the Maryland suburb of Bowie, where his wife had sat angrily but quietly reading the Sunday paper while he showered and shaved. He had sipped the coffee she brought to their bedroom while donning his Sunday casuals: a camel's-hair blazer, blue button-down shirt and silk tie, gray slacks, and a pair of cordovan loafers. He had offered Kitty the short version of the "Sorry, it can't be helped" speech. She was angry at having missed the Forrests' dinner party the night before and even angrier at having to spend another Sunday alone. But Jimmy also knew her well enough not to offer the long version, the one that reminded her of the nights and weekends she spent at her job as an accountant during tax season. That version would only have poisoned their relationship for several more days. And so he had kept quiet, kissed her on the cheek, and headed back to the city to meet

Eddie, a Mobile Crime Lab technician, and two crime-scene search officers from the Fourth District.

He had felt fine when he pulled into the parking lot of the Carter Barron Amphitheater a few blocks from Milton Higgs's home. He had even smiled when Eddie Nickles, wearing the same suit he had worn for the past four days, greeted his attire with a suspicious "You expecting maybe someone's gonna be serving brunch?" But he felt terrible now and wondered whether the pain and fatigue were clouding his judgment or whether there really was something wrong about the scene in the alley leading to the back of Milton Higgs's house.

Jimmy stood by a locked gate at the center of an eight-foot-high, wrought-iron fence defining the border between the crumbled pavement of the alley and the smoothed gravel of Milton Higgs's driveway, which led to a four-stall garage. From there he could see what from the front and side of the house was camouflaged by well-placed and manicured growths of holly and spruce. This short block of Eighteenth Street contained not two homes, as he had first thought, but a single residence made up of a large Tudor mansion and a second, smaller stone house that bent around the corner to the north. The two structures were connected by an enclosed walkway whose Palladian windows looked out onto the formal gardens comprising the rear of Higgs's property. Electric eyes at the corners indicated that the fencing that enclosed the entire rear of the compound was augmented by an elaborate alarm system. He looked back down the alley and tried to imagine how much one could see from inside Higgs's house. Although he had no idea where the kitchen might be, unless it was in the far north wing, he guessed that anyone standing there could easily see the entire length of the alley until it doglegged to the left and traveled a short distance to the side street. He could also see the backs of the four other houses that lined the alley, set two each on either side.

They had been there for more than an hour. The two crime-scene search officers had worked their way down to where Eddie Nickles and Mobile Crime Lab Technician Booker Hammond were slowly pawing through the overgrowth of the yard whose perimeter traced the bend in the alley. Jimmy nodded to himself, confirming his own suspicions, and walked down to where Nickles and Hammond had been joined by the two other officers.

"Is it just me," Jimmy asked of no one in particular, "or is there something really wrong here?"

Eddie Nickles, bent over his work and paying no attention to the others, suddenly looked up. "What?"

"Look around, Eddie," Jimmy said. "There's something wrong here."

Eddie looked around, frowning that he had no clue as to what the young detective was talking about. "Whaddaya talking 'bout?" he barked, and looked at Jimmy, whose expression was studiously curious. "Ya mean 'cause we're up here on the Gold Coast? You know, it wouldn't be the first time someone's got blown away for fuckin' with a man with a stock portfolio."

"No, no," Jimmy said slowly, his eyes scanning the whole scene, "I mean right now. There's something real wrong about right now."

Eddie Nickles stood up very slowly, his own eyes quickly surveying windows and corners, bushes and fences, his right hand easing back the flap of his rumpled jacket to expose the service revolver nestled next to his ample waist. Silently, and almost reflexively, Booker Hammond and the two crime-scene search officers formed a loose circle with Detective Nickles, their backs to each other like a small herd of musk-oxen waiting for the wolves. "What is it?" Detective Nickles asked quietly, alert for whatever had alarmed Jimmy.

"I mean look around," Jimmy said. "It's Sunday, the middle of the afternoon, the sun's out, and for more than an hour a Mobile Crime wagon and two cruisers have blocked off the entrance to the alley while five cops take pictures and peck along the ground like chickens looking for grain and not a single soul steps out of their house to see what's going on?"

Booker Hammond rolled his eyes as Eddie Nickles's stomach muscles relaxed and allowed the loose flesh to once again roll over his belt. "Maybe they're all watching the Redskins," Eddie offered with a shake of his head, and Jimmy Legget looked at him with a silent expression that said "Get serious." Eddie just shrugged in response and said, "Yeah, well, we're almost finished here and we'll tap on a few doors and see what happens."

Booker Hammond spoke up. "I don't know about you, but we're finished. I mean we've combed this place, and unless you got a warrant to get inside the fences there's nothing left to comb. There's nothing here, man."

"Wouldn't you think if a man got shot in the back and scraped half his face off falling on the pavement there'd be some sign of it?" Jimmy asked the Mobile Crime Lab technician.

"Not really," Hammond answered. "Look at the pavement. It's all broken up. Mostly gravel now. If they don't leave the body lying there for the blood to pool, one good pail of water'd wash away whatever might've been there. Outside, overnight and any skin fragments would just dry out and shrivel up. You couldn't see it for all the crap around here. You'd have to put the whole place through a sifter, and even then it'd be a miracle if you found anything."

"Nothing, huh?" Jimmy asked.

"Nothing," Hammond confirmed. "No shell casings, although we really didn't expect to see any since Eddie said the guy used a revolver, right?" Detective Legget nodded, and Hammond continued. "Yeah, well, even if it was an automatic and the casings were ejected, they're not in the alley now. Could be in one of those yards on the other side of the fences, but we got no warrants and I've tried all four of these houses for permission to search. Either no one's home or no one wants to answer their door. Besides, man, if someone was careful enough to get rid of the body—if there ever was one—and clean up the scene, you can bet they got rid of any shell casings. You've got nothing here. Sorry."

Jimmy's hand-held police radio crackled suddenly and he listened while one of the Fourth District detectives assigned to canvass the neighborhood reported that they, too, had turned up nothing. No one had heard or seen anything unusual in or near the area of Milton Higgs's house. As instructed, the detectives had covered every house between Seventeenth and Argyle, Upshur and Allison—every house, that is, except that of Milton Higgs and the four houses backing onto the alley. Detectives Nickles and Legget were to cover those personally. Booker Hammond had already determined that there was no response at any of the four houses bordering the alley, and that left only Milton Higgs's house. Legget and Nickles conferred briefly, agreed, and the Fourth District detectives were released.

"Well, dude," Eddie addressed Detective Legget as the other officers climbed into their respective vehicles and prepared to leave, "you ready to meet the biggest doper in town?"

"You ever meet him?"

"Never laid eyes on the man 'cept in some old photos Intelligence had on him."

"What's the book on him?"

"There is no book on him. Lots of rumors. No evidence. Piles big money into political campaigns, friends with all the right people, entertains a lot but all very quiet and behind the scenes. There's been talk for years the funeral business is just a front for his dope business. But as far as I know, no one's got shit on him. That's it."

"Maybe all the rumors are crap," Jimmy offered. "Maybe Wheatley was just trying to come up with a story he could sell to save his ass."

Eddie frowned curiously. "Changed your mind already? A few hours ago—"

"I know, I know," Jimmy broke in, "but last night seems like a long time ago. Maybe I'm just too tired to put any of this together. It just seems to me we better not be jumping to too many conclusions here. Y'know, it's not like we're going in to jack up some street slime."

"Yeah, well"—Eddie frowned—"we ain't going to tea with the Prince of fuckin' Wales, either."

Jimmy persisted. "What makes you so sure he's the Prince of fuckin' Darkness?"

Eddie Nickles had made a career of avoiding explanations of his instincts, uncomfortable with the effort of translating thoughts into words. But

Jimmy knew too much. He had been allowed inside and he had to be kept on track. And so, grudgingly, Eddie tried to explain.

"Look, forget all the snitches who say he's the man. Just look at Wheatley. The man was a stooge. Am I right? They didn't pick him for his brains. Just the opposite. People like Wheatley don't think. They react. They do what they're told and don't ask questions. That's what happened in the alley. They told him not to let the man get away and he didn't. If they told him 'Don't hurt him but bring him back,' he would've run the man down if it took him all night. You don't trust an Adrian Wheatley with judgment calls. And they knew it. Just like they knew he'd never hold up under a beef for killing a cop. He'd do time on a dope charge and never say a word. But killing a cop? No way. He'd react, just like he did. So he had to die, and fast. So far it looks like they've cleaned up pretty well. But it happened just like Wheatley said it did. He couldn't've made that story up. Not and fill in details we know are true. No, a phony story woulda stood out like a turd in a punch bowl. I'd stake my reputation on it."

Jimmy could not suppress a smile that said that wasn't much of a bet these days.

"Fuck you," Eddie responded. And then: "Forget the theories, man. Let's just play the hand we're dealt."

≫ ≪

They could not hear whether the doorbell had rung inside Milton Higgs's home, and Eddie was about to push the button again when the elaborately carved and elliptically arched wooden door swung open. A short, stocky, and very dark black man in a black suit and heavily starched white shirt stood before them and said nothing.

"I'm Detective Nickles of the Metropolitan Police Department's Homicide Branch. This is Detective Legget. We're here to see Mr. Higgs."

"Do you have an appointment?" the man asked.

"No, I don't," Eddie answered calmly, "but I'll have a grand jury subpoena within the hour if that would be more convenient."

The man's expression did not change. "Wait here," he said and closed the door.

"You love doing that shit, don't you?" Jimmy said, shaking his head, and Eddie just smiled. A full minute passed before the door opened again and Jimmy noticed Eddie's strong and negative reaction to the man who stood before them.

"You're getting a little heavy-handed in your old age, aren't you, Detective Nickles?" the man at the door said. He was tall and everything about him seemed thin. His hair, a soft, graying blond, was combed straight back, and there was little definition between his narrow and ascetic pate and the widow's peak. He had a face distinctive for its lack of substance. Even the pale green eyes seemed washed of their true pigment. Hands with long, effeminate fingers reached out from the sleeves of a gray pinstripe suit and were held up almost awkwardly, as if to display the gold linking the heavily starched cuffs. He had the look of a man who showered too often. "Detective Nickles, where are your manners?" The man smiled. "Aren't you going to introduce me to your associate?"

Detective Nickles remained silent for a brief moment, looking almost intimidated, not by the man so much as by his own reaction to him. Finally, Eddie spoke. "Jimmy, this is Victor Stearman. Victor used to be an Assistant United States Attorney here. About ten years ago, wasn't it, Victor?" The man barely nodded, as if he were offended by Eddie's familiarity. "But we don't see much of ol' Victor around here anymore. He hung around D.C. after leaving the DA's office just long enough to make some money off the department in some police-brutality cases. Civil rights, I think they called it. Then he went south—Miami, actually—and rumor has it he's made it big representing the importers of controlled substances. Is that right, Victor? You a big-time dope lawyer now?"

Victor Stearman ignored Eddie and offered his hand to Jimmy Legget, who shook it perfunctorily. "Detective James Legget," Jimmy offered, and Victor Stearman nodded pleasantly.

"What can I do for you, Detective Legget?"

"Actually nothing, Mr. Stearman, thank you. We're here to see Milton Higgs. Could you get him for us?" Jimmy's voice was pleasant but firm, and Eddie Nickles smiled.

"No, I'm afraid I can't," Stearman said. "Mr. Higgs is quite busy right now."

"You representing Higgs, are ya, Victor?" Eddie asked.

"I happen to be an old friend of Mr. Higgs, but for your purposes, Detective Nickles, you can consider Mr. Higgs to be my client. Now, if you would tell me what this is all about, I'm sure Mr. Higgs would be happy to schedule an appointment to see you at another time."

"Victor, do you really want us to haul your man down to a grand jury?" Eddie asked.

"No, Detective Nickles, I don't. And I'm sure the U.S. Attorney would be surprised to learn that detectives are now deciding when and for whom to issue grand jury subpoenas in his district. As I said,

Mr. Higgs is busy now, but I am sure that if he knew what you wanted to speak to him about he would be happy to schedule an interview without the necessity of any subpoena. Does that sound unreasonable to you, Detective Legget?"

Jimmy reached into his breast pocket and pulled out a small leather case containing his business cards. He handed one to the lawyer. "Mr. Stearman, I'm sure you have heard about the police officer who was killed yesterday. The man who killed Officer Arteaza appears to have been an employee of Mr. Higgs. We would simply like to speak to him to get as much background as we need to complete our investigation. My number is on the card. I'll be back in the office tomorrow morning. I'd appreciate it if you or Mr. Higgs could give me a call to set up an appointment. It shouldn't take very long at all."

"Thank you, Detective," Stearman said. "Someone will give you a call tomorrow, I am sure." He then turned to Eddie Nickles. "You know, Eddie, I would have thought you would have learned by now. It was that same attitude that got all your friends in trouble ten years ago." He smiled, then nodded to Jimmy and said, "Good afternoon, gentlemen," and closed the door.

As Jimmy got in behind the steering wheel of the cruiser, he slammed the door angrily. "What the fuck's wrong with you, man? I may be the new kid on the block, but that bullshit back there was lame. I mean, what the fuck? You in some contest to see how many people you can piss off just to piss them off?"

"Back off, Jimmy," Eddie said quietly. "It's no big deal."

"And that bullshit threatening grand jury subpoenas? Man, that lawyer ain't no muff off the street. You can't be running that game with him. Where's your fuckin' head?"

Raising his voice only slightly, Eddie said, "Look, I said it's no big deal. There's just a lot of history there. Stearman's not going to cause anybody any problems. Okay?"

Jimmy's hands clenched the steering wheel as he let his temper ease. "That history got anything to do with the investigation a coupla years ago?"

"No."

Jimmy waited for more, but when it did not come he stepped on the accelerator. As they sped off, Eddie Nickles stared out the side window and said nothing while Jimmy Legget began to wonder whose side he was on.

Seven

There were those who claimed that United States Attorney Thomas E. Joslin had not always been a drunk. But there were those who disagreed. The man did not have a reputation so much as a collection of histories and speculations so numerous and diverse as could support anyone's predisposition toward him. He had grown up six blocks from a meat-packing plant in Central Falls, Rhode Island, and apparently in the shadow of his father, a large, burly man who, before succeeding as one of the largest paving contractors in southern New England, had augmented his wages at the plant by playing right guard for the semi-pro Providence Steamrollers. Tom, the only one of five sons who had never played organized football, often joked that he had made more money in one month as a lawyer than his father had earned throughout his football career.

He was not always so open about his past. Although listed on the forms required for his FBI security check, Tom Joslin never mentioned—and, indeed, had been heard on occasion to dispute—that he had begun his legal career with the D.C. Neighborhood Legal Services Program. Neither did he refer to his nine months as a law clerk with a county prosecutor's office in one of the Maryland suburbs. According to the oral history, his professional career began when the then senior senator from Rhode Island recommended him to the Deputy Attorney General who personally administered the oath Tom took as an Assistant United States Attorney for the District of Columbia. Two years into his three-year commitment, Tom left the office when Devan Porter, the founding partner of Porter & Winston and Tom's future father-in-law, invited him to join the firm as a senior associate.

It was said that private practice had provided Joslin with an income that almost matched that of the trust fund of his wife, Whitney, and that he had managed to avoid the boredom of actually practicing law with long lunches at the University Club and the politics of jockeying for position and influence with this or that partner, client, committee, or congressman. But whatever the truth, it was clear that in his twenty years of private practice, Tom Joslin had prospered under the patronage of Devan Porter, gathering a full partnership, several committee chairs with the local bar association, moderate wealth, and more party invitations than Whitney could possibly reciprocate. He enjoyed a reputation as a competent if uninspired attorney, political but not particularly offensive about his ambitions, which were largely unknown.

Tom Joslin's appointment as United States Attorney had come as a complete surprise to everyone but those who actually had some say in the selection process. The former United States Attorney had been a holdover from the prior Democratic administration, and the Republicans wanted a change. However, there had been few, if any, high-ranking Republicans with significant name recognition who were willing to see their income cut by 50 percent or more to become the top prosecutor in a district that elected no senators or voting congressmen.

Most of the staff attorneys had predicted that Roger Evert, a sixteen-year veteran of the Department of Justice, would be their next boss. But the staff attorneys were notoriously naïve when it came to political predictions and had considered inconsequential the fact that Roger Evert had always registered as an independent. It wasn't much of a contest.

Seizing upon the opportunity to cut down on his firm's expenses and to place his son-in-law in a potentially helpful position, Devan Porter and a host of his Republican friends lobbied hard for, and eventually won, Tom Joslin his appointment. For those few who had voiced concerns about the business of actually running the largest U.S. Attorney's office in the country, an office of more than two hundred trial attorneys, Roger Evert was named Principal Assistant.

That was four years ago and, it was said, about the time that Tom Joslin found that he not only liked vodka, he needed it.

Vivian, Tom Joslin's secretary, blinked at Michael Holden as he walked into the executive suite on Monday morning. "Oh, hi, we've been looking for you."

"So I hear. I haven't seen your name on so many message slips since the days when no one cared where either one of us was."

Vivian laughed and then caught herself. She took her job very seriously. She had once been secretary to Michael Holden and two other trial lawyers, and even now, years after her promotion to the front office, she referred to them as "her attorneys." In her midforties, Vivian had the looks that caused men half her age to stop and take notice and the ingenuousness to blush deeply when they did.

"How's the latest charity ball coming along?" Michael asked, nodding toward the green print glowing above the keyboard on Vivian's desk.

"Stop that, Michael," she scolded, and turned off the word processor's screen with a sigh of relief as if she had just extinguished the dynamite's fuse. There were few in the office who were not aware of the time Joslin required his secretary to spend typing letters and arranging events for his wife and her many clubs and charities. Still, Vivian was embarrassed at being asked to type personal correspondence on government time and government stationery, and even more embarrassed at being caught at it. She immediately buzzed the inner office and announced, "Mr. Holden is here to see you." And, after a moment: "You can go in now."

Michael returned her smile and asked, "Who else is in there?"

"Just Hyskal and Dan McKeethen," she answered, then added, "I think you can handle it."

Michael smiled. "Thanks, Viv, I needed that. And just for you, I'll keep them busy so you can finish that list of invitations."

"Go!" she insisted in a whisper.

"Michael, me boy," Joslin boomed in his annoying affectation of an Irish brogue, "what a weekend, hey? I was just saying to Hyskal, here, you must've really put the fear of God in that man, him killing himself and all." Within the sanctum of his office Joslin too often stretched for camaraderie with jokes that consistently left his assistants uneasy. Hyskal Gaelen was an exception. He always laughed.

Gaelen sat in one of the four overstuffed leather chairs arranged in a loose semicircle in front of an overstuffed leather couch. What appeared to be the last of a danish was perched at the entrance to his already full mouth, while telltale crumbs sprinkled the shelf of his huge belly. "Yummph," he chortled, and several more crumbs were launched onto the carpet in front of him. Dan McKeethen, chief of the Criminal Trial Division, sat opposite him and looked up at Michael with a silent signal that said *Be nice!*

Michael had joined the office within a few months of McKeethen, and for years their careers had run a parallel course until McKeethen grew tired and began to angle for the supervisory positions and away from the trial work and the debilitating nausea and loosened bowels that had preceded his every courtroom appearance. Technically, he was Michael's boss, but the relationship was more personal than professional.

"You're a hard man to find," Hyskal Gaelen said to Michael. "Tom's been trying to get ahold of you since Saturday night." Gaelen seemed more caricature than real: a man with a curious bent toward emphasizing his own worst traits, his immense girth exaggerated by his short stature and an abundance of flesh that popped like blisters from every opening of his ill-fitted suits. He had spent years in the office, and, except for his constant recruitment of assistants to serve on various bar association committees, his years had been spent in relative anonymity. He had tried a share of unnoteworthy cases and had achieved an acceptable but hardly enviable percentage of convictions. Thus it was the subject of much speculation and no small degree of concern that when Roger Evert resigned to accept a partnership with a West Coast law firm after less than a year in office, Tom Joslin had snatched Hyskal from obscurity and appointed him to the position of Principal Assistant. While rumors about the reasons for his elevation ran the gamut, the favored theory was simply that "Hyskal's smoking the man's Johnson."

Michael ignored Gaelen completely and asked, "What can I do for you, Tom?"

Joslin looked uncomfortable and glanced back at the tall glass filled with ice and two fingers of clear liquid sitting on the far corner of his desk. "It's this mess with the officer getting killed on Saturday. Ortega or something?"

"Arteaza," Michael corrected politely.

"Yeah, right, Arteaza. And then his killer hanging himself. Christ! The press is all over us. What the hell went on? I mean, what are we doing about this?"

Michael wanted to ask Joslin if he had any ideas about where to start, but resisted long enough for Dan McKeethen to step in.

"We got a copy of the running résumé Jimmy Legget started. Obviously it's sketchy. Whaddaya think, Mike? Was this guy Wheatley trying to sell a story for a deal, or was he telling the truth?"

Michael hesitated, as if he were contemplating the question while he reminded himself of the agreement reached between him and Detectives Nickles and Legget over breakfast that morning. They would all stick to a skeleton of the truth, leaving out any mention of the Friday-night meeting at Milton Higgs's house or of the dignitaries Wheatley claimed had been there. So, too, would they describe Wheatley's acknowledging the killing in the alley and the shooting of Officer Arteaza, but would state that he had refused to supply a motive for either until he had secured a deal.

Jimmy Legget had been reluctant, at first seeing no good purpose to the deception. But both Eddie and Michael had convinced him that any mention of the mayor or of the "gov'ner" would be coun-

terproductive, generating the interest and interference of every official in both the police
department and the U.S. Attorney's office, not to
mention city hall. With Wheatley's death, his story
would be inadmissible hearsay for the purposes of
any trial, and therefore the burying of that part of
the story had little or no significance. Jimmy had
argued, however, and correctly, that although inadmissible at trial, Wheatley's hearsay could be used
in the grand jury or as the basis for a search or
arrest warrant and that by excluding those parts of
his story from the official reports and running ré-
sumés from the start, they were abandoning any
hope of using the information if they needed it at
a later time.

Michael offered a compromise. A skeleton report
would be prepared for inclusion in the official jackets and would form the basis of all their conversations with supervisors and others, including the
Internal Affairs Division. A second confidential report would be prepared that detailed all the information imparted by Adrian Wheatley and that gave
specific reasons why that information was excluded
from the official reports. The confidential report
would be signed, date and time stamped, and kept
secured but available if they ever needed it. It was
a charade, Michael knew, given the skepticism with
which any court would look upon such a document,
but it satisfied Detective Legget. Everyone was on
board.

Michael was not happy dissembling before
McKeethen, but no more unhappy he supposed
than was Jimmy Legget with their agreement. And
always, like a pebble in his shoe, was Michael's suspicion that something more than political expe-
diency had motivated Joslin's ordering closed the
grand jury investigation of two years ago—a sus-

picion heightened by Wheatley's parting comment. Someone inside belonged to Higgs.

"I don't know whether he was telling the truth or not," he answered McKeethen. "All we can do is try to check out what he said. But my guess is that even if his story was true, the chances of proving any of it are slim at best."

Michael watched Joslin move to his desk and drain his glass. He then started for his private bathroom and, Michael suspected, for a bottle of Stolichnaya stashed under the sink. "Go on, Mike. I'm listening," Joslin said. "It's just this damned high-protein diet my wife has me on. Have to drink water all day long." Michael waited for Joslin to return to the room before he continued.

"Well, like I say, I'm not sure what I believe. First of all, the detectives tell me this morning that they and the crime-scene people scoured the alley behind Higgs's house yesterday and found no sign of anything. Second, a canvass of the neighborhood turned up nothing. You'd think that if someone were gunned down in that alley and the body removed, somebody would've heard or seen something, particularly in that area. I mean, we're talking about a real quiet neighborhood. Again, we've got nothing but Wheatley's word that somebody was killed in that alley. There were no 911 calls, no missing-person reports. Nothing.

"On the other hand, you've got to ask yourself why Wheatley would make up a story like that. It hardly makes sense to implicate yourself in a second murder. And the shooting of the police officer makes no sense. There didn't seem to be any reason for it whatsoever if you discount Wheatley's version as a complete fabrication. Now, we can sit here and imagine the tactical advantage of conjuring up a big lie to sell a deal for killing a cop, but that seems to me to be giving Wheatley more credit than he deserved, particularly since we kept telling him we wouldn't deal away the killing of the officer."

"Absolutely right," Joslin pronounced, fortified. "We don't make deals with cop killers. Not in my district."

"Anyway," Michael continued, "the bottom line is I think it happened like he said it did, but I can't give you any corroboration. We spent half the night dancing around with him until I figured we just weren't going to get any more without making a deal. We just cut it off."

"You spent all night talking about whether he'd talk or not?" Gaelen asked.

Michael stiffened before McKeethen's look again advised calm. "You know how that goes, Hyskal. He was giving up enough to justify pressing him for more. We just kept going until it was clear the man wouldn't go any further. It was a standoff. Figured we could take another crack at him on Sunday, or today, but obviously we guessed wrong."

"You think it was suicide?" McKeethen asked.

"Again, I don't know. Like Eddie Nickles said, the man had had a real bad day."

"You don't think so, though."

"I don't know, Dan. I really don't. I haven't talked to Crowell. He's doing the post."

"The what?" Joslin asked.

"Postmortem. The autopsy on Wheatley," Michael responded. "But Nickles said there were no apparent signs of a struggle. Again, we can come up with a lot of theories to explain that either way. But unless IAD or whoever is going to look into it comes up with a witness or something definitive comes out of the autopsy, toxicology maybe, I suspect it'll be closed as a suicide."

Joslin's intercom buzzed and he moved quickly

to his desk. "Yes, of course I'll take it," he said into the phone and punched the blinking light.

Hyskal Gaelen strained with the effort of getting up from his chair and moving across the room to sit down next to Michael Holden. He leaned forward to speak, as if he had a secret to share.

"Why did this guy Wheatley call for you? Just because he knew one of your witnesses against the mayor?"

"Any port in a storm, Hyskal," Michael said.

Hyskal persisted. "What's this really all about?"

"What do you mean?"

"You know. The killing and all. The suicide. I mean, what's really going on?"

"Hyskal, listen. I've told you what I know. There's nothing more to tell. At least not now. Maybe the police will come up with something, and if they do, I'm sure you'll be the first to hear about it."

Michael glanced past Hyskal Gaelen and saw Dan McKeethen, resting his forehead in his hand, listening to the United States Attorney's end of the telephone conversation. "No, I can't right now. . . . No, I'll get Vivian to take care of that. . . . No, no, it'll be taken care of."

Hyskal leaned closer as Michael pressed back in his chair. "Are you investigating anything involving the mayor?"

Michael looked surprised. "What the hell are you talking about, Hyskal? Whatever gave you that idea?"

"I don't know," Gaelen answered, and straightened up a bit. "I was just wondering, that's all. You know, the guy calling for you specially. Him saying he had information about important people and all that. I don't know. I was just asking."

"Do you know something that I don't?" Michael

asked as he half listened to Joslin's muffled "Yes, yes, I'll let you know."

Hyskal Gaelen sat back and answered, "No, I'm not trying to tell you anything. I'm just trying to find out what's going on. Tom needs to be briefed."

"Well, I don't know what else to tell you."

"You know," said McKeethen, "it's kind of interesting that Victor Stearman just happened to show up at Higgs's house to run interference."

Hyskal Gaelen sat up and asked, "What's that supposed to mean?"

"I don't know what it means," McKeethen answered. "I just said it was interesting. Anyway, where do we go from here?"

"Well"—Michael shrugged—"with a cop dead and a suicide or a murder in the cellblock, we're gonna have to have a grand jury at some point. But for now, I'd suggest we low-key this. I mean, we'll call in Higgs and whoever else we can dredge up, but we'll do it informally. Play the gentleman role unless and until we've got some good reason to play hardball. If we don't have anything, no sense stirring up a lot of dust. And God knows I speak from experience."

Dan McKeethen laughed and Hyskal seemed embarrassed. Tom Joslin hung up the phone and drained his glass. "Well," he said, "I'm sorry for the interruption. There's just never enough time in the day. Look, Mike, I'm glad we had this chance to talk. We really appreciate the job you and Dan here are doing. Don't we, Hyskal? Listen, why don't we get together over lunch and talk this around some more? Give Vivian a call and set up a date when we can all get free. Hyskal's got all the details, right? Good, good. I'm glad we had this chance to talk."

Holden and McKeethen exchanged curious glances but took the signal to rise from their chairs. Michael shook Joslin's extended hand and followed Dan McKeethen out of the office.

As they walked down the hall, Michael asked, "What the hell was that all about? I mean, he calls us in for a meeting and then can't wait to get us out of there."

McKeethen shrugged and shook his head. "You got me. I've stopped trying to figure the man out." After a moment of silence waiting for the elevator, McKeethen asked, "You got time for a cup of coffee?"

Michael nodded. "Yeah, we oughta talk."

"Your place or mine?"

"Neither. Let's go down to the cafeteria."

In silence they rode the elevator to the basement, where they gathered coffee and doughnuts and moved to a table in the far corner, away from the defense attorneys and police officers killing time between court appearances.

The silence continued while Michael debated his divided loyalties. For a moment he looked away from the man who alone had been willing to deflect onto himself much of the internal sniping and second-guessing over the methods and outcome of Michael's prior investigation of the mayor. But Michael had made his pact with the detectives and both he and McKeethen understood the one simple rule that guided them through the often fuzzy distinctions between their personal and professional roles: *If you don't want to be part of the answer, don't ask the question.*

McKeethen finally spoke up. "Do I smell the stench of history here?"

"Uh-huh," Michael answered simply.

McKeethen shook his head slowly. "Are you gonna be able to keep control of it this time?"

Michael shrugged. "I hope so . . . if there's even gonna be a 'this time.' " He hesitated before adding, "Listen, I wasn't just blowing smoke up there. All right, I'm convinced that what little Wheatley said was the truth. The killing in the alley happened and somehow Higgs was involved. And Wheatley didn't kill himself. Someone got to him." Again, he looked away. "Shit, who knows? Maybe he did hang himself. But either way we lost our only leverage. What we've got is in Jimmy's report, and that's not much."

"What are you gonna do?"

"Pray for a little luck, I guess."

McKeethen chuckled a bit, again shaking his head. "You're gonna need it."

"I know. I'm also gonna need some help from you." McKeethen nodded. "I'd like to keep the decibel level down. Keep the politics and the meetings and the memos to a minimum. That's what killed us the last time, and we had a lot more going for us then."

"That won't be a problem, but I gotta tell you that you've got to stop letting your attitude show in front of Joslin and Gaelen. It only makes them nervous. Like you don't trust them or you're hiding something."

"Do you trust them?"

McKeethen shrugged. "If you're asking me if they know when to keep their mouth shut, no, they don't. Do I think they're corrupt? No, I don't. Just too political, too concerned about press relations and all that. Look, why don't we just keep this thing simple? We'll play it by the book for a while. Just give me enough to pass on to them so they'll feel involved. Okay? And if a problem comes up, we'll talk about it. All right?"

Michael nodded.

McKeethen frowned a bit and asked, "Is there something else going on? You've got that dark look."

"It's Katy. She's a little upset about all this. You know, history repeating itself."

McKeethen let out a brief sigh. "Yeah, I can imagine. Mike, listen to me. The bottom line here is that you and I have both been doing this shit too long to take it personally. It's just business, man. Just another case. You gotta keep your priorities straight."

Michael looked at him curiously. "Man, don't you ever get bored writing memos no one ever reads and going to meetings no one cares about?"

McKeethen smiled broadly. "Bored to death. But," he said, "every night I curl up with my wife and not just another case file. And I can talk to my kids without being distracted by the next trial coming up or cops calling me out in the middle of the night for a warrant or whatever. One of these days you'll wise up. You just better hope that when you do, Katy'll still be there."

"Well, on that cheerful note," Michael said, raising his coffee cup in toast. McKeethen, once again, just shook his head and returned the gesture.

Eight

The deaths of Officer Arteaza and Adrian Wheatley displaced nothing. They were simply added to the list. It was late Monday and Michael Holden was struggling to stay alert during the tale he had heard a half dozen times or more. The woman's voice came across his desk as solemn as her dark, blue dress and pillbox hat. In this her last witness conference before the trial set to begin the next week, Clarice Joyner looked just as she had at their first meeting a year before, just days after her daughter's funeral. Michael rocked quietly in his chair, his whole body nodding in sympathy. Only when Mrs. Joyner averted her eyes did he glance at the spread of reports and photographs and witness statements on his desk or to Detective Wallgren, who looked pleased with how well his witness was doing.

The door to Michael's office swung open suddenly and Jimmy Legget started in. "Sorry," he said, stopping abruptly, "I didn't realize you were busy."

"We'll be through in a few minutes," Michael said. "Don't go anywhere. We need to talk." Jimmy nodded and closed the door. "I'm sorry, Mrs. Joyner, please go on."

Mrs. Joyner took a deep breath and continued to recount for the prosecutor the details of finding her daughter lying facedown at the bottom of the basement stairs, the red-and-white-lollipop underpants stuffed in the child's mouth, which gaped so wide that it had seemed the only discernible feature of the bloodied face. The gray, checked skirt Mrs. Joyner had ironed for her daughter the night before was gathered about the waist, the body otherwise naked except for a torn and blood-soaked blouse, which covered only the upper portion of the right arm.

Michael was pleased that his witness's story remained clear and uneventful, that no surprises or gaps had surfaced since he had last spoken to her. Every aspect of this case had been reviewed and rehearsed, including the expected testimony concerning the twenty-six-year-old defendant's signed statement asserting that the twelve-year-old Rene had enticed him into the basement, a statement that the defendant now claimed through his attorneys had been fabricated by overzealous detectives.

Michael's expressions of shock and sympathy were equally well rehearsed. The details of violent death and imaginative brutality were neither new nor shocking, and he regularly received such details with no more fanfare than that which accompanied his morning newspaper or cup of coffee. He no longer cared why anyone would rape and murder a twelve-year-old. He dealt only with the reality that it happened and left the why's and how-could-theys to all those who had never spent a minute watching the coroner pick over a body with less reverence than his father showed for the Thanksgiving turkey.

Thus, as he had so many times before, Michael Holden repeated the rituals of preparing for trial. He knew exactly how his case-in-chief would go and, if asked, could parrot in advance the predictable cross-examinations of the public defender. He had spent days boiling the scientific evidence down to its essence so that the jury would only spend hours listening to the descriptions of the violence exacted upon the decedent's body: multiple contusions and abrasions of the face, chest, knees, and elbows; multiple fractures of the skull, right cheekbone, and nose; linear abrasions on both the right and left side of the neck and the internal hemorrhaging within the muscles that overlaid the thyroid gland and thyroid cartilage; the hemorrhaging within the posterior of the hypopharynx and in the muscles surrounding the horn of the hyoid bone on the right, although the hyoid bone itself was intact; the distended anus, its margins lacerated with associated hemorrhaging and the external presence of fecal material; the multiple lacerations and associated hemorrhaging of the labia and introitus and the presence of intact sperm in the anus but absent from the mouth or vagina.

They, the jury, would have no reason to doubt that the cause of death had been a combination of manual strangulation and blunt-force trauma resulting from the face and forehead having been bashed against the smooth cement of the basement floor, how many times it was impossible to tell, as the neck and throat were clutched in the killer's hands and the gagged mouth could emit no cry for help. Count One.

Counts Two and Three charging rape and sodomy seemed equally certain of proof, although the coroner could not testify to the order of the rape, sodomy, and trauma to the head. He could be certain, however, that at least some violent penetrations had preceded the child's death.

The coroner would also note that the victim was five-feet, one-inch tall and weighed eighty-six pounds. Mrs. Joyner would testify that she had no idea why her retarded but functional child had slipped away from the special classes for the mentally disabled and had gone home that afternoon. The school's principal had called Mrs. Joyner shortly after one o'clock to report Rene missing from school, and the mother had left her job at the Department of Transportation to rush home, where she discovered her daughter's remains. Mrs. Joyner would then be asked to look again at the crime-scene photographs, which showed a gold-colored bracelet lying on the floor a few feet from the body, the bracelet later identified by the defendant's girlfriend as a gift given in celebration of the defendant's return home from the Lorton Reformatory just three weeks before Rene had died.

Mrs. Joyner finished her tale with a deep sigh and an apology for the few tears she could not restrain.

"Please don't apologize, ma'am. Everyone understands that this is not just a case, it's your daughter we're talking about. And you remember that when you're on that witness stand you can take just as much time as you need, and at any time you can just stop and ask for a glass of water or to take a break if that will help you get through this ordeal."

Mrs. Joyner smiled weakly and nodded appreciatively. Michael nodded in return, not bothering to tell her that at just the right moment during her testimony he planned to offer her a glass of water whether she asked for it or not, a tactic often successful in bringing on a flood of emotion and tears that might help drown the defendant's last hope.

Several more minutes passed with the ministerial tasks of arranging for Mrs. Joyner's witness fee and Detective Wallgren's argument via telephone with his sergeant over whether he was to return the cruiser immediately to headquarters or whether he would be allowed to drive Mrs. Joyner home. "Asshole," Detective Wallgren muttered under his breath as he hung up the phone and then, embarrassed, apologized to Mrs. Joyner.

"That's all right." She smiled, and the detective escorted her out of the prosecutor's office.

Michael flopped in his chair and stared at the ceiling until his phone rang. He took the call from Dr. Arthur Crowell, Acting Chief Medical Examiner for the District of Columbia, just as Detectives Nickles and Legget walked into the office, each looking as tired as Michael felt. Eddie slumped in the leather armchair next to the window, while Jimmy mimed his question of whether anyone else wanted coffee. Eddie shook his head, and Michael, exchanging pleasantries with the pathologist, nodded yes and pulled from the bottom drawer of his desk a bottle of Wild Turkey. It was after hours. Eddie nodded appreciatively while Jimmy shook his head and left for the communal coffeepot down the hall.

Dr. Crowell was calling to follow up on his earlier conversation with the prosecutor, which had been cut short. The FBI laboratory, he reported, had preliminarily confirmed what he already knew from his own observation. A strand of hair found pressed into Adrian Wheatley's skin by the coiled shirt wrapped around his throat was from the head of a Caucasian. A second hair sample found on the shoulder of Wheatley's T-shirt was Negroid and appeared to have been treated with a commercial relaxer, unlike the known hair samples taken from Wheatley's body. Other than the ligature abrasions of the neck caused by the shirt, there were no signs of recent violence but for a mild contusion appearing as barely more than a short patch of redness of the skin in the area of the seventh rib on the left side. The bruising was barely discernible to the naked eye and could not be distinguished in the autopsy photos. There was no corresponding injury to the external oblique muscles. Dr. Crowell could offer no opinion as to whether an instrument such as an electric stun gun could have caused the bruise. There were no needle marks or other observable puncture wounds, and the toxicology report indicated no sign that Wheatley had been drugged by anything but the beer he had consumed at Carillo's. With a blood ethanol reading of only .037 that beer would have had little or no effect. Dr. Crowell had requested further tests for some of the more exotic and less easily detected substances but felt certain that Wheatley had not been drugged before the hanging.

Off the record he concluded, "The man either committed suicide in about as easy and painless a way as he could, given available resources, or someone put him under and hanged him. No drugs or rough stuff. Stun gun's as good a guess as any if you don't buy suicide. He could have gotten the bruise by being jabbed with the stun, but he could just as easily have gotten it bumping into something, or even when he was arrested. To tell you the truth, I'm surprised there wasn't more, given the circumstances of his arrest. The hair samples don't help me. They could have come from any number of sources. You're going to need a lot more to show it wasn't suicide. Like I said, if the man wanted to commit suicide, it's as clean and painless a way to do it as any other. Just lower yourself down slowly. The blood to the brain gets cut off, you pass out, and, after a short while, bingo! Not much, I know, but it's all I can give you."

"How are you going to rule it, Doc?" Michael asked.

"Asphyxia by hanging. What else?"

"No, I meant are you going to rule it suicide?"

"For now, 'undetermined.' Maybe toxicology will come up with something more. So far he's clean. Not even any dope. I'm not going to rule it one way or the other unless you guys can come up with something more. Like I said, the stun gun's a nice theory, but it's only a theory, and that's all it'll ever be without a witness. You know that. By the way, you'll be interested in the reason I had to get off the phone before. The body was claimed."

Monday afternoon, twenty minutes before the medical examiner's office had closed its doors, Ada Wheatley appeared to claim her son's body. She held all the required papers identifying her as the next of kin and stared hollow-eyed as they were reviewed by the medical examiner's staff, who in turn gave her the required releases to be signed before the body could be given over to the representatives of the Higgs Funeral Home. Mrs. Wheatley had not said a word. All questions that were asked and the answers that were given, including those attendant to the identification of the body, were relegated to a woman who stood next to Mrs. Wheatley, supporting her physically throughout the process. The woman spoke softly but distinctly and left no doubt that she knew precisely what was to be done. Her name was Elizabeth Henning and she was, according to Dr. Crowell, "a striking woman."

"Elizabeth Henning?" Michael asked, writing the name on a yellow legal pad tattooed with doodles and notes.

Detective Legget looked up from his coffee cup,

his expression stretching into a wide grin. He turned to Detective Nickles, who also smiled and offered his palm for Jimmy to slap silently.

"Thanks, Doc," Michael said, as he watched the two detectives. "No, there's no hurry on the report. Just let me know if anything unusual turns up with toxicology. Thanks."

He hung up the phone.

"Okay, I'll bite," he said. "Who's Elizabeth Henning? I mean, I'm assuming she's the ''Lizbeth' Wheatley was talking about, but who is she?"

"You first, Counselor," Eddie said, raising his Styrofoam cup of bourbon.

"Nothing, except that one Elizabeth Henning, who by the way Doc Crowell says is a real looker, shows up today with Wheatley's mother to claim the body. She does all the talking. That's it, except his funeral's Wednesday at Mount Olivet Cemetery. What have you got?"

"Elizabeth D. Henning," Jimmy Legget said with satisfaction, "1723 Walburn, Northwest, which, by the way, is the house next door to Higgs and backs onto the alley. Anyway, DOB, March 26, 1944. Black female. Employment, Higgs Funeral Homes. And doesn't that raise a lot of interesting questions?"

"How'd you find her? Go up to the house again?"

"Yeah, well, we did, but nobody was home," Jimmy answered. "Really odd. Nobody home in any of those four houses on the alley. So anyway, while Eddie works the streets for a while I sit down at the computer and start tracking back through DMV records for the street addresses on those houses and come up with a driver's license for one Elizabeth Henning. Then I go over to check out the property tax records and find out that the house

Henning's in belongs to Higgs, or at least to his business."

"Okay. So?" Michael asked. "What's the punch line? We've got a forty-some-year-old black female who works for Milton Higgs and lives around the corner from him in one of his houses. So what?"

"Lawyers," Eddie said to Jimmy. "They want everything handed to them on a silver platter. Michael," he addressed the prosecutor tutorially, "what we've got is a real possibility at a weak link. You got a lady obviously tight with the boss. Otherwise she's not gonna be in the big house when the boss is doing business with the governor, whoever the fuck he is, and Roscoe Barbosa. Am I right? Second, Higgs is lettin' the lady live in a house that's gotta be worth two, two-fifty at least."

Michael shrugged. "Yeah. So?"

"Man," Eddie persisted, "Higgs ain't letting no yard niggers live up there. She's gotta be trusted. Am I right, Jimmy?"

Jimmy's silent stare lasted a second or two before he nodded.

"That's right," Eddie said without missing a beat. "So what's she doing with a lame like Wheatley? Who the fuck knows? But there's obviously a relationship. I mean Wheatley couldn't wait to dump on Higgs, but he wouldn't even let us ask about this lady. And now her man gets hung by the boss. Where's her loyalties? Point is, we've got to snatch the lady up and do some talking before she forgets her grieving, if you know what I'm saying."

Michael just shook his head. "Eddie, what makes you think there was anything between this lady and Wheatley? Maybe the man just liked her. Maybe the lady was just polite to the chauffeur—you know, went two or three days in a row without calling him a cocksucker and he appreciated it. Maybe he kept saying she had nothing to do with this because she has nothing to do with this. I mean, I've got no problem pulling her in, but I think you're stretching a bit to think she's gonna switch sides over Wheatley."

"The kid," Eddie said triumphantly. "You forgot the kid."

"What kid?"

The two detectives looked at each other and Jimmy shrugged and said, "I thought you told him."

"What kid?" Michael insisted, and Jimmy explained.

"In the appointment book we found in Wheatley's pocket. After you left we were going through it, asking him about any names that we saw until we came across this name Christian Henning. Suddenly, the man just clams up again, just like he did when we asked him about Elizabeth. Got angry again. Refused to talk about it. And the more we pressed him, he just started acting like he couldn't stay awake, just rambling and not making any sense. But he wasn't that tired, he just didn't want to talk."

"What was the name again?" Michael asked.

"Christian Henning. The address was some school up in Rhode Island. Wait a minute. I've got it in my notes here." Jimmy flipped through his note pad while the prosecutor suppressed his impatience. "Yeah, here it is. Christian Henning, St. Anselm's Academy, Newport, Rhode Island. It sounds like some kind of prep school."

Michael noted the information on his pad as Eddie said, "Think about it. It's gotta be Elizabeth Henning's kid, and what's the chauffeur doing with the name and address of her kid if there's no relationship?"

"Interesting," Michael said. "What else is there that you thought you'd told me?" Neither detective said anything. "Okay, I'll give you a subpoena for Elizabeth Henning for Thursday. If you can't catch her at home she'll probably be at the funeral Wednesday. But wherever you find her, be nice. Tell her if she wants to come in for an informal interview, that's fine. We can put off her grand jury. But be *nice!*" he emphasized again. "The boss got a call from Victor Stearman this morning. Then the boss gives me a call." The prosecutor stopped for a moment and looked at Eddie Nickles, then went on. "Anyway, Higgs is coming in for an interview on Friday. So when you serve Henning, be sure to let her know that Thursday's the day. Either come in for an informal interview or for a grand jury. Whichever. But it's got to be before we see Higgs. And Jimmy, tomorrow how about bringing in everything the police recovered from Wheatley? You know, his wallet, any papers, whatever was in his car, everything—particularly that appointment book. I want to go through the stuff myself."

> ≪

The detectives' attempts to serve Elizabeth Henning with a subpoena both at her home and at the main office of the Higgs Funeral Homes had failed, and so, on Wednesday morning, they were reluctantly going to Adrian Wheatley's funeral. They did not relish the idea of having to serve a subpoena in front of the press, whom they expected would be there in force, not to grieve but to provide some counterpoint to Tuesday's funeral of the slain police officer, an almost garish affair replete with officials competing with one another in their expressions of mourning to an army of reporters.

The rain had stopped hours before the detectives

turned off Bladensburg Road into Mount Olivet
Cemetery. A bright sun was drawing a mist from
the sodden earth as they spent nearly twenty minutes wandering through the cemetery before finding the grave site at the far corner near Montana
and West Virginia Avenues. The ceremony was almost over.

No more than a dozen mourners stood near the
casket draped with a single, large arrangement of
flowers. Several reporters and photographers stood
a discreet distance apart, packing away their note-
books and cameras and preparing to leave. One of
the two photographers still taking pictures was an
undercover narcotics officer who owed Eddie Nickles a favor. The Homicide detectives stood apart
from the others and under a tree about thirty yards
from the grave site.

In front of the grave two people sat in folding
chairs listening to the final words of an elderly minister who held in one hand a Bible and in the other
an unopened umbrella. On the left was a very thin,
elderly woman who leaned forward, staring into
the dark hole before her. The man to her right,
appearing even older and dressed in a dark suit
and white shirt whose oversized collar was gathered
in folds around his thin neck by a narrow tie, held
her hand. "Nate's father?" Eddie wondered. Several young men stood behind the elderly couple,
looking, it seemed, at everyone but the minister,
who was concluding his tribute.

Next to the seated woman, whom the detectives
presumed was Wheatley's mother, stood the
woman they presumed from Crowell's description
was Elizabeth Henning. Both men immediately and
silently began to assess her. Had they not known
her age, Jimmy Legget would have guessed her to
be no more than thirty-five, while Eddie Nickles

would have guessed even younger. Whatever, both
men would agree that she was remarkably attrac-
tive. Approximately five-feet, six-inches tall, she enjoyed a pleasant roundness that was demurely
accented by a straight, navy skirt and fitted jacket.
Her light-gray blouse and blue-and-red scarf
Jimmy would have wagered, even from his distance, were silk, and he was impressed. Her me-
dium brown complexion was clear and smooth, her
face framed by jet-black hair pulled back and woven
in a tight bun, more businesslike than matronly.
There seemed to be no obvious imperfections; even
the slight wrinkles at the corners of her eyes hinted
at a pleasant smile.

Several minutes passed before Elizabeth Henning's gaze turned from the minister and settled
on the detectives. Jimmy Legget returned her stare
but felt uncomfortable doing so. She did not look
away until the minister completed his brief sermon
and the mourners stood and began to walk toward
the cars parked along the street behind them. Elizabeth Henning trailed behind as the others passed
the detectives without notice. She approached them
slowly, confidently.

"Can I help you gentlemen?" she asked simply.

"Elizabeth Henning?" Detective Legget asked.

"Yes."

"Ms. Henning, I'm Detective Legget and this is
Detective Nickles from the Metropolitan Police
Homicide squad. We're sorry to have to bother you
at this time, but we have a subpoena for you."

Elizabeth Henning looked at him carefully but
without expression. "This is hardly the time or the
place for such matters," she said finally.

"Yes, ma'am, we're sorry. But we have tried to
reach you for two days now, both at your home
and office. We really had no choice. This subpoena

is for the grand jury tomorrow morning. We've talked with the prosecutor, and he's agreed that if you'd prefer, tomorrow's session can be informal. Just an interview rather than a formal grand jury appearance. His name is Michael Holden, and his telephone number is at the bottom of the subpoena. If you have any questions you can call him at that number. But in any event, your appearance tomorrow will be required."

Elizabeth Henning took the subpoena and read it slowly. When her eyes lifted from the paper, Eddie Nickles said softly, "You might want to ask yourself which side Christian would want you to be on."

She was clearly startled, and her eyes showed the first hint of an emotion. Defiance. Without saying a word, she turned and walked to the long, black Cadillac that awaited her.

Part II

Nine

Alton Kimbough was on edge. He had warned the governor that attending the meeting at Milton Higgs's home was both unnecessary and a mistake. But for all his admonitions, the governor could not resist the fawning attention accorded him at such gatherings. It was a weakness that Kimbough understood could one day destroy them both. Having spent the last four days in hastily called meetings in St. Thomas and Washington and New York and now Rome, he wondered if that day had come.

Kimbough had survived and succeeded in the world of international drug trafficking by caution and limited ambitions. A man of articulable intelligence and, when necessary, ruthless ingenuity, he had kept both his ego and his greed in check. He was satisfied to play the role of *consigliere*, a facilitator willing to accept as his due a minority share of the business that over the years had allowed him to accumulate substantial but not ostentatious wealth. The business had taken its toll, however, and what had once engendered a sense of reckless excitement now produced only tension. At the age of forty-five Kimbough's reserves of adventure had been spent and he wanted out. If he never worked again, Kimbough could live elegantly and for the rest of his life on the income of his carefully masked investments. But with his share of the reinvested profits from this one transaction, the jobbing of two hundred kilograms of 95 percent pure heroin, his biggest problem would be spending the income generated in the future without attracting the attention of the Internal Revenue Service. The governor had agreed that, if successful, this deal would be their last. But the events of the weekend before had threatened to disrupt their carefully constructed plans. It was now Kimbough's job to repair the damage.

He was not enjoying Rome. In fact, he wondered if he had ever liked the city: the incessant echoes of impatient horns blaring more out of habit than necessity; streets too narrow and crowded, bordered by buildings of stone and marble darkly coated with what looked to him like a millennium of grime. It all offended him. Crossing the street to the small piazza at the top of the Spanish Steps, he thought of bougainvillea and oleander, of hibiscus, morning glories, and flowering vinca and of the sweet, warm air that washed his home in Judith's Fancy on the island of St. Croix. Rome was warm but not sweet and he felt a disappointment that approximated anger. Not once in all his visits had he ever seen the waterfall of flowers that draped the ancient steps in the photographs of every tourist guide and promotional pamphlet. What he saw now was what he had always seen and what he could not look beyond: stone steps and walls that were old, bruised, and pitted, strewn with bodies sweating, sleeping, staring, nodding, and adding with felt-tip markers their own obscene chapters to the history of the city.

He looked with disdain upon the congregation of tourists and hucksters and lamented silently the despoliation that inevitably followed the discovery of something worth seeing—like his native islands, where the cruise ships daily regurgitated wave upon wave of full-grown men in little-boy shorts and their pale, flaccid women who lacked the decency to conceal it. As he crossed the plaza at the bottom of the steps, he was drawn to a tired, old woman who stood hunched over, silently seeking charity from the tide of people moving toward the McDonald's up the street. He dropped a five-thousand-lire note in her basket and walked away, wondering if he had been scammed. It had been a particularly bad week.

He took a deep breath to settle his stomach and turned into the shadows of the Via Borgognona, heading for a small caffè near the end of the street. As he entered, Kimbough looked to the single table at the rear of the room and recognized Tim Carmody by the shock of red hair. He moved confidently toward the man sitting stiffly in a gray wool suit and open shirt, drumming his fingers impatiently on the table. Carmody acknowledged Kimbough with a nod and barely stood to greet him.

The two men sat as Carmody signaled the waiter with a tilt of his head and a muffled "*Prego.*" His every gesture was as thin as his physique, and he asked Kimbough, "What'll you have?"

"A cappuccino," Kimbough answered.

Carmody repeated to the waiter, "Cappuccino. *E mi dia una birra. Perroni, molto freddo. Grazie.*"

The waiter moved away and Carmody turned to Alton Kimbough. "I hope your news is better than the first reports we got."

Kimbough, annoyed that his host had dispensed with the familiar chitchat that usually preceded their getting down to business, shrugged indifferently and spoke in an even voice that gave no hint of the West Indian patois he abandoned off-island. "I thought that Bertini would be here," he said, referring to the man Carmody served as he served the governor. Kimbough preferred Enzo Bertini, a man who masked the harsh realities of their business with a certain antiseptic gentility.

Carmody, on the other hand, was not given to such pretense. "You speak to Bertini through me," he said. "Now tell me your news."

Kimbough, as he had so many times before, suppressed his ego. "The problem is all but resolved. The immediate threat was removed and there is no reason to alter our plans."

Carmody's brief smile signaled his skepticism, and he said, "The immediate threat, as you call it, does not concern us. What does concern us is the future. From what little we know, one of Higgs's people spent an entire night being questioned by the police and a prosecutor. That concerns us a great deal. Higgs's problems are his own but we cannot let them become ours. You understand?"

Alton Kimbough hesitated, watching the expressionless face of the man who kept his right hand forever stuffed in his jacket pocket.

Carmody broke the silence. "What happened?" he asked. "Exactly."

Kimbough scanned the room, wishing to keep his voice low but unable to do so in the din of crowded conversations and jostled china which rattled off the tile floor and metallic furnishings. The setting seemed the very antithesis of secrecy and caution. But he had no choice. This was where they met, always in the same bright corner of the same caffè, always at the same table and at the same time, late in the afternoon as Rome reawakened for the second half of its business day. No, he had no choice. The governor had made that clear. There would be no second chance. Time was working against them, and their arrangement with Bertini was essential. Kimbough suspected that Carmody knew that.

"Last Friday," he began, "there was a meeting at Milton Higgs's house. The governor was there but the meeting had nothing to do with our project here—"

"And what was it about?" Carmody interrupted. "Casinos, perhaps?"

Kimbough attempted to conceal his surprise. Carmody was disturbingly well informed. "Casinos?" he deadpanned.

"Doesn't matter," Carmody said, having already established his advantage. "Go on."

Kimbough welcomed the interruption of the waiter's delivering the cappuccino and a bottle of beer in a small ice bucket. He waited for the waiter to retreat before starting again.

"In any event, the governor stayed with Higgs overnight and the next morning saw a man watching Higgs's house from an alley behind it. Turned out that he was a private detective from St. Croix. From what we have tracked down he was small-time. Mostly peep work, divorces, things like that."

"What was he doing in Washington? Who hired him?"

"We don't know. He was shot before he could be questioned." Carmody sat back with a frown and Kimbough explained. "One of Higgs's security people was sent to bring the investigator in, but he ran and Higgs's man shot him. Killed him instantly."

"What has all this to do with the man the police talked to?"

"It was the same man," he said quietly. "The one who shot the investigator shot the policeman later that day. Apparently, Higgs was meeting with one of the last people to bid on some of our merchandise. That man also went out to help bring the investigator back. But when the man was shot, he took it upon himself to send the killer away from Higgs's place. Under the circumstances, it was understandable. He didn't know if anyone might have seen the shooting and didn't want the killer seen going back into Higgs's place. So he sent him off to some bar he knew until they could figure out how to handle the situation. Anyway, when a policeman showed up in the bar, the man must have panicked and shot him. He was captured just outside the bar."

"And did this policeman belong to Higgs?"

"I didn't ask," Kimbough lied.

There was a moment of uncomfortable silence before Carmody spoke. "Your American friends," he said, shaking his head. "We warned you. Too damned careless. Too quick with stupid violence. That's why we won't deal with them directly, why we have always insisted that we deal through you. We've always trusted your caution. But I'm beginning to wonder. You tell me this man gets arrested for murdering a policeman and then spends all night with the police before he is silenced, and you say we need not worry?"

"Look," Kimbough said, "I understand your concern, but we are confident. We have been thoroughly briefed. We have seen copies of the police reports of the interviews. First, the killer was nothing more than a bodyguard. He had no knowledge of us or our plans. And, of course, no one, not even Higgs, knows the delivery plans. What this man gave the police was useless. His only knowledge was outdated. We haven't used the pickup points he knew of for years and we have no intention of using those networks again. Correct? If anything, his information will send the police in the wrong direction. In fact, we should hope that they take a great deal of interest in all that and spend all their time on it. It will only divert them from us."

"And what about your friend Higgs? What about all the attention of the police and prosecutors on him?"

"We can deal with that. Listen, neither one of us is a virgin here. We've always known that Higgs sometimes gets too close to the edge. That's precisely the reason why we have so carefully planned each of our transactions, why neither Higgs nor anyone else in his organization is told anything until the last moment. Everything has worked smoothly in the past and will work again this time. I am confident of that."

Carmody looked away with a slow shake of his head. "The last time someone argued confidence over caution it cost me a hand and two good friends. I don't intend to make the same mistake again." He looked back, his eyes narrowing, and said, "Tell me, Kimbough, this prosecutor. What does he think?"

Kimbough quickly but carefully weighed his choices. He could feel their plans unraveling. How good was Carmody's information? Could he know that the prosecutor was the same man who had come so close to Higgs two years ago? If not, to tell him would only make him too nervous, too cautious. But if he did know, was Carmody testing him? Trust was a very thin commodity in this business and Kimbough decided to walk the wire. "I don't know, but again I must emphasize that we have read the police reports. We know what they know, and it is nothing. In fact, there is considerable question in the minds of the police whether the killer was even telling the truth about the incident in the alley, whether he might well have been making up the story to secure an agreement. Also, remember that Higgs's man spent most of his time trying to secure a deal by talking in hints. There was no mention of the Friday-night meeting or of anyone that was there. The man was holding back information with which to bargain. The prosecutor, luckily for us, would not bargain without specific information. It was a standoff. And Higgs assures us that we will continue to have access to their files. We can monitor everything they do, everything they know."

"I hope that you're not relying on the assumption that this prosecutor or the police are stupid. It would be a mistake. You may be placing too much faith in the information your friend Higgs says he has. I'm sure you've considered the possibility that the police have purposely not included everything in their reports."

"Whether they did or not isn't important. The point is that the man they questioned could not have divulged our plans because he could not have known them. And other than the target dates and the agreed-upon weight, even Higgs has no knowledge of the delivery plans. We are safe now and will be even more cautious until the deal is completed. And before you say it, I do agree that Higgs may have more attention paid to him at this time than we would like, but that cannot be helped. We cannot avoid him. He has the network to distribute the merchandise quickly and quietly, and for the prices that will support what we have all agreed upon."

"We're not concerned with Higgs's network or what you do with the product after it's delivered. That's your problem. But as for us, we're gonna have to rethink our plans. Wait and see how things develop."

"You're not backing out of our arrangement, are you?"

Tim Carmody leaned forward and spoke slowly. "I said we must wait and see. Bertini will make the decision, but I can guarantee that there will be some delay. New plans will have to be made."

"How much of a delay are you talking about?" Kimbough asked, and leaned forward himself to press a bluff. "You understand that time is critical here. If there's too much of a delay we may have to look elsewhere."

Carmody smiled. "We're not worried about losing a customer. If it's not you, then it'll be someone else. If not this year, then next. But the bottom line is that we are going to take as much time as necessary to be sure we are not delivering ourselves to the police along with the merchandise." And then as an accommodation, Carmody said, "In any event, we weren't scheduled to deliver for another six weeks. Perhaps we will know enough in the meantime. But whether it is one month or three months is of little consequence. If you insist, we will be happy to deliver the merchandise on schedule. But it'll be delivered here, in Europe."

Kimbough had to concede. "You know we're not prepared for that."

"Yes, unfortunately. And we're not prepared to walk into this foolishness created by your friend Higgs."

Kimbough nodded slowly while Carmody took a long swallow of beer and suddenly changed moods. He invited Kimbough to join him for dinner. Kimbough thanked him but declined. "I have a flight to catch," he said. And then: "You know we want this deal. We don't want to have to shop for another one."

"We know that," Carmody said. "We can work this out. We just have to take a little more time and a lot more care about the plans we make. Neither one of us can afford to be rushed into mistakes. The governor will understand."

Kimbough nodded but he wasn't so sure.

Ten

Without thinking, Jimmy Legget flipped on the fluorescent ceiling lights and Michael looked up abruptly.

"Oh, right. Sorry, I forgot," Jimmy apologized, rolling his eyes a bit at the prosecutor's aversion to bright lights, and he flipped the switch to return the room to the somber, yellowed incandescence of a single brass desk lamp. Michael was hunched over a scattering of papers and seemed indifferent to the detectives' presence as Eddie Nickles moved to the leather armchair and turned on a second lamp, sitting next to it. Jimmy sat uncomfortably in the long silence that followed, watching Holden's face gesture confusion, then a glimpse of understanding, then confusion again. He turned to Eddie and shrugged a question, which Eddie answered with an expression that said "Relax, it's nothing personal."

Finally, Michael looked up and said, "Tell me about the gun and whatever we've heard from the lab."

Jimmy Legget sat forward in his chair. "Well, the gun's an Israeli Military Industries Desert Eagle. First one our people've seen. A .357 Magnum, semi-automatic. Takes ten rounds, nine in the clip and one in the chamber. Serial numbers were all filed. Can't be traced. One round missing. They found one shell casing behind the bar, and Firearms says both the firing and ejection marks match the gun. They pulled a bullet fragment out of the wood above the kitchen door. It got pretty well mutilated blowing through Arteaza's skull even before it hit the wood. They say there are some similarities between the fragment and the test fires, but the best they can give us on a match is a possible. Joe's gonna run some more test fires to see if he can raise it to a probable, but positive's not possible." Jimmy grinned but Michael wasn't looking. "Anyway, I checked with the Bureau's lab on Wheatley's clothing. There's nothing there but the hairs the doc told us about."

Michael nodded. "How carefully did you guys look at all this stuff?" he asked, referring to the items recovered from Adrian Wheatley that were now scattered on his desk. On one corner was a wallet that had contained a driver's license and car registration in the name of Joseph W. Bryant; a dry-cleaning receipt; a D.C. lottery ticket; and three hundred twenty-seven dollars in ones, tens, and twenties, which had been separately bagged and marked. Three more drivers' licenses in three different names found in Wheatley's pants pocket were laid out separately. Directly in front of Michael were Wheatley's pocket-sized appointment book and a few odd scraps of paper containing notes in the decedent's scribbled hand.

"We looked through it," Eddie said. "You know, copied down anything that looked like a name or an address or something like that. Why?"

"What do you make of this?" Michael asked, and the two detectives stood and walked over to look at the yellow pad filled with notes and lists of numbers annotated with brackets and asterisks, question marks and arrows. "Did you notice these?" Michael

asked, holding up the pad with a list of numbers
compiled from Wheatley's appointment book:

```
1673051211215
5284670155107
213156322365
51195257888875
1491627622672
31831766713
1102449488494
```

"Yeah," Jimmy answered slowly, almost defensively, "we saw them. Doesn't make much sense,
though. Wheatley faded before we could ask about
them."

"Look again. There are seven different numbers
on seven different dates in this book. Right?" The
detectives looked at each other as if they were
checking on the answers to a quiz. "They aren't
phone numbers or dollar amounts or addresses or
anything that I can decipher. At least not by themselves. They even seem too long to be account numbers. But look at this. In every number the last four
digits repeat in reverse the prior four digits. See?
Five-seven-eight-eight. Then eight-eight-seven-
five. And here; two-seven-six-two. Then two-six-
seven-two. It's the same for all of them."

"And?" Eddie asked.

"*And,*" Michael emphasized, "look at something
else. Either on the same day as these numbers appear or on the day before—each time—you see
these notes that I thought at first were names. See?
'Rich' and then 'Fred' and 'Phil' and this one looks
like 'Bill.' But the more I look at them, they just
don't strike me as names. You know what I mean?"

Jimmy Legget started to concentrate on the notations while Eddie shuffled his feet impatiently.
"The periods. Aren't those periods after the
names?" Jimmy asked, staring at the elementary

scrawl that Wheatley had left behind. "Looks more like he was abbreviating."

"That's what I think," Michael said, pleased that at least one of the detectives was interested. "What if that's not Bill but Bal? What if all of these are abbreviations of places? Like Richmond, Philadelphia, Baltimore, Frederick, or maybe Fredericksburg."

"And the numbers?" Eddie asked.

"Could be anything," Michael answered. "Combinations of amounts, weights, addresses. Who the hell knows?"

"But Wheatley said he hadn't been making pickups or deliveries for what, almost two years? Not since he started driving for Higgs personally. And all these notations are for this year."

"Maybe he wasn't telling the truth, or only half the truth. Maybe he was running his own game."

"Counselor," Detective Nickles offered, "you may be right. But I'll tell you one thing to keep in mind, just like I told Jimmy the other day. Wheatley was simple. Whatever those numbers mean, don't go looking for anything too sophisticated. I mean, if that's some kind of code, either he was just copying down what someone else gave him or it's a really simple code. This was a guy who had to have the same initials for all his aliases. A genius he was not. You know what I'm sayin'?"

Before he could answer, Michael's intercom buzzed. As he took the message from his secretary he began to smile at Detective Nickles.

"What?" the detective asked as Michael hung up the phone.

"Well, you can kiss your weak-link theory goodbye. Elizabeth Henning is here for our ten o'clock appointment and she has brought her attorney with her. Victor Stearman."

Several minutes passed before Eddie Nickles's mumbled obscenities and presumptuous instructions to the prosecutor on how to handle "this toe cheese" ran their course and Michael was able to clear his desk of the exhibits and suggest that the detectives take a coffee break while he talked with the defense attorney alone.

> <

The first meeting between prosecutor and defender is not unlike the rituals of a singles bar, a dance of seduction between two rivals, each speaking with the voice of a virgin and the soul of a whore. The inexperienced or naïve often find themselves pregnant before they realize they've been seduced: a defendant bluffed into a plea with an agreement to testify under the mistaken belief there is enough evidence to convict; a prosecutor dealing too generously too early only to learn too late that his star witness is more culpable than his target. Michael Holden and Victor Stearman were neither inexperienced nor naïve. They had lost their innocence years before and enjoyed the dance all the more for it.

Michael did not send his secretary out to escort Victor Stearman and his client back to his office but walked out to the visitors' waiting area to greet them personally. "How are you, Victor?" Michael effused. "It's been a long time." Elizabeth Henning remained seated as Victor Stearman stood. Michael recognized her immediately from the detectives' description. He made no gesture of recognition but waited for Victor Stearman's introduction.

"I'm well, Mike, thank you," Stearman greeted him. "It has been a while. Three, four years, I guess, since we tried our last case together."

The two men had known each other as coworkers

before Victor left the office and later moved his practice to Miami. Victor still maintained an association with a local law firm and every once in a while returned to Washington to represent a client. Four years before, he had defended one of three men Michael prosecuted for a drug-related contract killing. The fact that the trial had turned into a bitter and often rancorous contest did not prevent either man from indulging in the collegial aphorism of having "tried a case together."

"Mike, I don't believe you know Ms. Henning." Stearman turned to his client, who stood up. "Ms. Henning, this is Michael Holden, the Assistant U.S. Attorney who is handling this matter today."

Elizabeth Henning offered her hand in that curious way some women have, palm down, leaving uncertain whether they expect it to be shaken or kissed. Michael shook it, once. "Ms. Henning," he said.

And she replied, "Mr. Holden."

Michael turned back to Victor Stearman and suggested that they speak briefly and alone in his office before the interview began. Stearman agreed. It was part of the ritual. Elizabeth Henning was escorted into an interior office and seated next to a small table piled with months-old magazines opposite Michael's secretary. She was offered coffee, which she declined, and was assured that the attorneys would not be long. She did not object or ask any questions but maintained a silent poise that was betrayed only slightly by her eyes. She was nervous, Michael thought, as he and Victor stepped into his office and closed the door.

Michael did not sit behind his desk but directed Victor to the leather easy chair as he sat in one of the higher-seated side chairs, allowing him to look down at his opponent. "Business must be booming,

Victor," he started. "You look like you haven't been out in the sun since I saw you last."

Victor Stearman looked like he had always looked, as if he had never been out in the sun. His pale features clothed in a finely tailored, light gray suit and a tie that only hinted at pink, Victor seemed like a wraith of smoke hovering in the soft light of the office. Michael knew this man as much by type as he did personally. He guessed that no one appeared more successful to Victor than a man who had no time for himself.

Stearman smiled at what Michael knew he had taken as a compliment. "Booming's an understatement, Mike. We can't keep up with the work. I keep telling you, you should come down to Miami. There's more business than you can handle and the clients pay up front. There's always plenty of room for someone with your experience."

They continued to stroke each other for several minutes, catching up on the news of mutual friends and feigning interest in their respective fortunes. It was then time to begin.

"Well, Victor, I have to admit I'm surprised to see you. I wouldn't have thought a local matter like this would have caused Milton Higgs to call in a big gun from Miami."

Victor Stearman laughed as best he could and said, "Our firm has handled a number of Mr. Higgs's corporate concerns, and I just happened to be in town when this matter came up. This is just a courtesy to a client. What is this all about, anyway?"

"A policeman was shot and killed in a bar Saturday night, and the man who shot him ended up hanging himself in the central cellblock Sunday morning. He happened to work for Milton Higgs. A chauffeur, I think. Anyway, the police simply want to get a background on everything to close the case out. That's it."

"Then what was all this about some shooting in the alley?" Stearman stopped, then quickly added, "Or whatever it was they were nosing about there for."

Michael wondered whether Stearman's question about a shooting in the alley had come from seeing the Homicide detectives searching the alley or from his having been briefed on the contents of Jimmy Legget's reports. He guessed the latter.

"What shooting are you talking about?"

"I just assumed that whatever shooting the detectives were speaking about must have happened in the alley since there had been a whole group of policemen scouring the alley for an hour or more before they came to the door to ask for my client. What has that to do with the shooting of a policeman in some bar?"

"That's what we're trying to determine."

"Well, are you going to tell me what was supposed to have happened there? In the alley, I mean."

"I'd rather hear what your clients have to say."

"Well, I can tell you that they're just as baffled as I am about this business. Do you have some indication that my client would know anything about the death of the officer wherever it happened?"

"Which client are we talking about here, Victor?"

Victor Stearman was visibly irritated by Michael's refusal to answer his questions but at the same time careful to step around the issue of a potential conflict of interest—ethics dictating that he could not represent one client who might have an interest in testifying against another. "Milton Higgs, principally. I'm here with Ms. Henning as a favor to Mr. Higgs. She works at the main office as a bookkeeper. At any rate, she has no experience in these matters and was understandably hesitant to come down here alone. Is there any reason why that would be a problem?"

"None that I know of," Michael lied.

"Anyway, I take it you're not prepared to tell me what it was the police were looking for in the alley. Am I correct?"

"For now, yes. There was some talk of an incident that was supposed to have occurred in the alley, and we're simply asking all the neighbors what, if anything, they know. Your clients seem to be the only ones who insist on turning this into an adversarial process rather than simply answering the detectives' questions. Should I be reading anything into that?"

"No more, I suppose, than I should read into your detectives' rather silly attempts to Bogart these people," Stearman said. "What is all this about Ms. Henning's son, anyway?"

"I don't know what you're talking about. What about Henning's son?"

Victor Stearman proceeded to embellish Eddie Nickles's remark to Henning at the cemetery as if the reference to Christian Henning had been a veiled threat. "You really should put a lid on that man," he concluded. "You know he barely escaped that civil rights complaint himself a few years back and he doesn't seem to have learned from the experience."

"Victor, Eddie Nickles doesn't work for me. You know that. And I don't know anything about that case and, frankly, don't want to know anything about it. As far as what he may have said to your client, I am sure she could very easily have misinterpreted the remark. I'm certain that you've told her that if she has done nothing wrong and simply tells the truth, she has nothing to fear from me."

Stearman ignored the stock assurances of fairness and said, "I would think in your position you would want to know when your detectives step over the line."

"Victor, when was the last time you asked a client whether or not he really did it?"

"Well, that's hardly the point. The point is that your detectives seemed to have implied that Ms. Henning has something at stake here. Is that true? Has anyone accused her or Milton Higgs of anything? Anything that I should be aware of?"

"I'm not prepared to make any accusations."

"Are you prepared to say whether either one of them is or is not a target or subject of the grand jury?"

"Neither," Michael said without hesitation. However misleading, the answer was literally true if only because no case had yet been opened before a grand jury. "Target" and "subject" were terms of art defined by the level of evidence that might or might not point to a particular suspect. Outside the courtroom, even experienced lawyers rarely used the terms except in the context of the simple question "Are you after my client?" Michael chose to define his terms strictly no matter what targeting might have been in his or the detectives' minds. He had decided, even before Victor Stearman's phone call to arrange the appointment for the proposed interview of Milton Higgs the next day, that candor with the defense would be a tactical mistake.

Michael knew Stearman was not misled. Victor understood the codes as well as he, and more than likely had already gleaned from Michael's responses or lack of them that whatever hammer might have been poised over his clients' heads on Saturday night had disappeared with Adrian Wheatley on Sunday morning. Victor tested his thesis by asking whether the prosecutor intended to put Elizabeth Henning before the grand jury that day.

Michael answered, "No, there's no need for that right now." He had no reliable information with which to confront Elizabeth Henning, nothing that could be used either to encourage her cooperation or set her up for a perjury prosecution if she testified falsely. Putting Elizabeth Henning before the grand jury and under oath at this time, prepared only for maintaining the story line established and rehearsed at least with Milton Higgs, if not with Victor Stearman as well, would jeopardize any value she might have as a witness if for some reason she decided later to switch sides. It was the nervousness in her eyes that let Michael indulge the thought that her switching sides was at least a possibility. But it would take time and luck to find the right incentive.

Satisfied that neither posed a threat to the other, the two attorneys were prepared to go forward with what promised to be a sterile interview. Having no expectation of hearing the truth, Michael's only curiosity was as to the inventiveness of the lies about to unfold, and his only concern was that neither he nor the detectives reacted outwardly to them. The detectives were called in while Victor Stearman spoke briefly and in private with his client. An extra chair and cups of coffee for everyone but Elizabeth Henning were gathered, and for the next forty-five minutes gentle questions were politely asked.

Henning had worked for the Higgs Funeral Homes as its bookkeeper for almost nine years. For the past four years she also had acted as Milton Higgs's executive assistant. Her compensation included living rent-free in the house at 1723 Walburn Street, which was owned by the corporation.

She had been present in Milton Higgs's home on the preceding Saturday morning when Adrian Wheatley was fired by Mr. Higgs for repeatedly showing up for work late and with alcohol on his breath, as he had that morning. No one else was present in the house at the time except Henry Fasoon, Mr. Higgs's butler. Henry, however, was not actually in the room during their conversation with Wheatley. She had been called to the house in order to give Wheatley a check representing thirty days' severance pay. She had been present in the house for less than fifteen minutes before Wheatley left. He seemed angry but had made no threatening or abusive comments. She was not aware of anything unusual occurring in the alley that morning or at any other time. Nor was she aware that the police had searched the alley. Neither Mr. Higgs nor Mr. Stearman had made any mention of that. She had left Washington shortly after noon on Saturday to visit friends in New York and had not returned to the city until late Sunday night. Her relationship with Mr. Higgs was purely professional and she had neither been invited to attend nor had attended Mr. Higgs's dinner party on Friday night. No, she was not aware of whom the guests may have been.

"I can answer that," Victor Stearman said, to Michael's surprise. "Besides myself and Mr. Higgs, the mayor was there. His wife was out of town, I believe. Charming woman, Hazel. And there was Thaler Bernard and his wife. Thaler's with Capital City Bank and Trust, you know. And Ora Fisher and Carlisle Morris."

"Who's Carlisle Morris?" Michael asked.

"He's Congressman Ottley's administrative assistant. Otis Ottley. And, finally, Cecil Belleman and his wife. You know Cecil, don't you?"

Michael did know the attorney who owned a half

dozen restaurants in the Washington–Baltimore area, but only by reputation, much of which centered around Belleman's wife, D'Avonne, an ex-model and sometime actress. Michael nodded and returned to Elizabeth Henning.

Henning answered all their questions without hesitation or emotion, her words spare but direct. Her eyes remained almost entirely on the prosecutor, even when responding to questions of the detectives. It was as if she understood that to be the protocol. Michael was bothered by her stare, not that it was directed at him, but that it was unnaturally concentrated. She averted her eyes only once when Michael asked her what, if any, relationship she had had with Adrian Wheatley.

"I knew him, of course," she answered after a barely perceptible pause, "but only as an employee of Mr. Higgs. I guess I got to know him better in the past year or so when he began driving for Mr. Higgs personally. He would also drive me on various business errands if necessary. But that was all."

"Were you aware of any problems he was having or trouble he might have been in?"

"No, other than I knew that he seemed to be developing a drinking problem in the past few months. We . . . that is, both Mr. Higgs and I—and perhaps others, I don't know—we mentioned to him, warned him, in fact, several times, that if he didn't straighten out his problem he would lose his job."

"Do you have any idea why Wheatley might have needed drivers' licenses or other identifications under three or four aliases?"

"No, I don't. I never knew him as anyone but Adrian Wheatley."

"Did you know that he was carrying a gun on Saturday?"

She looked almost shocked at the question. "No, of course not. I cannot imagine why he would be carrying a gun."

"You've never known him to carry a gun?"

"No," she emphasized. "If I had any suspicion that he or anyone else—except, of course, a police officer or someone like that—was carrying a weapon I wouldn't stay in their presence. Not for a moment."

"Mr. Higgs has no security people who are armed?" Jimmy Legget asked with surprise in his voice.

"The business has a contract with a private security firm, which guards the offices at night. I am sure those guards must have weapons. Other than that, I am not aware of any employee who is or would ever be allowed to be armed. We are a funeral business with various interests in real estate. There is no need for weapons in our business."

"What connection or relationship do you have with Wheatley's family?" Michael asked.

"None, really," she answered. "I suppose you are asking about my handling the funeral arrangements for the family. That was nothing more than Mr. Higgs would insist be provided to the family of any employee. Even though he had been fired and in spite of the tragic circumstances of what he had done, Mr. Higgs still felt that we had some duty to the family. I hope you understand that our providing for his burial in no way was meant to condone what he did or diminish our deepest regret at the death of the police officer. It was simply a matter of trying to help his family through a very difficult time."

Michael was growing impatient with the meaningless questions and answers and knew by Eddie Nickles's obviously tightening jaw muscles that he was having difficulty maintaining his silence. They had agreed before the interview began that no questions would be asked about the notations in, or even the existence of, Wheatley's appointment book. Nor would they ask any questions about Henning's son or in any way suggest Wheatley's hesitancy to talk about them. Michael decided to end the interview. After several minutes of his and Victor Stearman's thanking each other for their cooperation and each assuring the other that if either had any questions or further information they would feel free to call, the defense attorney and his client started out of Michael's office. Elizabeth Henning stopped suddenly and turned.

"I'd like to ask one question, if I may," she said to Eddie Nickles. "How did you know my son's name?"

Before either detective could speak, Michael said, "I don't recall how Christian's name came up. Am I correct? It is Christian, isn't it?"

Stearman stepped in and took her elbow gently to discourage any more conversation. "We'll discuss this outside," he said to Henning, then turned toward Eddie Nickles. "I'm sure the detective's remark was intended only to impress you with how thorough they can be, justified or not."

Michael let Stearman's comment pass and looked at Eddie so that he would do the same. Henning's question interested him. It seemed born of more than simple pique at Eddie Nickles's remark in the cemetery. It signaled vulnerability. It was something to look into.

Eleven

Within an hour of Elizabeth Henning's leaving his office, Michael had Clifton St. John, the headmaster of St. Anselm's Academy, on the phone. St. John was hesitant to speak, even to a federal prosecutor, about one of his students or how the child's education was being financed. Michael understood the headmaster's concerns and indicated that the matter could await his personal appearance before the grand jury.

"Is that really necessary?" St. John asked in a voice that suddenly had lost some of its edge.

"No, sir, it's not. As I explained, it's really up to you. We can take care of this over the phone. But if you're uncomfortable doing that, I'll simply issue a subpoena for you to appear before the grand jury here in Washington next week and to bring with you the school's financial records."

"Well, I suppose it would be easier to do this . . . uh . . . less formally, and we certainly want to cooperate."

Armed with the assurance that a subpoena was on its way, that his personal appearance in Washington could be waived, and with the understanding that it was in everybody's best interests that the prosecutor's inquiries and the headmaster's responses be kept confidential, St. John hurried off to the business office to collect the information he would need when he called the prosecutor back.

Forty-five minutes later, Michael learned that Christian Sevard Henning was a fifteen-year-old sophomore whose yearly expenses for room, board, tuition, and books exceeded twenty-two thousand dollars. Those expenses, plus a two-hundred-dollar-per-month petty cash allowance held on account for the student by the school, were paid by a bank check issued on a trust account in the young man's name.

"No, there's no payor signature as such," the headmaster reported. "You see, it's from one of those bill-payer or telecheck accounts or whatever one calls them. The checks come as a bank draft to the school with the notation that it is to be applied to young Christian's account. . . . Oh, yes, the payments are quite regular and always prompt. . . . Yes, yes, there is an account number listed." The account number at Washington's Commerce Bank and Trust was given. It was the beginning of the trail.

Over the next six weeks, Michael's indifference to the processes of the investigation into the deaths of Officer Arteaza and Adrian Wheatley became increasingly apparent. The detectives spent long days seeking out and repeatedly interviewing witnesses thought necessary for the grand jury—the eyewitnesses to Carl Arteaza's murder, the people in the cellblock at the time of Wheatley's hanging, officers and prisoners alike, the coroner and firearms examiner—only to have Michael shuffle them through the grand jury with little or no preparation of his own. Neither Eddie Nickles nor Jimmy Legget said much, but on occasion they commented to each other on Michael's obvious lack of interest and his growing impatience with the many witnesses they gathered to his office.

The detectives' impatience, too, began to show, and with increasing frequency they voiced their concerns. This was a murder investigation, they argued, and the relevance of Henning's paying for her son's education or Wheatley's scribbled notations seemed at best attenuated, not matters that deserved the priority Michael had given them. At first there were only suggestions, but as time dragged on they began to question openly whether Michael was wasting both his and their time. But Michael ignored their comments, concerned more with another phone call to another bank and with the numbers and notations scribbled on his ever-expanding file of paper.

Over the years Michael had accumulated a Rolodex filled with contacts within scores of banks: security officers, branch managers and records custodians, all of whom were accustomed to the informal processes by which prosecutors could get account information quickly so long as at some point a grand jury subpoena was delivered to cover the bank from any liability for disclosing the information. They were also accustomed to honoring the so-called "nondisclosure letters" by which prosecutors formally requested the banks not to disclose to the account holders the fact that their records had been subpoenaed.

Careful not to deal with any bank at which he did not have a personal contact or a firm assurance of non-disclosure, Michael proceeded to track backward from Christian Henning's trust account. That account, he discovered, was primarily funded by deposits from Elizabeth Henning's personal checking account, which, in turn, was funded by the direct deposit of her paycheck from Higgs Funeral Homes. In early September, however, just before Christian's tuition had been due, there was a short-fall in the trust account. The next day the account received a total of twelve thousand five hundred dollars in deposits from various business accounts in four separate banks. None of the names on any of those accounts was familiar to Michael or to either of the detectives. The only similarities among the accounts were that each was a so-called bill-payer or telecheck account, whereby the account holder, using any touch-tone phone, could call the bank, dial in the account number and a personal identifier code, and direct the payment of monies to whichever creditor the depositor had previously listed with the bank. Once having established such an account, the customer need never appear at the bank or sign a check.

Each one of the accounts in turn led to more accounts, all in different and unfamiliar names, all showing the same pattern of interbank transfers. It seemed clear to Michael that he had just scratched the surface of a money-laundering sys-tem; but it was a system that seemed almost too complex to be useful. It was a maze, and the deeper into it he delved, the more engrossed he became and the greater were the tensions developing among the three men.

The detectives pressed harder and argued with increasing vehemence their objection to the course Michael was following, particularly to his decision not to put either Henning or Milton Higgs before the grand jury. Both were dissatisfied with his re-fusal to follow up on the office interviews of either subject, interviews that had seemed to them obse-quiously polite and devoid of any attempt to do more than allow each to parrot the other's version of events. Eddie Nickles was particularly upset about Michael's refusal to issue grand jury subpoenas for either Roscoe Barbosa or any of the people who had attended Higgs's dinner party the night before Carl Arteaza died, and his adamant objection to the detectives' even approaching them.

Feeling stymied, the detectives chose to follow their own course, focusing their attention on the suspicion that Adrian Wheatley's hanging had been either at the hands of, or with the collaboration of, someone in the police department, and by early December they thought they might have identified a weak link. With Eddie's guidance, Jimmy had begun to concentrate on Simon Taft, the officer who had been on duty in the cellblock the morning Adrian Wheatley died. Although his story, both to Jimmy and to IAD, was simple—he had not seen or heard anything—he had seemed unusually nervous about being approached and had tried to avoid Jimmy's questions with the statement that he had been instructed by IAD not to discuss the matter with anyone. Jimmy persisted, dropping by Taft's house to ask just one more question, suggesting that each was the result of some other tidbit of information they had uncovered, assuring him that they were working directly for the U.S. Attorney and that nothing he said would be passed on to IAD. Jimmy served him with a grand jury subpoena, then immediately postponed the date of his appearance, saying that some other information had surfaced that needed to be checked out before Taft actually testified. After receiving two more phone calls and another visit to his house, Taft began to waver on just how certain was his memory that no one had entered the cellblock after Wheatley had been placed in his cell. It was time to apply pressure.

Officer Taft was again subpoenaed and told to report to Holden's office preliminary to his grand jury appearance. He also was directed not to check in with the police department's court liaison office. On the appointed day, Jimmy met Taft in the outer lobby and escorted him directly to Holden's office, which they entered without knocking. Eddie Nickles sat slouched in the leather easy chair and simply nodded to Taft as Michael introduced himself from behind his desk without bothering to stand or offering his hand.

The plan was simple. Jimmy would conduct the questioning, leading Taft through his story, while Eddie and Michael suggested their skepticism based on information they would not reveal and emphasized that this was Taft's last and best chance to secure with the truth whatever favors or forgiveness he might need from the prosecutor.

"These logs aren't complete, are they?" Jimmy asked almost forty-five minutes into the interview when he dropped a sheaf of papers on Taft's lap.

Taft looked surprised as he flipped through cellblock entry and exit logs seized by IAD shortly after Wheatley's body had been found. "I don't know," he said quietly, and, looking back and forth between the two detectives, "I thought—"

"I know," Jimmy interrupted, "you thought IAD had everything and wouldn't release anything. Right?"

Taft did not answer.

"Look through them," Jimmy directed. "There's a sheet missing, isn't there?"

"Man, I can't tell you that. It's, you know, been a while. I can't remember everything."

"Sure you can," Eddie said. "You know that Wheatley and I weren't the last people to enter the block that morning, don't you? Someone else—a cop, a marshal, or someone signing in as one, maybe someone you had never seen before—came in after I put Wheatley in his cell. And you did your job, right? You signed them in. Whoever they told you they were, you signed them in. Right?"

"Look, you guys are coming in and out of the block all the time. You know, going back to talk to a prisoner or whatever. Happens all the time. I can't remember everyone."

"But you do remember that morning, don't you?" Jimmy pressed. "It's not every day you find someone hanging in his cell. And no matter what these logs or IAD say, you remember that morning. And you know there was one more log sheet that somehow got lost. Isn't that right?"

"I'm telling ya, man, it was a crazy morning. I had that PCP freak in the isolation cell screaming and shoutin'. I couldn't've heard a thing back there."

"No one's saying you did," Jimmy assured him, "but maybe since then you've figured out that the freak could've been a cover, put there to make a lotta noise so no one could hear anything in Wheatley's cell. I mean, even you must've thought it strange the man's case got dropped the next day. And then IAD grabs the logs, tells you not to talk to anybody, and later insists that nothing's missing. I mean, who are you to say, right? It's your word against theirs. Maybe your memory's not so good. You got a wife and kids. Who are you to make waves? Am I getting close?"

Simon Taft sat motionless but his eyes drifted over to the prosecutor. But Michael wasn't looking. His attention was buried in the paper on his desk that he was quietly annotating with penciled check marks.

The silence was broken by the buzzer on Michael's phone. "Yeah, I'll take it," Michael said, while Jimmy looked over to see Eddie's jaw tightening. Michael turned his back so that his voice was barely audible. "Hey, Harry, thanks for calling back. Listen, on that last subpoena, have you got the names on the signature cards handy?"

Eddie turned to Simon Taft and said, "Have a seat outside for a coupla minutes."

Taft stood up and moved to the door. He stopped and turned to Jimmy. "Look, if someone has a log sheet that shows somebody coming into the block after Wheatley, then it happened. All I can tell you is that I don't remember it."

The door closed and Jimmy could see Eddie swelling with anger as Michael ended his brief conversation. "What's the matter?" Michael asked, looking up.

Eddie exploded. "What's the fucking matter? I'll tell you what's the fucking matter! I mean, is our working here bothering you? I hope we didn't interrupt your schmoozing with your stockbroker or whoever."

"Easy," Jimmy murmured.

"Easy, bullshit!" Eddie huffed and started pacing the floor as Michael sat back in his chair, holding his thoughts. Eddie stopped and planted both hands on the desk, leaning toward Michael to voice his frustration. "Man, just tell me what's going through your head. I mean, Christ, you been softshoeing this case from the beginning. You veto just about every suggestion we come up with. You won't let us kick any ass and I don't see where it's getting us. For almost two months you been running this circle jerk with all these banks and you still haven't come up with a single name that means anything or traced a dime to Higgs or anyone else that matters except Henning. And the only thing you got there is that someone's helping her pay for her kid's school. What's that do for us? Shit, maybe you'll find something, I don't know. But in the meantime, you're pissing away any chance we got with these witnesses."

Michael spoke slowly. "Are you talking about Simon Taft?"

"Yeah, for one."

"First of all, I was listening to what went on and it's clear that either he really doesn't know anything, or, if he does, he's not gonna come off it. You guys've been working him for weeks and the most he'll say is 'I could be mistaken. I don't remember.' He knows we can't do anything without the missing log, if there ever was one, and if one does show up he just said he'd agree with it. What's the point?"

"The point is that if we had any chance to squeeze him, your sitting there like you don't give a shit didn't help."

"No, the point is that I put him in the grand jury and we go on to the next step."

Eddie turned away, shaking his head. He stopped just before the door, turned back, and said, "Man, I'm not accusing anybody of anything, but if I didn't know you, I'd be hard-pressed to say you didn't wanna just shove all this shit under the rug. I just can't believe that. Not after all the crap we've been through. Not this time." And he stalked out.

Michael stared at Jimmy. "And what do you think?"

"I don't know," Jimmy shrugged, looking a bit embarrassed. "But it sure seems like all we're doing here is going through the motions."

Michael sat back and took a deep breath. "You're right," he said finally. "That's exactly what we're doing."

"But I don't understand. Why?"

"Because, right or wrong, I'm convinced that's the only chance we have," Michael said to Jimmy's blank stare. "We've been talking for weeks about dead ends, and I keep telling you this isn't a street case. Those methods aren't gonna work. Wheatley's dead and the chances of proving he was murdered or that there ever was someone shot in the alley are virtually nonexistent. And the truth is that we're not gonna get Higgs or Barbosa or anyone at that level unless we catch them in the act or on paper, or with something concrete that doesn't depend on a witness's memory or willingness to testify. And, yeah, I think all these interviews and grand jury sessions are a waste of time—except for one thing. They give us a good cover." Jimmy sat back with a puzzled frown. "Look," Michael emphasized, "I want Higgs to think we're going nowhere. My gut tells me that the answer is somewhere in these bank accounts, and until we find it, I want them to think we don't have it and don't have any idea where to look. Don't underestimate how stupid they think we are. It's one of the few advantages we have."

Jimmy had no answer, or at least none that he voiced.

≫ ≪

It was the third week of December, when Jimmy Legget was about to accept the futility of their efforts, that the first break came. Jimmy walked into Michael's office just before noon, prepared to complain about being relegated to the ministerial tasks of serving useless subpoenas. His voice was flat as he announced, "Tarble went rip-shit when I handed him the subpoena."

Detective Sergeant Ernest Tarble had been put in charge of the Internal Affairs Division investigation into the death of Adrian Wheatley. He had tried to schedule a formal, on-the-record interview of the prosecutor but Michael had refused, saying that he had already briefed two of Tarble's investigators and if Tarble wanted any more information he could talk to his own detectives. Purely as an exercise in one-upmanship, Michael had subpoenaed Tarble to the grand jury, an invitation Tarble could not refuse.

"Fuck him," Michael said with a wide grin on his face and a sheaf of papers in his hand. "Jimmy, we may have finally stumbled onto something."

"Yeah? What is it?" Jimmy asked, encouraged by the first smile he had seen on the prosecutor's face in weeks.

"Wheatley's code. I think we've broken it. Look at this. I just got this stuff from Industrial National in Baltimore. It's the first account to match up with anything in Wheatley's book." He laid out the papers on the desk for Jimmy to see. "The account's in the name of Jervis W. Banyon. Remember that name? One of Wheatley's aliases? The name on one of the drivers' licenses he was carrying?" Jimmy nodded. "Anyway, look. The account was opened on July 10 with a one-thousand-dollar cash deposit. Now go back to that date in his appointment book. See? Here. 'Bal. 1673051211215.' Now look at the account number. '67–3051–21.' See? He's making a note of the opening deposit, 1 for one thousand dollars and then the account number. See?"

"Yeah," Jimmy said, "I see what you're saying, but why the last four numbers?"

"It's the personal-identifier code to call in transfers. It's got to be. The banks won't give that out even under subpoena, but that's what it's got to be. The account holder picks his own and it's an easy way to remember without using the same number for every account. Just reverse the last four digits.

Just like Eddie said. A simple system for a simple man. Where is Eddie, anyway?"

"Hell, I don't know. He shows up for roll call and then splits. I haven't seen him for days."

"Drinking?"

"I don't think so. I really don't. I think he's just off doing his thing. You know."

"Want to give it a shot?" Michael asked, smiling and holding up the papers as if he were showing off a new toy.

"Let's do it."

Michael dialed the Industrial National Bank as he looked down the list of standard function codes he had requested from each bank subpoenaed. Jimmy moved to the second extension and picked up the receiver.

On the second ring, a mechanical voice answered. "Thank you for calling Telecheck. Please enter your account number."

Michael dialed in the numbers 67–3051–21.

"Please enter your secret code."

He entered in reverse the last four digits of the account number, 1215.

"Please enter payee code or function code." And Michael dialed *7#, the function code that called for account balances. The computer's soft staccato reported, "Available balance is thirteen thousand five hundred forty-five dollars and fifty-seven cents."

"Goddamn!" Jimmy murmured to Michael, who hung up the phone looking very pleased with himself. "What's next? What's this all mean?"

"I don't know yet. The whole thing has been bugging me. I mean it's obviously some kind of laundering scheme, but somehow it just doesn't smell right. Considering the kind of money you'd expect Higgs's organization to be generating, these accounts are peanuts. Five thousand here, ten thousand there. And there are so many accounts with transfers back and forth, it's an awkward and inefficient way to go about laundering money. It'd be a lot easier and leave less of a trail to just take it to the casinos in Atlantic City, you know? And the other thing, I really can't believe Higgs would trust information about his accounts to someone like Wheatley."

"That leaves Henning."

"That's right, but what the hell is she doing? And is she doing it on her own or for Higgs? I'll tell you one thing. We've got a lot of paper to chase, but once we find it we might be able to seize all of Higgs's assets just sitting here and dialing the phone." Both men laughed. "Where the hell is Eddie, anyway?"

"I don't know, man. C'mon, let's get some lunch. I'm buying." And the two men walked out, the tension lifted.

> ≫ ≪

It was quiet in the corner where the two men sat hunched over a table talking in voices barely above a whisper.

"I thought maybe you didn't love me anymore."

"I been busy, man. Y'know? Like what can I say?"

"You can tell me why for more'n a month I've been calling you and you won't call me back. And after all I've done for you. Man, I'm hurt."

"Shoot, man, whatjou talkin' 'bout, all you done for me? Ain't done nothin' but run my ass 'round doing shit could get me kilt, threatenin' me with my parole. Man, that's some bullshit. Like you owe me, man, all I done for you."

"What is this? You coming to collect? That why

you called me up all of a sudden? You've got trouble you can't handle and you're coming to me?"

"You owe me, man."

"I thought so." Detective Nickles smiled. "Something's got you nervous and you want a favor. Is that about right? 'Sthat why we're old pals now?"

The man seated across the table from Eddie looked around to the few customers in the chicken joint near the Metro stop on upper Connecticut Avenue, a long way from the haunts where his friends and associates might pop up. He looked uneasy. It was sometimes hard for the man to be taken seriously, his high-pitched, birdlike voice sounding almost comical emanating from his muscular, light-skinned body. He had been tagged "the Peeper" in his early teens and the name had stuck. But few called him that to his face. The Peeper had learned to compensate for his effeminate voice with an aggressive disposition. The official record only hinted at his experiences but included convictions on three armed assaults and a manslaughter as a juvenile; an armed robbery, several drug possessions, and a second-degree murder as an adult.

"Man, I can't go back to the joint," he whined. "I'm tired of fightin' alla time. Lookit these hands, man. I can't hardly make a fist no more. Lookit that."

His hands were badly swollen, the skin rough and appearing about to split, the effects of a heroin habit that had gone on too long. In his midthirties, the Peeper could easily have passed for fifty, and Eddie understood his concern. He had survived solely on his well-deserved reputation for pure meanness. But if he went back inside in this condition, that reputation would be quickly tested, and without the heart or the muscle to remain on top, he would be relegated to a life of doing favors that just the thought of doing would make most men lie awake in a cold sweat. Detective Nickles was enjoying his advantage.

"I heard the Dip took you off the street. That you're at the table with him now. What, you bagging, weighing, mixing? What?"

"Man, like I'm just trying to stay cool. Do my little job and don't bother nobody. Y'know?"

"I understand," Eddie said, nodding agreeably and starting to get up. "Listen, good luck with your little job and let's hope no one bothers you."

The Peeper reached up quickly and put a swollen hand on Eddie's arm. The detective looked down at it, and the hand was slowly withdrawn. "Look, man," the Peeper said, "you right. I need some help. Bad. You know all they gotta do is convict me on any ol' bullshit and I'm in the joint for fuckin' ever. I got a lotta backup time, you know?"

"I could've helped you maybe a month ago when I needed you. But you weren't there. Wouldn't even call me back. Give me a reason not to tell you to go fuck yourself."

"What about that time I gave you the man that gut-shot that old lady, and the time y'all didn't know shit from the guy you found inna trash can. Am I right? You wouldn't a found shit 'cept for me. You owe me, man."

Eddie just shook his head. Some men deserved sympathy but the Peeper was not one of them. "That's ancient history. Unless you got something to say I wanna hear, I got an appointment for a shoeshine."

The Peeper leaned lower, almost into the chicken sitting in its plastic basket, looking intent. "The police was by my place with some papers. My lady told 'em I left town, you know. They left this." The

Peeper pulled a folded piece of paper from his jacket and handed it to Eddie. "Man, you know I can't take another fall. Whatja gonna do for me, man? Whatja gonna do?"

Eddie unfolded a subpoena issued in the case of *United States* v. *Henry J. Coleman.* Below the case number was the notation: "Violation of D.C. Code Sections 22–501, 3202." Eddie recognized the code citations for an armed assault with intent—to kill, rob, rape; could be anything. He also saw immediately that Adonis Smith, aka "the Peeper," was being subpoenaed as a witness, not as a defendant. But the Peeper was too strung out, panicked, or just plain stupid to have made that connection himself.

Eddie put the subpoena in his pocket and asked, "Who'd you shoot?"

"I ain't shoot nobody. Why you gotta say that shit? Lookit these hands. I ain't shoot nobody. You say yourownself the Dip took me off the street. Man, I don't do that shit no more, for real."

"Who'd you shoot, Bo Peep? 'Sthat what they're gonna be calling you soon? Bo Peep?"

"Look, man. Like I didn' shoot nobody 'cept maybe this one dude. And that was personal, man. Just 'tween him and me. Had nothin' to do with business."

"Personal?" Eddie smiled, and the Peeper squirmed in his seat, irritated and nervous.

"Man, like it weren't about nothin'. Like it don't make no difference what it's about. The man was playing the dozens with me. You know what I'm sayin'? It's like the man was disrespectin' me, so like I had no choice but to pop a cap on him. And that's that. Like that's the way it is on the street."

"Well, hell, no problem then. I'm sure the DA will understand as long as it was just personal. Why don't we ride downtown and talk it over with him right now?"

"Man, ain't that some shit," Adonis Smith said, his head hung low and shaking. "I mean, I don't even kill the man. Hell, I don't even try and hit the man and now he's talkin' to the muthafuckin' *police*. Ain't that some shit." He looked up at Eddie. "Man, you gotta help. I'm tellin' ya I can't stand no more time."

"Let me make a call or two," Eddie said, and stood up and walked to the pay phone, not believing how easy this was going to be. The prosecutor listed on the subpoena was in his office and confirmed that Adonis Smith was wanted only as a witness, although no one knew what, if anything, he could say. His name had been given by another witness but no one had been able to locate or serve him for any of the grand jury or pre-trial witness conferences.

"You need him?" Eddie asked, hoping the answer was no. It was. The defendant had already agreed to plead guilty to a simple assault and no one had bothered to notify Adonis Smith to ignore the subpoena. Eddie smiled to himself. He told the prosecutor that he would take care of that little detail and returned to the table at the far corner of the room.

He held up the crumpled subpoena. "Assault with intent to kill while armed, asshole. That's life on top of your backup. You're gonna be somebody's sweet Bo Peep for a long time."

"Man, how's that 'tent to kill? Never even shot the muthafucka. I mean, I just fired off a round to scare the man. I mean, I coulda chase the man down, blowed his head off, you know? But I just let the muthafucka run. How's that 'tent to kill?"

"You're right, man. It's a fucked-up world. You

go ahead and fight it. You got rights. With your record, the DA, the jury, everybody's gonna be on your side."

"Man, ain't that some shit?"

"You wanna go downtown now? Get it over with?"

"You gots to help me, man. All I done for you."

"I haven't heard anything makes me want to help. You're just sitting there feeling sorry for yourself. Maybe thinking about how big a diaper you're gonna be wearing in a year or two. But I don't hear you saying anything makes me wanna sit around eating greasy chicken with you."

Adonis Smith sat silently for a moment. "Whatjou wanna know?"

"Same thing I wanted to know a month ago. What's the word on what happened in the alley behind Milton Higgs's place. They say your boss, the Dip, was there. Is that right?"

"You gonna help me out?"

"You do good and you'll see this paper disappear."

"For real? You can handle it?"

Eddie nodded and Adonis began to relax. "I don't know it all, but yeah, the Dip was there. S'pose to be some other dude got shot by one of Higgs's people. The same man that shot the police. Yeah, the Dip was there. They say it was the Dip's gun ended up shootin' the police. I don't know 'cept the Dip was some kinda pissed off losin' that piece. I 'member him talkin' one night at the table, saying he should never had given up that gun."

"Since when is the Dip working for Higgs?"

"He ain't working for the man. It's more like they's going in together on a deal." Eddie frowned with skepticism, and Adonis said, "Hey, man, like I'm only telling you what I hear. The Dip says he's got a line of some heavy weight at bottom prices, y'know, through Higgs and his man, but the whole deal got put off 'cause of all that went down. Things been kinda quiet since then."

"What man? What're you talking 'bout?"

"The dude Roscoe's there ta meet. El Jefe, man. Like they's all goin' in on a deal, y'know?"

"El Jefe? Who the fuck's El Jefe?"

"Don't know. Like alls I 'member was the Dip sayin' he was ready to go big time, and if ever'body stays clean, we can go with him, y'know? I mean, like that's why you gots to help, man. Like I gots a opportunity here."

"El Jefe, man. Who is he?"

"Like I say, I don't know no names. Just sound to me like not the man's bigger'n Higgs, y'know? And that's some heavy shit."

"What kinda weight are we talking about?"

"The Dip's sayin' he's gonna do ten keys hisself. S'pose to be good shit. I mean really good shit. Ninety, ninety-five percent."

"Don't bullshit me, man."

"I'm tellin' ya. That's what he's sayin'. Ten keys, ninety-five percent."

"Jesus Christ," Eddie said slowly, impressed. "Even at bargain prices ten keys of that stuff's gotta run him two and a half, three mill. Where's the Dip gonna come up with that kinda cash?"

"He's been doing good lately. With all the coke, peoples is needin' more dope to bring themselves down, y'know? So's he 'spanded. Runnin' more people and sellin' only big packages. You know, a hun'red quarters or more. Let somebody else handle the street."

"How many quarters is he doing a day, average?"

"Two thousand, fifteen hun'red maybe."

"Are you at the table?"

"Yeah, sorta, not really. You know, like I'm de-liverin' the packages and collectin'. I ain't doing no cuttin' or baggin'. But I knows what I'm deliverin' and far's I knows it's only me and Moor Man doing that and they's nights I'm dropping off ten, twelve packages, y'know, like a hunnerd quarters each. And I been working steady, man. Six, seven nights a week. That's why I say just leave me be. I's just doing my little job and ain't botherin' nobody. Make my little piece a change and get a billy to boot. Can't get no better. The Dip's been good to me."

"Is Higgs taking the Dip in or what? He getting all his dope from Higgs?"

"Man, Roscoe don't tell me his business like that." Eddie's jaw tightened and his eyes showed impa-tience and the Peeper responded. "Look, all I knows is that it used to be Roscoe's buying half keys or no more'n one key at a time and having to go to New York or Chicago or whatever. And the best he's gettin' is maybe forty, forty-five percent. Even went down Mexico once and picked up some of that brown shit, y'know, tar, but couldn't sell it. You know, nobody knew what the fuck to do with it, y'know, whether to cook it or to chew it or what. Anyways, the last year or more the Dip's not trav-elin' 'cept to take his ladies or somethin' to Atlantic City or Vegas or whatever. And he's gettin' good stuff. Ninety percent. Pure powder. Coupla keys at a time."

Eddie looked straight at Adonis Smith, his eyes narrowing as he calculated in his mind. "Shit, two keys of that stuff'll last him six months at least. What the fuck is he gonna do with ten? He trying to take over the city?"

"I dunno, but ever'body's happy. Nobody fightin' over it 'cept the Chinese once t'awhile. Everybody gettin' good powder and the price's steady, man.

Still gettin' thirty-five, sometimes forty dollars a quarter on the street and the Dip's lettin' 'em have packages for twenty a bag."

"And no problem with Higgs's people?"

"No problem from nobody. 'Cept after that policeman got shot."

"Yeah, and what happened then?"

"Nothin', 'cept the powder's gettin' scarce. The Dip's puttin' in more cut now, y'know, stretchin' what he's got. I guess he ain't got but less'n a quarter key. Been addin' a little sleepin' powder with the bonita tryin' to keep ever'body happy. Y'know, he's got a rep for good dope."

"It's not gumming up on him with the sleeping powder?"

"Yeah, a little. Been gettin' some complaints, but he's gotta stretch what he's got for his customers till the big load comes in."

"When's that?"

"I dunno. For real, I dunno. But the man's been makin' a few calls trying to line up a half key to tide him over, you know?"

Eddie picked up a chicken leg and took a bite as he looked at his snitch in silence. He chewed the meat slowly and watched the Peeper's eyes constantly scan the room and the front door for any sign of someone who might recognize him or, worse yet, recognize him *and* the detective with whom he was eating lunch. Almost a minute passed before Eddie spoke. "Who else was there with Higgs and Roscoe when the man was shot?"

"You mean 'sides this El Jefe dude?"

"Yeah. What else you hear?"

"Nothin' particular. They say Roscoe's there makin' his deal but that's all I hear. The Dip ain't much for braggin' on who he's dealin' with, y'know? Smart 'nough to mostly keep his mouth shut. 'Cept

I's tellin' ya, the man's talkin' some shit 'bout goin' big-time."

Eddie took another bite of chicken. "What's the word on the police and the grand jury?"

Adonis Smith smiled. "That y'all ain't got shit. The word is no one's worried. That's covered. No problem."

"Any word on who's covering for them?"

Nah, no one's sayin' who, just it's covered. The Dip's sayin' y'all can't shit what they don' know when and how much. Y'know, it's no problem."

"But there is a problem, isn't there?"

"What's that?"

"You. You're gonna let me know everything you hear, isn't that right? And you're gonna let me know it as soon as you hear it. And you're gonna find out who El Jefe is. When the load's arriving and where. And any shit about the police or the DA's office or anything else. And you're gonna return my calls just like the old days, isn't that right?"

"You gonna handle my problem for real? No plea, no time? You know the Dip's got peoples watchin' the courtrooms seeing who's coppin' on a deal 'n' all."

"I gotta stretch some on this one 'cause of the charge and your record. But you do good and this thing'll go away. No court at all."

"For real?"

"For real."

"My man! . . . You gonna eat that short leg?"

Twelve

Three days before Christmas, Officer Carl Arteaza's widow gave birth by Cesarean section to a five-pound, eight-ounce baby girl whom she named Alicia and whom the doctors declared would need a heart operation if she were to survive her first year of life. The event was not heralded by the press, which had swarmed over the rituals attending the death of Alicia's father. Indeed, except for family and a few friends, none of the people who had been so concerned about Carl Arteaza's death were even aware of his daughter's birth, not even the prosecutor charged with the investigation of that death.

Within hours after the infant first bellowed her disapproval of the cold world into which she had just been lifted, Michael Holden leaned back in his chair, propped his feet on his desk, and took several quick swallows from a bottle of beer that had sat cooling for a week in a small icebox in a corner of his office. His intercom buzzed and thoughts of ignoring it were raised and rejected in the time it took him to reach for the phone.

"Yeah, Becky. What's up?"

"The front office wants to see you."

"Now?"

"That's what Vivian said. I told her you were back from court but weren't in your office. Thought I'd give you a few minutes to finish off that beer."

He looked at his watch and frowned. It was after six-thirty, long past the time Tom Joslin usually held any meetings. "Did she say what it's about?"

"She just said it was about your case. They want to know what's going on."

"How about calling her back and telling her the jury just went out?"

"I already did. She just said that the boss wanted to see you before you left. Oh, and Dan McKeethen called. He wants to see you, too."

"Okay, thanks."

"Sure. By the way, I've got to work late to finish these pleadings so I might raid your fridge later. Mind?"

"Help yourself, darlin'."

Michael was mildly perplexed by Tom Joslin's interest. His seventh murder trial of the year had been a routine affair of little interest to anyone but the parties involved. The facts were simple enough. Early one January morning, the defendant, Ernest Cooksey, age twenty-three and angry that one of his runners had been robbed of a small package of cocaine, walked up behind the reputed thief, twenty-year-old Antwan Humphrys, and fired four rounds from a nine-millimeter automatic into Antwan's back. Several hours later, while enjoying a haircut and a manicure at a local barber shop, Ernest learned that in fact the real culprit had been Antwan's cousin, Bey Brother. No matter, Ernest had made his point. By local standards, the murder had not been unusually brutal and had involved no one worth noting. The case had no hook to interest the press, which did not attend the trial. Even the courtroom personnel, long since inured to tales of death told by and about an endless stream of anonymous sociopaths, had busied themselves with irrelevant paperwork and muffled phone calls while the witnesses testified and the lawyers argued.

Michael tried to imagine what about the case might have piqued the U.S. Attorney's interest, but quickly gave up the effort as wasted energy. He finished the last swallow of beer and dialed Katy's office before remembering that she was in Chicago on business. There was a certain hollowness to having no one to tell that he'd be late, and so he called her hotel. She wasn't in, and he had to satisfy himself by telling the hotel operator that he'd be late for dinner. He then called Vivian to make sure Becky hadn't confused the message from the front office, and, assured that she had not, he took the back staircase to the executive suite.

Dan McKeethen was seated in Tom Joslin's outer office when Michael walked in. "Are we here for the same meeting?" he asked McKeethen.

"Yeah," McKeethen answered, as he stood and took Michael quickly by the arm and led him out to the hallway. "Did Becky give you my message?"

Michael's expression darkened from one of curiosity to concern. "Yeah, she said you wanted to see me. I just thought I'd drop by your office later. What the hell's going on? Why so serious?"

"Hyskal called me a couple of hours ago to set up this meeting. They want to shitcan the Arteaza-Wheatley investigation."

"*What?*"

"Yeah. That's why I wanted to see you before this meeting. I didn't want you walking in blind, but you've been in trial all day."

"Why? What the fuck's going on?"

Before McKeethen could respond, Vivian walked out of Joslin's office and saw the two men standing in the hallway. "Oh, good, you're both here." She smiled. She picked up the phone and buzzed the inner office.

"Mike, look," McKeethen said quickly and very quietly, "they've been talking about this for weeks. I keep telling them this thing's gonna take time, but the department's really putting the pressure on Joslin. And from what you've been telling me, things look stalemated. Right?"

"Gentlemen?" Vivian called out, signaling that the boss was waiting.

"Just stay cool," McKeethen advised, "but if you can come up with anything to convince them to keep this thing alive, now's the time."

As they walked past Vivian, she spoke just above a whisper. "Now don't you two drag this meeting out. I need to get out of here at a reasonable time tonight." And then to Michael alone: "How's your murder trial going?"

"Okay," he answered, as if to some other question.

It was a relaxed atmosphere that Michael walked into, the overhead lights turned off and the large, expensively furnished office softened to the look of a living room in the mixed light of brass and Chinese-porcelain lamps. Tom Joslin lounged in his shirtsleeves at the end of the sofa, his suit coat draped over the back of his desk chair, twenty feet away, his feet resting on the coffee table in front of him. Hyskal Gaelen sat slumped in the armchair opposite Joslin, his suit coat on but opened to the shirt straining at its buttons. Both men appeared to have just shared a joke, and Joslin raised his tall glass to the two men who had just entered.

"Gentlemen! Thanks for stopping by this late. I appreciate it. C'mon, have a seat. Can Viv get you a drink? Some coffee? Anything?" Both Michael and Dan McKeethen declined, and Joslin turned his attention to Michael. "You've been real busy, I hear, what with this rape trial and all."

"Murder."

"Beg your pardon?"

"It's a murder trial."

"Right, right. Of course. You're gonna get 'em for us, hey?" Joslin was annoyingly upbeat. "Everyone says you're pretty good in court. I used to do a fair amount of trial work myself. Loved it. I miss it, the courtroom. That's what it's all about, right?"

Michael nodded politely along with Dan McKeethen, who had not tried a case in eight years. "It's been so long, I'm not sure I'd know which side of the courtroom to sit on anymore," McKeethen joked.

Tom Joslin laughed and said in a tone that implied serious consideration, "You know, one of these days I'm just going to have to make the time to try a case or two myself. Show the troops how it's done."

"I'm sure the troops would love to see you in action." Michael smiled.

"It's just so hard to break away from all this, you know?" Joslin's arm swept the expanse of office toward his empty desk, and Michael wondered what it was he was gesturing to.

"Anyway, I don't want to keep you too long. What we need to talk about is this Ortega mess. You know, the policeman shooting. Anyway, Dan's been keeping Hyskal and me briefed on how it's going and we're just wondering if it isn't time to wrap that up."

"Wrap it up?" Michael asked evenly. "I'm not sure what you mean, Tom."

"What Tom means," Hyskal Gaelen interjected, "is that from what we've seen so far, the investigation is going nowhere and it seems like it might be time to close it down."

Michael glanced at Dan McKeethen, who took his cue, leaning forward in his chair. "Mike, why don't you just review where we are on this thing?"

Michael nodded stiffly before turning back toward Tom Joslin. "Well, officially, you're right, we're nowhere right now." He regretted immediately the word *officially*.

"What do you mean, *officially*?" Gaelen asked. "Is there something *un*official going on that we don't know about?"

"No, I didn't mean that at all, Hyskal. All I meant was that on paper, it's true, we don't have anything. It's just that we're also convinced that there's more to this than Adrian Wheatley going off the deep end over getting fired and killing a cop and then hanging himself. And I can't tell you that we'll ever find out what really happened or turn up any evidence to prove it, whatever it is, but we're just convinced Wheatley was telling the truth and that his death wasn't a suicide." He proceeded to outline in some detail the information imparted from the many witnesses, conceding that no one had yet admitted having seen or heard anything in the cellblock on the morning of Wheatley's death and that the autopsy and toxicology exams had been inconclusive, at best. He repeated their suspicions concerning the missing log sheet from the cellblock and the two foreign hair samples found on Wheatley's body, but again conceded that without their being able to turn someone like Simon Taft, their prospects were dim.

All three men sat silently for a moment until Hyskal Gaelen spoke up. "And what about all those accusations about some shooting in the alley behind Higgs's house? What about that?" he asked.

"Bottom line is right now we have the word of Milton Higgs and his bookkeeper against the word of a dead cop-killer," Michael answered.

"No one who lives in any of the houses backing on the alley saw or heard anything?" Gaelen persisted.

"The only other person besides Higgs and the bookkeeper who lives there is an art dealer who has a gallery near Dupont Circle. Specializes in African art and he was out of the country on a buying trip the whole month of October. The other two houses are vacant. Actually, one belongs to Higgs that he sometimes uses as a guesthouse. The other one's a rental. The owner said he didn't have any tenants in there at the time. No one saw or heard anything."

"Well, forgive me for saying so, Mike," Gaelen began, "but I'm having a hard time figuring what we've been doing for the past coupla months. I mean, this sounds like just what we had a week or so after this thing started."

Michael bristled visibly. "*We?*"

There was a sudden uncomfortable silence, which Joslin interrupted. "Mike, I don't think Hyskal meant that as a criticism. We understand how hard you and Dan here have been working on this thing." Michael looked again to McKeethen, trying to control his temper. "I guess our question is whether it merits any more of your effort. I know it must be a burden handling this matter on top of your trial schedule."

McKeethen took the lead. "Tom, let me ask you something. I think what Mike and I are wondering is why we need to close it down. No one's being held in jail here. No one's rights are being stepped on. I agree that we've got nothing now, but who knows, something may turn up."

Tom Joslin smiled diplomatically. "Well, the truth is the police department's pushing this. I mean they've got a point here. A police officer was killed and the killer ends up hanging himself in their cellblock. They've completed their investigation and everyone comes up with the same thing. There's no evidence pointing to anything but the fact that Wheatley shot a policeman for reasons no one will ever know and then committed suicide. They want to close it out publicly."

Hyskal Gaelen added, "They particularly want to put to rest any suspicion that Wheatley might have been hung in retaliation for the officer's death."

"Hanged," Michael said.

"Pardon?"

"Hanged, not hung."

"Whatever," Hyskal snapped. "Look, as I understand it, you've already interviewed or put in the grand jury everyone who should have any connection with any of this—and some, like Sergeant Tarble, who don't." Gaelen stopped, distracted by McKeethen's jokingly raised eyebrows and Joslin's chuckling. It was apparent that official complaints about Michael's treatment of the IAD detective had been voiced. "Anyway, what you and the detectives are doing now is just waiting for someone to turn up, a snitch maybe, to see if you can put anything together. Is that right?"

"Well, not entirely," Michael said without thinking. "I've come across a couple of strange bank accounts." The room turned silent, and Michael's stomach tightened immediately with regret.

"What bank accounts?" Joslin asked.

Michael shook his head, allowing his thoughts to regroup, and he formed his lie as he spoke. "I don't know what they mean, if anything. We came across two accounts in the name of one of Wheatley's aliases. But they're all cash in and out. Maybe Wheatley was being used to wash some of Higgs's money. To be honest, we can't trace anything, but who knows, maybe something else will turn up."

Both Joslin and Gaelen pressed Michael for the specifics of the accounts and how they had turned up.

"Just by chance, actually. One of Eddie Nickles's snitches told him he knew Wheatley—actually, he knew him by the alias Joseph Bryant, and that he had an apartment over in Alexandria. When we checked it out with the landlord, we found bank references on the rental application. But again, all we found were cash deposits and cash withdrawals. We can't trace it any further."

Joslin nodded. "Interesting. Hyskal, whaddaya think?"

Gaelen shrugged. "Well, I don't see where that looks any more encouraging than the rest of it." He turned to Michael. "Look, Mike, I'm not trying to second-guess you here, but it seems to me that we don't have any real good reasons to buck the department on this. Basically, we're still left waiting on the possibility of something turning up out of the blue—a snitch or something like that. If that happens, we can always reopen. Right? In the meantime, the department's got a legitimate interest in publicly putting Wheatley's hanging to rest. The question is: Why not?"

Michael sat in silence for several moments, then shrugged and allowed a slight smile. "Because I don't feel like spending the holidays writing up a declination memo."

Joslin laughed heartily and boomed out, "Agreed! I like a man with a sense of humor. No memos. What the hell we need a memo for? We all know what went on. We'll just let the department know. How's that?"

"That's fine, Tom," Michael said. "But I'd like to ask one favor. I'd appreciate it if we could hold off until the first of the year. Jimmy Legget's on leave right now and won't be back until New Year's. He and Eddie Nickles have worked pretty hard on this and I'd like to sit down with them and explain it before they hear it from someone else."

"I don't see any problem with that," Joslin said confidently. "I'll just tell the chief we'll have an answer for him right after the first. Agreed?"

Everyone nodded.

In the hall waiting for the elevator, Michael turned to Dan McKeethen. "What do you read in all that?"

"I don't know. Like I said, they've been leading up to this for weeks." Then, with a frown, he added, "I get the feeling you think those accounts of Wheatley's could lead somewhere."

Michael shook his head, knowing McKeethen was upset that he had not been informed earlier of the accounts. Michael decided not to upset him further. "I don't know, Dan, not really, not with what we've got now."

McKeethen's voice contained no accusation. "I was just surprised, you know, since you hadn't said anything about them before."

Michael averted his eyes with a hint of embarrassment. "I'm sorry if I bent your nose a bit. The only reason I hadn't said anything is that they don't lead to anything. I was just getting a little pissed in there, that's all."

"Yeah, I know. Look, let's just let this ride for now. The case'll be closed down. But if anything turns up, we'll just reopen it quietly. Put it under another heading until we've got something solid. If that happens, I'll cover for you. Tell them it was my idea to keep things quiet. Just let me know what's going on, all right?"

"Okay." Michael nodded.

"Enough said." McKeethen's serious expression lightened suddenly. "By the way, are you and Katy gonna make it New Year's Eve? Rachel's dying to see her again. She always thought you were a jerk to have broken up with her in the first place."

"Yeah, well, tell Rachel I'm dying to see her, too."

"Good. We'll see you about eight," McKeethen said as the elevator door opened and Michael stepped in. McKeethen reached over to hold the door while he remained in the hall. "Relax, man," he urged with a smile. "We can handle this."

"Merry Christmas, Dan."

"Yeah, you, too."

≫ ≪

Milton Higgs's small frame was swallowed by the deep, red-leather chair in his study. Henry Fasoon stood beside him, holding the body of the black telephone as Higgs held the speaker very close to his mouth, puckering curiously between sentences. His voice carried a sense of urgency. "We need this deal to be consummated. Two months may be too late. We have had to go to some lengths and considerable expense to keep our customers happy. . . . Yes, yes, I understand, but we cannot keep control for long without the product. Whatever you can do. . . . Yes, everything is under control here. We have information that the investigation will be closed down by the first of the year."

Elizabeth Henning sat stiff-backed in an upholstered side chair, maintaining a steady gaze at her boss. His gray, almost white, hair was cut close and bordered his bald crown, the narrow skull accentuating his large, black eyes, whose stare at her seemed all the more concentrated by round, rimless glasses. He did not move until he finished his conversation and looked for an instant to Henry Fasoon. The butler hung up the phone, then retired from the room.

"Elizabeth," Higgs addressed her directly, giving a light tug to one of his French cuffs, "have you heard about any subpoenas for bank accounts in Adrian's name or in the names we had given him to rent those apartments?"

She looked surprised and hesitated in thought as one hand moved slowly to her white silk blouse and absently closed the material over a hint of cleavage. "No," she said carefully, "I haven't heard a thing. I don't know about any accounts he may have had except for the little ones we set up to pay the rents. All but one of those were closed long before he died, and the one that was open, I left open. I thought it best not to touch it after the police got involved."

Higgs rose from his chair and moved to a crystal decanter sitting on a sideboard at the back of the room, allowing Henning to draw in a deep breath and let it out slowly. "Yes, I agree," Higgs said, his back still to her. He then turned. "Would you care for a cognac?"

She smiled. "Thank you, no."

He replaced the decanter's top and held the glass to his nose, smiling in that relaxed fashion that she knew signaled concern. "I've been given to understand that this man Holden has come across some account in the name of one of Adrian's aliases. I don't know what that means, do you?"

Henning shook her head before saying with confidence, "I don't think it means anything that we should worry about. Those few accounts were carefully masked. I made sure that every transaction was in cash. I'll check again, but I'm certain that they can't lead back to the business. The one account that was left open was at a local bank—Penn National, I think. I'm sure it's nothing more than that they may have been following up on whatever Adrian might have told them about renting the apartments and how the rents were paid. But it can't lead back here. Adrian made all the contacts with the landlords, and all the deposits in those accounts were in cash. Without his testimony, they won't be able to trace it back."

Higgs spoke carefully. "I depend on you, you know that." Henning nodded. "I know how careful you have been in all this, but I would like it if you could check around as discreetly as possible. . . ." Higgs stopped himself. "Of course you will be discreet. I did not mean to imply that you wouldn't. At any rate, I would appreciate it if you could check around. See if maybe our friend Adrian may have decided to go off on his own . . . if there's anything that could cause us any concern."

"I understand," she said, and began to rise. "Did I hear correctly? The investigation is to be closed down soon?"

"Yes, that's what I am told. But frankly, I'm not sure that solves all our problems. This man Holden seems capable of mischief on his own no matter what his boss may say."

She nodded. "I will check and let you know."

He lifted the snifter in a light toast. "And Christian will be home tomorrow. I know you are anxious to see him."

"Yes," she smiled. "I am."

"And you'll of course join us for Christmas dinner? I hope Christian won't be bored with all us old folks."

"No, not at all. He asks about you often."

"Yes, he's a fine boy. No plans to get away over the holidays?"

"Well, no, I thought with all that was going on you'd want me to be available."

"I do appreciate that. When this little transaction is completed I want you and Christian to take a long holiday. A month, at least, wherever you choose."

"Thank you," she said. "You're very kind."

Thirteen

It was a bitter-cold Christmas morning. The snow that had fallen the day before remained crisp and dry, so dry that the sound of Michael's footsteps as he retrieved the morning paper had an almost annoying squeak about it, like that of a dentist mashing silver compound into his teeth. The sun had not yet reached the kitchen where Michael returned to brew some coffee and heat a raspberry strudel while the old dog lay by the warming oven, her ears cocked at his muttered complaints of the layabout still nested in his bed. A tray was finally loaded with the breakfast offerings and the two went upstairs to the bedroom, where Katy lifted her head and smiled at Michael's "I'm sorry. Did I wake you?"

By nine A.M. they had exchanged their gifts, shared their strudel with the dog, and were on the road to Ijamsville and the farmhouse where Katy had grown up forty miles northwest of the city. The heater in Katy's Porsche did little to cut the chill as they passed in silent mourning the sprawl of suburbs along Route 270, the flat, glass facades of business parks, and the rash of town-house developments erupting more and more on what once had been a smooth skin of pasture and farmland. As the sprawl receded, they returned to their chatter and eventually Katy banked right, exiting onto a two-lane road. For another ten miles they coursed through the back country while the old dog whimpered until allowed to crawl from the rear jump seat to Michael's lap, where she fogged the passenger's window and watched the Maryland countryside pass by.

Approaching Ijamsville from the south, they bounced across a one-lane bridge and turned left just before the village to follow a creek bed bordering the family's farm, known locally as "the old Taliafero place." Except, perhaps, for the new families that had settled in the development that had once been Otho Curren's dairy farm, there were few in the village who did not measure their distances by reference to the farm to which Carl Taliafero had brought his bride in 1873. " 'Bout quarter mile past the old Tulliver place," they would say, Anglicizing the pronunciation as it had been for generations. Or: "Turn left before you get to the old Tulliver place," as if a stranger should know precisely where that place was before he got to it or, even if he got to it, would recognize the long-faded letters TALIAFERO on the top rail of the fence, just below the mailbox, as a sign that he had gone too far. There had not been a Taliafero on the farm since Katy's grandfather was shot by a deer hunter in 1943. But in this part of the country it was the bloodline and not the name on a mailbox that defined the property.

They rolled along the narrow road for another half mile, then turned right onto the hard-packed dirt-and-oystershell drive that climbed a long hill of apple orchards leading to the house. Clearing the bend where the orchard gave way to an expanse of open ground just before the house, Katy spied thick billows of smoke rising to streak the sharp, blue sky.

"Momma's run out of good wood already," she said.

"What?" Michael asked.

"The smoke. They've got a fire going in the new kitchen."

Michael smiled at Katy's unconscious habit of mimicking her mother's description of the kitchen as "new." Although it had been more than forty years since it had been added as a separate wing to the house, to Katy's mother, at least, the kitchen was new, the kitchen of her childhood having been part of the main house since her grandfather first acquired the two-hundred-acre farm and built his home among the oaks and beeches and maples on the crown of the hill.

"What makes you think the wood's no good?"

"The smoke. It's thick. The wood's wet or still filled with sap. She's just getting too old to pay attention to what she's buying. But I'm surprised Vera Lee's letting Chester get away with delivering unseasoned wood."

"Jesus, Kate, Vera Lee's even older than your mother."

"Yeah, but she's as sharp as she ever was. Not like Momma."

Vera Lee Jordan was eighty-one years old and had been working on the Taliafero farm since 1944, when her husband had returned from the war, his right arm amputated above the elbow. Katy's father, the late Colonel "Mad Jack" Reynolds, had returned a year later, physically intact but mentally scarred, and he had spent the next twenty years until his death swapping war stories with Willy Jordan as if they had fought side by side in the same campaign. Willy had the good grace never to point out that while the colonel's tank command was motoring about Europe, he was slogging through the jungles of the South Pacific in a segregated infantry unit. Willy and Vera Lee had lived peacefully and childless in a five-room cottage beyond the high pasture about three hundred yards from the main house until Willy died of cancer on New Year's Day, 1977. By then, Katy and her older brother, "Little Jack," had long since moved away, and her mother, Miss Evelyn, otherwise alone in the huge house, kept hinting that Vera Lee could move into the main house if that would be more convenient. Vera Lee never found it more convenient and remained in her cottage—except when winter came, and the cold and Miss Evelyn's arthritis told her that she might be needed. Vera Lee would then move a few of her things into the guest room at the top of the stairs and stay awhile, almost to April in the past few years.

"Lord, child, you get in here and stand by this fire," Vera Lee ordered Katy as she opened the back door to the kitchen. "Merry Christmas to you, Mr. Mike. Come on in here and bring that raggedy old dog with you."

The kitchen smelled as warm as it felt, and Katy hugged the old woman who barely came up to her shoulder. "Merry Christmas, Grammy. I'm sorry I couldn't get out here yesterday to help out, but I didn't get back from Chicago until last night."

"Don't you mind all that. I got everything cooking and your momma's still upstairs fussin' with her hair. Lord, she's so excited I had to give her extra bourbon last night just to get her to sleep. Don't you go up there just yet. You know she wants to come down those stairs like she was Scarlett O'Hara." Vera Lee laughed and then turned on Michael. "When you gonna marry this woman and take care of her so she don't have to be flying all over hell and gone just to support herself? You're gettin' a mite long in the tooth, you know, and you'd best start thinking about sharin' your bed with somethin' besides that old dog. . . . Get away from there!" Vera Lee snapped at Babe, whose nose was inching toward the four pies resting on the counter. She shooed the dog and then handed her a sliver of country ham, as if no one could see. "Now don't you go lookin' at me that way, child," she said to Katy. "You know what I'm saying is right. Ain't natural for young folks like you to be living that way."

Michael smiled his encouragement to the old woman as Katy protested, "Grammy, please."

"Honey," Vera Lee said, her clear brown eyes fixed on Katy as if Michael weren't there, "I may just be a dried-up old lady, but I remember like it was yesterday, me and my Will. A woman needs a man. You know, in that special way. I'm not talking about workin' and supportin' her. That ain't nothin'. Why, if it weren't for us women, the men-folks'd still be livin' in trees." She nodded at Michael, as if to emphasize her point. "But they sure are nice to have around when you need them. Lord, sometimes I think I can still feel my Will, and that's comin' on to ten years." She drifted a moment with her memory and then said, almost secretively, "There's nothin' wrong with him, is there? You know, as a man? He's not so handsome as your daddy or my Will, but he's not so bad. There's nothing wrong with him, is there?" Vera Lee turned her head to inspect Michael as a deep blush high-lighted the few freckles on Katy's cheeks, and Mi-chael waited for her answer.

"Grammy, can we talk about this later?"

"Child, you ain't got time to be talkin' later. You got to be doing now. I'll go call your momma."

It was a Norman Rockwell day. Michael spent an hour or more splitting firewood beside the barn, not because it was needed, but because he enjoyed it. He had tried to get Babe to join him, but she refused. She had been to the farm before, many times. Too old to romp, she still liked to waddle through the fields sniffing the air for birds, reminding Michael of the winters when she crouched in a blind, shivering in wait for the shotgun's blast and the fallen geese she retrieved from the icy waters of the Choptank River. But today she wanted no part of winter and stayed in her quiet corner of the kitchen near the fireplace.

"Something's not right with that dog," Vera Lee said several times as she'd bend over to scratch an ear and furtively offer a scrap of food.

The women fussed about the kitchen and the final preparations for Christmas dinner. There wasn't much to do, really. The dining room table had been set two days before, and since Christmas Eve morning Vera Lee and Miss Evelyn had been cutting and chopping and peeling and stuffing and baking and brewing until all was ready for the family's arrival. And so mostly they talked. Miss Evelyn brought her daughter up to date on all the gossip around Ijamsville, including the scandal of the antiques dealer from New Market, just across Route 40, who had sold his shop and moved to Alexandria to live with his gay lover. That, of course, only encouraged Vera Lee to question Katy again about whether Michael was, as she put it, "a healthy man."

"Yes, Grammy," Katy said, exasperated, "he is a very healthy man. Too healthy sometimes."

"Has Richard been sick, dear?" Miss Evelyn asked, again confused and forgetting that the man out by the barn was not the man her daughter had divorced more than five years before.

"No, Momma, we're talking about Michael."

"That's good," Vera Lee said, "you marry that man and quit all this flying around and that nonsense in your head, trying to be something you don't want to be. You marry that man and be happy. I know that look in his eye. It's not him that's hidin'."

"It's just not that simple, Grammy."

"Child, it's as simple as you want to make it. You just make up your mind to what's gonna make you happy and you take it and hold on to it and be satisfied."

"Now, Kate, you listen to Vera Lee," Miss Evelyn said. "You married that man and you have to stand by him even if he is sick. When your daddy got sick and when Willy Jordan got sick, you didn't see me or Grammy running off to Chicago or Baltimore or wherever, now, did you? If Richard is sick, why, maybe after dinner Vera Lee and I'll make up some nice soup for you to take back. How would that be?" And so it went.

Dinner was scheduled for one o'clock, and Katy's brother, his wife, and three sulking children arrived at a quarter to. "Little Jack" was six-foot-three and weighed no less than two hundred forty pounds. His wife, Libby, was fully a foot shorter, bone-thin, and wore her gray-blond hair in a bouffant that looked as if it had been freeze-dried in the fifties. Their children, all in their early teens, a boy and twin girls, were three of the homeliest children Michael had ever seen. It was the first time Michael had ever met Jack, a stockbroker in Baltimore. Katy rarely spoke of him except to complain about how difficult it was for her to get him to visit his mother and to help with repairs to the old house. "He's always talking about how fucking busy he is," she had said the only time Michael had ever heard her use that word.

Dinner was served and Little Jack sat at the head of the long table, where the colonel once sat, his mother at the opposite end. Vera Lee sat to Miss Evelyn's left. It had taken several years after Willy Jordan's death and she had begun to spend the winters in the main house before Vera Lee felt comfortable enough to sit with her employer for Christmas dinner. Even now she was unusually quiet. As the dinner wore on, the conversation grew more animated, Jack and Katy and Miss Evelyn trading tales of their youth, laughing at themselves, their friends, and neighbors. They recalled the year Billie Fay Coggins went into seclusion for a month after audibly breaking wind in the middle of her Christmas pageant solo of "Silent Night." And the time Katy caught Reverend Picknel and the widow Armstead skinny-dipping in Luther Powell's fish-pond, and how Miss Evelyn had tried to explain to the seven-year-old child the Baptist rite of total immersion. Even the three sullen children soon warmed to the occasion as the talk flew simultaneously across the table, each person carrying on his own conversation with the others, no one particularly caring who was listening to what. Every so often Katy would turn to Vera Lee beside her and softly share some thought. Once Michael heard Katy mention Uncle Willy, and the old woman smiled and reached over to squeeze Katy's hand.

The table fell silent only once when Jack announced that he had been talking to some Baltimore developers who were looking for large sections of land in the area. Katy stiffened, but before she could speak, her mother said quietly, "My daddy and your daddy and my firstborn son all died in this house and so will I. After Grammy and I are gone you all can sell this place for a drive-in movie if you like. All we ask is that you bury us next to our husbands, and that's all we'll say about that. Now, who wants pumpkin or apple or mince pie?"

The children started calling their choices while Katy and Vera Lee quarreled over who was going to get the coffee and who was going to remain at the table. They compromised and both went to the kitchen. Jack turned apologetically to Michael. "Christ, you'd think I was putting them out on the street. Development's going to come and we can't stop it. Hell, this kind of life died fifty years ago. They just haven't figured it out yet. Might as well be in on the profits while you can and live comfortably from it. You know what I mean?"

"Well, it's none of my business," Michael said, "but I can understand why your mother wouldn't want to leave this place."

"Sure, but you're young enough to take care of yourself. They shouldn't be out here all alone. God knows what could happen to them. Most of the neighbors we knew are gone. The nearest one's almost a half mile down the road. And you know, if anyone, about all the crazies there are out there. Why, just this morning as I'm driving up, I see this man sitting in a car just down the road from the house. Just sitting there, right by the tree line, the engine running and all. And I stop to see if everything's okay, you know? I mean it's Christmas Day and some guy's just sitting by himself in a car. He didn't look like a local or a hunter or anything, so I stopped to see if he was okay. And he just looks at me like I'm the one who's crazy and drives off without a word. I mean with people like that running around, it just isn't safe for them to be out here alone."

"What did he look like?" Michael asked, furrowing his brow slightly.

"Oh, hell, I don't know. Black guy. Not too young, y'know, maybe forty or so. I didn't pay much attention."

"Did you notice the car?"

"It was a Ford or a Chevrolet or something. Nothing special. You know, nothing fancy. Looked kinda like a rental car or something. Why?"

"I don't know. Just curious. Did you see the license plates? I mean, whether they were Maryland plates or not?"

"I didn't pay any attention. Why? Do you think it could've been somebody—"

"Who's having coffee?" Katy interrupted. "And who besides me and Momma and Grammy wants a little brandy?" Everyone volunteered for coffee and brandy, including the children, who laughed, and Miss Evelyn began for the third time her story of the "homo" who had moved to Alexandria. As Katy sat down, she said to Michael, "Grammy wants to see you in the kitchen for a minute."

Michael excused himself and went into the kitchen. Vera Lee was sitting on the floor holding Babe's head in her lap. "This old dog's dying, son. You can call for Doc Pritchard over to Urbana, but the truth is she's just tired and ready to move on."

Michael kneeled down and gently scratched the dog's ear. "Hey, Babe," he whispered, his eyes beginning to fill. Babe's breathing was quick and shallow. She tried, but could not lift her head. Her tail thumped weakly on the pine floor, twice, and her lungs emptied their final breath.

"She's gone, son. With a full belly and by a warm fire. I pray God I die as peaceful." Vera Lee stood up slowly and put her hand on his shoulder. "You set here a while," she said, and returned to the dining room, where Michael could hear the chatter die suddenly. "Leave him be, child," he heard Vera Lee say. "There'll be plenty of time for helpin' in a bit."

Michael had no idea how long he had sat stroking the dog's head before Katy stepped into the kitchen holding an old cuddle blanket she had once clung to as a child. "Do you want us to help?" she asked, as they wrapped the dog's body in the blanket. "No," he said. He'd bury Babe alone.

Katy's mother directed him to a spot near a maple at the edge of the pasture. "The ground's soft there and we grow our flowers just south of that tree. That'll be a fine place to bury your dog." Michael lifted the body and carried it to the spot near the tree. Katy brought a pick and shovel from the barn and then left him to his work. Once he broke through the frozen crust, the earth was soft. He dug slowly for more than a half hour and then placed the body in the earth. He stood silent for a few minutes before he filled the grave with the rich soil, then returned to the house.

"That's done," Vera Lee said. "Now let's sit us down and have some brandy."

The mood lightened, and Michael was glad for it. Soon they were trading old dog stories, Vera Lee taking particular delight in recounting the battles between Katy's father and the stray basset hound her Will had adopted. "That old hound'd hold his water all day just waiting for the colonel to drive up in that brand-new Oldsmobile. Soon's he'd hear that car coming up the hill he take off to running from wherever. No sooner'd the colonel turn his back, he'd just lift his leg and pee all over them new whitewall tires."

By seven-thirty, Jack and his family had left to return to Baltimore. "A big day ahead of me tomorrow," he had announced, as Katy had predicted he would. She and Michael and the two old women retired to the kitchen for more coffee and brandy and to gab while they washed dishes and stored away the mounds of food left over from the feast. An hour later Miss Evelyn and Vera Lee were both worn out and a little tipsy. They agreed that it had been a fine Christmas. Even the dog's death was a good sign, they thought, that they, too, might look forward to just such a passing. As they were saying their good-nights, the phone rang and Vera Lee answered it.

"It's for you," she said to Michael, who took the phone as Katy hugged her mother and Grammy good-night.

It was a woman's voice on the other end of the line. "This is Elizabeth Henning," she said. "It's time for us to talk. Not now but tomorrow. I think we can help each other. You don't need to say anything, but just listen. You must know you're being watched. Just the fact that I know how and where to reach you must tell you something. I'll be at the arboretum tomorrow at two. At the entrance to the bonsai exhibit. Do you know where that is?"

"Yes," Michael said simply.

"I think we should talk," she continued. "I think you should meet me there. Just us, no one else. We can help each other, Mr. Holden, but if you show up with anyone else, that's the end of it." The voice was controlled, almost soft, and gave him no opportunity for a response before it hung up.

Michael was frozen. It took him a moment to slow his breathing and to say good-night to Katy's mother and Vera Lee.

"What was that?" Katy asked after the two women had retired.

"I don't know . . . wrong number," he said, trying hard to sound unconcerned.

"But Grammy said—"

"No, it was just a wrong number."

Katy started a frown but let it go as she pulled Michael into the living room and sat him down on the couch while she stoked the fire. Returning to the couch, she sat down, pulled her feet up, and rested her head on his chest. "I'm so sorry about Babe," she said, and a tear fell to his sweater. "I hope Momma and Grammy didn't upset you talking like her dying just capped off a perfect Christmas. But you know what they meant, don't you?"

"Yes, I know. They were sweet. And they're right. What better way to die than that? I'm okay. Really."

"I'm going to miss her," Katy said, then paused. "Do we have to go back to the city tomorrow?"

Michael took his time before answering her with a question. "Do you ever think about someday not going back to the city at all?"

She sat up a bit and looked at him. "What do you mean?"

"I don't know. Sometimes I think it's time to move on. Do you ever think about that?"

"Not really. Should I?"

Michael stared at the fire and nodded slowly, not so much in answer as in thought. "Listen," he said finally, "I've got to go back to take care of something tomorrow afternoon. Why don't you stay here and

I'll just drive in for the afternoon and come back out tomorrow night."

"We'll talk about it in the morning," Katy said, again resting her head against him. "If I let you go back there alone, I might not see you again. You have a bad habit of disappearing on me."

Fourteen

Aaron Yozkowitz cursed the cold Christmas night as he leaned back in his chair, his long legs bicycling in an attempt to keep the arthritic knees limber. And he cursed himself for not remembering the space heater that would have kept the van warm while it sat just outside the range of a streetlamp, its engine turned off and silent, its driver's compartment sealed off from the rear by a thick, black curtain. The oversight seemed all the more exaggerated by its uniqueness. It was his strength, attending to details, a strength upon which both his livelihood and safety depended. Only twice in the past eighteen years had anyone discovered one of Aaron Yozkowitz's listening devices or hidden cameras, and both of those times had been during the early years with the FBI, when it had not mattered. His defensive record was even better. Since leaving the Bureau, not a single client had ever been arrested or prosecuted on the basis of information gathered by electronic surveillance. He was one of the best, known in the trade as the Wizard of Yoz.

"C'mon man, enough talk, let's get on with it," Yozkowitz murmured impatiently to the images on one of three small television screens mounted above a console glowing green and red with the digital readouts of his multiple recorders and monitors. He reached over and lightly adjusted several dials, enhancing the recording level of the target's voice while muffling the interference from the sound-track of the pornographic video playing on the television inside the apartment's bedroom. The target, fascinated with the film he was watching, stared directly and obliviously into the lens of a video camera that captured his every expression. Nor was he aware that his obscene supplications of the young man beside him were being recorded with exceptional clarity.

Satisfied that all recording levels were properly set, Yozkowitz removed his earphones and reached for the remains of a pepperoni pizza and a dog-eared paperback novel. He had no interest in watching the pathetic sexual aberrations that the short, fat man was about to practice upon the young man hired for the occasion by Yozkowitz's client. In fact, he had little interest in this type of peep work. It offered no real challenge and little satisfaction—not like the time he had placed a device inside a prosecutor's office and listened while the FBI swept the office for bugs and declared it clean. *That* was satisfaction. But with hefty mortgages on his home in Potomac and the condominium in Miami, two children in college, and an ever-increasing cocaine habit, he could not afford to turn down the work.

A dozen pages passed before Yozkowitz glanced casually at the silent screen. The target was pacing the room, agitated, and Yozkowitz noticed that the audio readout for the television microphone was still. The tape counter had stopped at 1648, indicating that the film *Lucky in Lust* had been turned off mid-delictum. For a brief moment he returned to his book, but only for a moment, before his eyes were drawn back to the screen. Focusing now on the target's silent movements, he tossed the book aside, slid the headphones over his ears, and turned up the volume.

"Oh, fuck, please talk to me," Yozkowitz heard the target plead as he paced the room, pulling at his undershirt on which appeared a smeared stain where he kept wiping his right hand.

The target's young companion was not within camera view and Yozkowitz quickly flipped the switches that activated two other video monitors, giving him a fish-eye view of the interior of the bathroom and a wide-angle view of the apartment's living room and kitchenette. No one appeared on either monitor. Yozkowitz flipped the audio switches for all six secreted microphones. There was no sound other than the target's frenzied monologue.

"Talk to me. Please, I didn't mean it. Please talk to me, please." The target's face glistened with perspiration as he moved toward the primary camera and dropped to his knees so that Yozkowitz could see only the top of his head and shoulders. "Talk to me, you whore!" the man shouted angrily. "Talk to me or I'll kill you. You want more? You want . . . ?" But he could not finish his thought, his speech swallowed by heavy, sucking breaths as his hands pounded toward the floor and out of view of the camera. Yozkowitz could see the man weakening with each successive strike until he sat back on his haunches and raised his hands in front of his face. The fleshy fists were clearly bloodied.

"*Oh, shit,*" Yozkowitz groaned, cupping his own hand over his mouth. He reached for the phone on the console and dialed quickly. "You've got serious trouble at the Southeast apartment," he reported nervously, watching the target stumble from camera one to camera two and scoop water to his mouth. All the cameras and microphones were activated and the flashing bars of red and green danced with every movement within the apartment—with the flushing of the toilet and the rush of water washing blood from shaking hands and a heavy glass ashtray left on the sink, with the man's frantic, half-weeping mutterings as he swept through the apartment wiping down the smooth surfaces with a towel, with the rustle of a suit donned hurriedly and the heavy thumping of footsteps through the living room and the final green blip of the front door closing before the monitors were stilled by the dead silence left behind.

"No!" Yozkowitz barked into the telephone as he stuffed a pair of surgical gloves and paper booties into his coat pocket. "It's too late for that. The kid's down and there's no sign of life. He's out of view of the camera, right in front of the TV. . . . I don't know what the hell happened. I only record this shit, I don't watch it. My guess is you're gonna need a clean-up crew. I'm going up there, and if it's clear, I'm getting what I can of my equipment out." Yozkowitz slammed down the phone and stopped to think. From beneath the console he retrieved a mirror and a small case from which he pulled an adhesive-backed mustache, beard, and heavy eyebrows. While he donned his disguise, he previewed every detail of his intended route through the building's rear service entrance and up the stairs to the fourth-floor rear apartment. He checked his pocket for the apartment key, slipped a small .25 caliber automatic from a gym bag into his belt, and pulled a black knit cap low on his forehead. He then reached for the Nikon camera loaded with high-speed film and stepped out of the van. He did not head for the rear of the apartment building but instead hurried to the middle of the block where he slipped into an alley across the street

from the building's front entrance. Dressed entirely
in black and pressed against the cold brick wall that
steadied his telephoto lens, Yozkowitz was invisible
to his target. In less than a minute, the camera's
power drive began to click off twenty-four shots of
the short, fat man turning the corner from the rear
of the building and walking quickly past the front
entrance and to the end of the block where he got
into a white Saab and drove off. Yozkowitz stepped
slowly out of the alley and for an instant thought
he heard a siren in the distance. He did not wait
to confirm the sound but hurried back to the van,
abandoning his plan and his equipment. Tossing
the camera on the passenger's seat, he looked back
to the still-lighted window of apartment 4C, then
to a soft shadow of a figure in the paler light of a
window one floor below. He started the engine
quickly and drove away.

≫ ≪

Eddie Nickles had endured a number of grim
Christmases in the eight years since his wife had
ordered him out of the house and filed for divorce.
This Christmas was proving to be no different. He
had called to talk to the kids but the conversations
were strained and self-conscious. They thanked
him for the gifts he had dropped off in the middle
of the previous night, and Priscilla, the youngest of
the three and just turned thirteen, asked if he was
coming by to get his present. He told her he was
sorry but that he had to work. Maybe he could come
by tomorrow night.

Eddie was sorry. And he wondered why he had
volunteered to switch shifts with Dwayne Hillis, as
if Dwayne, who wasn't divorced, had a superior
claim to Christmas. Now standing over the lean

body of a young man whom he guessed to be no more than nineteen and who was lying naked on the floor by the television, the orbital ridge and bone above the left eye socket crushed, the face swollen and masked with a dark, almost black coagulate, the city's three-hundred-twenty-third reported homicide of the year, Eddie wondered if the kid's father had called to wish him a merry Christmas.

"*Hold it!*" he suddenly shouted at the uniformed officer who had just walked into the bathroom and held a lit cigarette poised over the thick glass ashtray sitting on the counter next to the sink. "What the fuck are you doing?" Eddie asked, rushing to grab the startled officer's wrist, preventing him from snubbing out the cigarette.

"I was just gonna take a leak," the officer said. "What's the problem?"

Eddie was not in the spirit of the holidays. "The problem is, asshole, this is a crime scene and not a public toilet. You were just about to put your fuckin' garbage in what could be the murder weapon." The officer looked skeptically at the ashtray. "See the moisture on the bottom? Think maybe someone mighta just washed it for some reason? Maybe washing the blood off? Think maybe they might not've got everything, like maybe the lab might be able to find something if some mindless fool like you doesn't fuck everything up?" The officer just stared, not saying anything. "Now, you gotta piss, you go down and piss in the alley or piss in your shoe, I don't care. But you don't piss on my crime scene. Understand? And take that fuckin' cigarette outta here!"

The officer hurried out of the apartment, crowded with too many officers, including a few officials just looking for a break in the boredom of the quiet Christmas shift. Eddie pulled Sergeant Rissoli aside.

"Sarge, you gotta clear everybody outta here. You got people tramping all over the scene, dropping ashes and touching shit. By the time Mobile Crime gets here, you're not gonna have a scene."

"Yeah, I know. I'll take care of it. By the way, Communication's got the lady who called this in on the phone again. Turns out she's in 3C, just below us here. But she won't open the door. Sounds like a head case. How 'bout you see if you can talk your way in while I clear this place?"

The building was a small, four-story brick structure that stood at one end of the block. There were three apartments on each floor but the first, where the stairway met a hall traveling from the front door to a rear utility room with a washer and dryer and a doorway to the rear alley. The only people home on either the third or fourth floors were in 3A and 3B, located at the front of the building. None of the people the police had questioned thus far had heard or seen anything unusual. 3C had not responded to their knocks.

Eddie walked down the one flight of stairs and returned to apartment 3B, where Lisa McCarthy, who lived alone, was probably having another drink to recover from his first visit. When Eddie had spoken to the thirty-four-year-old secretary thirty minutes before, she had said that she had spent the entire day with friends across town and had returned home shortly after nine. Not more than ten minutes had passed when she saw the flashing lights of the first police car to arrive. She had no hint that anything was wrong before that. She did not know who lived in 4C but a couple of times in the past few months she had run into a young, light-skinned black man climbing the stairs to the fourth floor. She recalled having one very brief conversation with him several weeks before, about the same time at night, around nine o'clock. It was the second or third time she had seen him, and she asked if he had moved in. He had said no, he was just meeting a friend. He was cute, she said, and she blushed slightly when she admitted that she had wondered if he was gay. "He kinda had that look, you know. But I wasn't sure. He was real nice, but kinda nervous and shy."

Eddie had asked if she would mind taking a look at the victim to see if it was the same young man she had met and she agreed, a little too readily. He knew from experience that it wasn't curiosity that allowed her to agree so easily. It was her naïveté, her failure to realize exactly to what she was agreeing.

Eddie had held her elbow gently as he escorted her through the living room filled with police officers milling about with an almost social casualness. He had warned her gently that the victim's face had been pretty badly beaten and that it was important just to take a deep breath and remember that the man was dead and beyond feeling any pain. It had taken no more than a few seconds in the bedroom before Eddie felt her body stiffen and begin to rock with the waves of nausea that were quickly building. He had rushed her out of the apartment and to the hallway where she vomited on the short gray nap of the carpet.

Back in her apartment, shivering, sipping Scotch without ice, she had said she was pretty sure it was the same man. "I can't be positive, you know, his face was . . . Jesus, his eye!"

• • •

"I'm sorry to bother you again," Eddie said as Lisa McCarthy opened her door a crack and looked at him with sad, red eyes.

"No, that's all right," she said. "It can't get any worse. Come in." She was still holding a glass of Scotch but was now dressed in a thick bathrobe that went down to her feet snuggled in white-cotton athletic socks. "Can I ask you something?"

"Sure, anything," Eddie said, feeling sorry for her and seeing his daughter in her paled complexion.

"Why didn't you let me throw up in the bathroom right there instead of pulling me out into the hallway?"

"I'm sorry about that but I couldn't let you touch anything until after the apartment's processed by the lab. You know, fingerprints or blood or whatever."

She nodded that she understood. "I guess I was a little embarrassed. I just wasn't . . . I don't know." She shook her head. "It's not like it is on TV, is it?"

Eddie smiled. " 'Fraid not," he said, then asked her about the woman in 3C.

"Mrs. Dalton? You haven't talked to her yet?"

"She won't open the door for us."

"Oh, yeah," she nodded slowly, "you've got to call her on the phone first. She won't answer her door otherwise." Lisa McCarthy proceeded to tell the detective what she knew of the woman in 3C. Mrs. Ella Dalton was old, well into her eighties, she guessed, and constantly in fear of eviction. Two years before, the landlord had evicted a family on the first floor—for what reason Lisa McCarthy did not know—and ever since, Mrs. Dalton had lived in fear that she, too, might be evicted from the apartment she had lived in for fifteen years. She had children somewhere who sent her money, but Lisa had never known them to visit. She liked the old woman, whom she thought slept most of the day and stayed up most of the night.

Whenever she was out late, Lisa said, the old woman would call as soon as she got home. "Just checking to see if I'm okay, you understand," Lisa chuckled. She said with a hint of shyness, "You know, even if I have a guest. Really, she's the eyes and ears of the building. Her apartment looks out on that little parking lot across the alley and onto the side street. Or she'll stand at her door and look out the peephole whenever she hears someone on the stairs. She pretty much knows when people are coming or going. I think it's the only entertainment she's got. She's sweet but a little dotty. Her latest thing is"—and Lisa's voice lowered with mock foreboding—" 'the man in black.' "

"The man in black?"

"Yeah. I don't pay real close attention to what she's saying but she's been talking about the man in black who's been hanging around the neighborhood. I don't know what she's talking about." Lisa paused suddenly as if a thought had just occurred to her. "You know, I wonder if she's all right. She didn't call me tonight, even with all that's been going on. You mind if I call her?"

"Please. Maybe you could help me get in to talk to her, if you wouldn't mind."

She called the old woman and after a minute or two of quiet conversation, Lisa hung up and said, "I'll go over there with you. It might be a good idea if you told the officers out in the hall to disappear for a while. They kinda make her nervous. She's scared to death the police are going to tell the landlord she was the one who called them and he'll evict her for causing so much trouble. Also, I don't think she knows anyone was actually killed upstairs. If she doesn't know it, I wouldn't tell her. You know, she's liable to get real upset."

Mrs. Dalton stood behind Lisa McCarthy and peeked around her while Detective Nickles was introduced. The apartment was barely lit by two antique lamps and a small plastic Christmas tree that sat on a table and whose lights gave the room a warm and comfortable feeling. The apartment was neat, everything in its place, the only sign of celebration being an empty glass coated with a milky film and a few crumbs left on a plate sitting on a table beside the sofa whose billowed arms were covered with lace antimacassars.

"Mrs. Dalton, I don't believe you ate all those cookies I brought over just this morning," Lisa McCarthy scolded. Eddie didn't believe it either; the old woman looked too thin to hold more than one or two. He could see that the woman had once been tall but was now stooped over. Her loose brown skin had an almost gray cast to it and her flesh concealed no more of her bones than did her eyes conceal her fear.

"Is he going to tell Mr. Vincent that I called the police?" she asked the young woman.

"Mr. Vincent's the landlord," Lisa McCarthy explained.

Detective Nickles spoke softly. "No, ma'am. We're not going to tell Mr. Vincent who called the police if you don't want us to. And if it will help, here's my telephone number so if anyone gives you any trouble, including Mr. Vincent, you can just give me a call. We'll take care of it."

The old woman stepped out from behind Lisa McCarthy, took Eddie's business card, and inspected it carefully. "It's the man in black you're looking for."

"Beg your pardon, ma'am?"

"The man in black. He's the cause of all this. He's the one you should be looking for. You don't need to be worrying about that young boy. He's too young to know what he's doing. But the man in black, he's the one."

Lisa McCarthy rolled her eyes as if to say "I told you she might be a little dotty," but Eddie thought differently. "Tell me about him, this man in black."

The old woman looked surprised and pleased that someone wanted to hear her story. She insisted that they each have a little eggnog and warned Lisa that it had "a little something" in it. It took several minutes while the old woman creaked back and forth from the kitchen, bringing one glass at a time, refusing any help from her guests. Once they each had their eggnog, spiked with a healthy portion of bourbon, Mrs. Dalton fell back into an easy chair, ignoring a dollop of nog that splashed on the front of her red dress, and began her story.

It took more than an hour, the old woman taking great relish in the telling of her tale. Often a word or phrase would divert her to memories of her youth on a tobacco farm in the Piedmont of North Carolina, or her son's high school graduation, or the night Harley Baskin ripped her dress by mistake. "But y'all don't want to hear about that," she would say after a lengthy aside and bring herself back to the story of the man in black.

Midway through the second glass of eggnog, Lisa McCarthy's eyelids began to flutter with the effort of staying awake. Eddie remained alert and patient, sitting still throughout the woman's tale. Not once did he interrupt her, but waited for her to pause before asking the next question. Filtering out the surplusage, Eddie found Mrs. Dalton's tale both credible and remarkable for its detail.

For the past two months, apartment 4C had been visited by a number of strangers, young women and men who usually arrived first, before the older gentlemen in suits would arrive. They would stay in the apartment no more than a couple of hours and then the older gentlemen would leave, followed shortly thereafter by the young people. She never said it directly, but Eddie knew the old woman understood exactly what was going on in that apartment. Only a few of the older gentlemen were repeaters, but several of the young people, including the young boy who was there that night, had come to the apartment as many as a half dozen times. The apartment was used once or twice a week, sometimes more, most often in the middle of the afternoon when all of the residents but her were at work, but sometimes late at night. But no matter when the apartment was visited, the man in black was there.

"You mean in the apartment?" Eddie asked.

"Oh, no, not in the apartment. Outside, in his truck. It's a black truck and he usually parks it right over there, across the street or in that little parking lot." She gestured with her hand without getting up from her chair as Eddie walked to both the rear and side windows. He could see that the woman had a complete view of the building's surroundings except toward the front. "He's always there before the people come and leaves after they leave. Sometimes he'll come up to the apartment for a bit before the others come, but he's never there with anyone else."

"What's he look like?"

"I told you, he's the man in black. He's always in

black at night, but once, when I saw him in the day, he was wearing things like he was a workman. But I know he's not."

"White or black? I mean his skin, not his clothes."

"He's a white man. Tall, looks like that fella in the story about the headless horseman. You remember?" Eddie thought for a moment and looked to Lisa McCarthy for help but she was asleep. "You know, that Ichabod fella?" Eddie just nodded. He did remember; he just couldn't remember that Ichabod fella's last name. " 'Cept, this man'll wear different things on his face, like a beard or something. Depends on when he's here. Like tonight. He was wearing his beard and everything. Saw him jump out of the truck after all the shouting and thumping stopped."

That's why she had called the police. Whatever the visitors usually did in that apartment, she had never heard any disturbing noises or commotion. An occasional creak of people moving about or muffled laughter and an occasional loud voice. But tonight was different. The loud and mean-sounding shouts, the terrible thumping on the floor.

"I got scared, I'll tell you. Live and let live, I say, but I got real scared. You won't tell Mr. Vincent that I caused all this commotion, will you?"

"No, ma'am, I sure won't. But you didn't cause any commotion. You did the right thing."

"Is he all right, the young boy?"

"Well, he did get hurt. That's why you did the right thing."

"He's dead, isn't he?" she asked, and Eddie nodded. "I knew he had to be. I got so scared."

"Do you think you'd recognize the man who was with him in the apartment if you saw him again?"

"Lord, I hope I never see him again. I don't know. Maybe, but I hope not."

"Had you ever seen him before? The short, fat man? Was he a repeater?"

"Just once before. About two weeks ago. But it was a different young man who was with him. Young black fella like the one tonight. But different."

"You sure you wouldn't recognize him again? The short man?"

She looked down. "Probably could. Just don't want to."

"What about the man in black? Would you recognize him?"

"I'd know him. He's the cause of all this. Don't think he'll be back here though."

"Why not?"

" 'Cause as soon as I heard the sirens, I saw him running back to his truck and hightail it outta here."

"He was out of his truck?"

"Oh, yes! When I heard all that noise and called the police, I went back to the window and saw him get out of his truck and sorta run to the front of the building. It seemed like forever before I heard the police coming, but when I did, I saw him scoot back to the truck. He won't be back here, I'll wager."

Eddie continued to press for details. How old would she guess the man in black to be?

She didn't know; forties, fifties maybe. How tall? "Tall, but not real tall. Over six feet, probably." Any scars? She didn't know. Odd clothing, fancy watches, unusual jewelry, a limp—anything? She couldn't be specific. The same for the short, fat man. What about the truck? Make? She didn't know. Year? She didn't know. "Looks new. It's always shined up. Not like most trucks."

Eddie nodded and, with a light shrug, asked,

"Can you think of *anything*—any little thing that might help us find the man in black?"

"No, not a thing . . . unless maybe the license number of his truck would help."

Eddie grinned and shook his head at the one obvious question he had not asked. "How about you and I sharing another glass of Christmas cheer?" he offered with a broad smile.

Mrs. Dalton nodded happily and agreed that he should wake Lisa McCarthy and escort her back to her apartment and tell the other officers where he would be.

Back in the hallway outside apartment 4C, Eddie briefed Sergeant Rissoli on his conversation with Mrs. Dalton. "I'm betting the whole fucking apartment's wired for sound and cameras. The bastards are probably watching and listening to everything we're doing. I'm going back down to hold hands with the old lady for a while, but tell Mobile Crime to start looking for bugs. If we've got to, seal the place off and get some technical people in here. Who knows, we might end up with a videotape of the killing."

Eddie returned to apartment 3C and shared another hour and two glasses of bourbon without eggnog with the old woman. He listened to her memories, not paying attention to the words so much as enjoying the sound of conversation about something other than death. It was very late when he finally crawled into bed, alone, and thinking that this wasn't the worst Christmas he had ever spent.

Fifteen

Some nights are darker than others. And longer. Michael's whole body ached from the effort of not moving, stiff with the fear of waking Katy, of her asking questions he did not want to answer. He wondered if he had slept at all. All he remembered was the sound of her breathing and the creaks and groans of the old house giving up the warmth of its Christmas fires to the chill of just another December day. Each creak, each groan, had stabbed him with an unreasoned fear, tightening his skin with the imaginings of half-conscious dreams that the meeting was starting here, in the dark. It was his sudden consciousness of just how tired he was that signaled that the night was nearing its end. He looked for confirmation to the window where the first weak light of dawn crept in. Relieved, he dismissed his dreams as too much food and brandy and looked to his watch. His eyes, accustomed to the dark by long hours of wakefulness, could barely see its hands set at six-forty. If only he could get up and out without waking her.

He slipped out of bed and to the bathroom where he washed and dressed quietly. He penned a short note to Katy before carrying his shoes down the hall to the top of the stairs where he sat to slip them on. Then he heard it, a muffled chatter coming from the kitchen, accompanied by the aroma of coffee. He abandoned his stealth and quickly descended the stairs.

"Good morning, ladies," he announced as he stepped through the swinging door.

"Why, good morning, Michael," Miss Evelyn said, sprightly but obviously surprised. He was pleased that the day had begun with her recognizing that he was not Katy's ex-husband.

"You're up awful early for a city fella," Vera Lee observed.

"Well, I thought I was going to be able to sneak down here before anyone else was up and raid the refrigerator," Michael said with a wink. "I was up half the night thinking about all that good food in there."

Miss Evelyn beamed. "Well, you just sit down there at the table and have a cup of coffee. Vera Lee's making the best creamed turkey and biscuits you'll ever eat, and after breakfast I'm just going to fix up a basket of things for you and Kate to take back. I surely do wish you children weren't always running around in such a hurry. I just know y'all don't eat properly."

There was no escape, and so Michael passed the time while breakfast was being prepared banking the fire in the kitchen fireplace, filling the woodboxes in the kitchen and living room, and topping off the stack outside the kitchen door. Soon the ladies forced him to sit down to what in fact was the best creamed turkey and biscuits he had ever had. All three agreed to let Katy sleep. The ladies were concerned that she had looked "bone-tired." Michael was concerned that she would not let him return to the city alone, at least not without an argument.

"That was a fine breakfast. Thank you," Michael said, leaning back in his chair and holding his stom-

ach appreciatively. "That'll hold me till dinner.
Speaking of which, I would be pleased if you would
allow me to take you all to dinner tonight. I thought
maybe, if you'd like, we could go over to the Bruns-
wick Inn in New Market."

The two ladies looked at each other in silence,
and Michael could not read their reaction.

"But you'll have to join in a little conspiracy with
me," he continued. "I have to go back to the city
for a while, and you know Katy. She'll insist on
going back with me, even though she'd rather stay
here. But if I leave before she wakes up, I can finish
my business and be back in plenty of time for all
of us to go out to dinner this evening. How does
that sound?"

The two ladies seemed oddly embarrassed, but
Katy's mother soon overcame her hesitation. "Why,
thank you, Michael," she said finally, "that would
be nice, wouldn't it, Grammy?"

"Yes, ma'am." Vera Lee nodded, turning nervously to the stove and fiddling with her rack of
spices. "I just don't know," she said to herself. "This
turkey needs something. I just don't know."

Michael was not sure but he felt as if he had just
stepped on a toe. He ignored the feeling as just his
imagination. "Good," he said. "How about if I make
reservations for seven? We'll plan to leave here
about a quarter to."

≫ ≪

It was just after eight-thirty A.M. when Michael
pulled up to the first phone booth he found and
called Eddie Nickles at home. He thought he heard
in Eddie's voice that his Christmas had not been a
sober one. He got straight to the point. "I'm sorry
to be calling this early but Elizabeth Henning called

me last night. She wants to meet this afternoon, at two o'clock."

"Whaddaya talking about?" Eddie asked, as if he could not have heard correctly, and Michael repeated slowly the telephone conversation from the night before. Eddie did not respond for a few moments and Michael did not press him. Finally the detective asked, "You been up to something I don't know about?"

"What do you mean?"

"Man, no one comes in without a reason. And as far as I know, we haven't been doing jackshit to make them nervous—with all due respect." Michael ignored the comment as Eddie continued. "So why now? What's spooked her?"

"I have no idea, but who cares? Why look a gift horse in the mouth?"

"You better start looking this horse in the mouth," Eddie said. "This lady's not calling you out of any sense of civic duty. And unless you know something I don't, I can't see why she'd want to switch sides."

"And?" Michael challenged.

"Hasn't the possibility occurred to you that you're being set up?"

"For what?" Michael asked defensively. The thought had occurred to him, but he did not want to admit to the fear.

The detective did not answer but said in a voice of exasperation, "Look, I've got some things to take care of. Come by my place around eleven. We'll talk then. And wear bulky clothes."

The phone clicked dead before Michael could respond. He wasn't insulted. He was familiar with Eddie's hangovers. Michael returned to his house in the city and distracted himself by calling for dinner reservations, reading the paper over several cups of coffee, and trying to ignore the thought of being set up, whatever that meant.

By the time he was finally buzzed through the entrance door and began to climb the steps to Eddie's third-floor apartment, Michael's chief concern was hiding the nervousness engendered by all the thoughts he had tried to ignore.

"It's the bank accounts," Eddie said, as he poured the two of them a cup of coffee. "That's gotta be it."

Michael thought for a moment as he looked around the apartment. He had been there before, but not sober. He considered the room as if it were his first visit and was struck by its air of impermanence, the absence of anything personal except for small framed pictures of Eddie's children that sat on a table in the corner. Even they looked transient, like three people waiting in an empty train station. Michael started to ask Eddie about his Christmas but stopped himself. "I thought you said chasing those accounts was a waste of time," he said.

"No. I said ignoring everything else just to chase paper was a mistake. But whatever, it's gotta be those accounts. There's nothing else."

Michael shook his head. "I'm not so sure. How is she going to know we've been into those accounts? Everyone's agreed not to disclose the subpoenas—"

"Easy," Eddie interrupted. "Higgs has more bank contacts than the fuckin' Federal Reserve. You're only the government. He represents big bucks. And tell me something. Who else knows you're looking at those accounts besides Jimmy and me?"

"No one."

Eddie's eyes narrowed.

"Well, the front office, but I only told them that

I had found two accounts in the name of one of Wheatley's aliases and I emphasized that we couldn't trace anything from them. You know, nothing but cash leading nowhere."

"Why'd you tell them anything? What is it that you're not telling me?"

"They're closing down the investigation right after the first. Joslin and Gaelen. I was looking for some reason to convince them to leave it open. It was a fuck-up."

Eddie stared out the window as he took several sips of coffee. "Why are they closing it down?" he asked, and Michael repeated the details of the meeting. "What about you, Counselor? You closing down?"

"Not unless you and Jimmy do. But we'll be on our own. Completely. McKeethen will cover us if we really need it. But for now it'll just be us."

Eddie turned back from the window. "Assume that she does know about the subpoenas—" he started.

Michael jumped in. "Yeah, and assume they're going to cause her or Higgs or whoever a problem. Why come to us and end up having to explain it all? Why not just clean out what you can and run? Anyone who can set up a wash operation like this one could easily figure out how to hide herself and the cash. No, I can't tell you why, but she needs us. It doesn't make sense to come in to bullshit us. She'd just run."

"Higgs ain't gonna run," Eddie said. "And Henning can't run from Higgs. Not with her kid. And you keep assuming that this is her idea. I'm not so sure about that."

The two men went on with their debate for twenty minutes, succeeding only in convincing themselves that they had no idea what had prompted Elizabeth Henning's phone call. Whatever the reason, they had to be cautious.

"Enough bullshit," Eddie said finally, cutting off the debate. "Take your clothes off."

"I beg your pardon?" Michael's eyes widened, and Detective Nickles rolled his with the impatience of having to deal with an innocent.

"You didn't think you were going to go in there without a wire, did you?"

"Oh, right," Michael said, as if he had just forgotten for a moment. "Where are you going to be?"

"Doesn't matter where I'll be. I couldn't get a transmitter. All we've got is a body recorder, so you're gonna be on your own. But don't worry, if they've decided to snuff you we'll have some really dramatic shit for the courtroom. Course, it may be a problem getting a DA off his ass long enough to indict it."

"You're getting a big charge out of all this, aren't you?"

"Well, Counselor, I have to admit it is nice to have you play by my rules once in a while."

≫ ≪

By the afternoon, fatigue had started to cloud Michael's mind. He shut out the noise and slipped back to quieter times, before Babe had grown too old to hunt, before his divorce, and before he had moved to the city whose impatient traffic now herded him eastward along New York Avenue, past the rail yards and fast-food joints, past the crowd of gas stations and motels that rented their rooms by the hour, past the old brickyard to the National Arboretum, an idyll hidden amid the industry near the city's northeastern boundary. His thoughts sped through images, diverse and disjointed, like flash cards of memories of a sun-brightened face and the sound of the river when the geese were there, of the smell of boxwoods and the taste of fresh-caught fish. His musing died suddenly when he turned into the park and his brain was flooded with the noise of caution.

Leaving the comfort of indifferent crowds behind him, Michael wound slowly through the empty meadows and quiet woods of the arboretum, past the creek and pond, both stilled by their cover of ice. His eyes darted everywhere looking for anything. He saw nothing until he approached the stucco-walled structure that enclosed the bonsai exhibit. He passed it slowly. There were no cars parked in the spaces provided across the street, and there was no one in sight near the entrance. It was only one-thirty. He had a half hour to kill and continued up the hill to the parking lot by the administration building where he pulled in and saw Eddie Nickles, dressed in a Park Service jacket and cap. Eddie ignored him. There was another man with him, also in the uniform of a Park Service workman, whom Michael did not recognize. The prosecutor smiled to himself and turned around to drive back to the front of the bonsai exhibit where he parked and waited.

Twenty-five minutes passed before Michael first saw Elizabeth Henning, alone in a bright red Mustang convertible, slowly make her first pass by the exhibit. She looked over as she drove by but gave no sign of recognition. Michael enjoyed the thought of her mimicking his caution. He reached into the small of his back to turn on the tape recorder and noted the time and circumstances of her arrival. Several minutes passed before Henning's car again appeared, and again she looked at him without gesture and drove past. He again activated the tape and noted the time. To him they seemed ridiculous, a pair of loons bobbing and weaving through some absurd mating ritual. On her third pass, Elizabeth Henning did not look over but drove directly to the visitors' lot where she got out of her car and walked the fifty yards back to and through the entrance to the exhibit. Michael took a deep breath, again activated the tape, and followed her inside.

She was leaning over to read the descriptive plaque on a one-hundred-eighty-year-old Japanese red pine when Michael's footsteps crunched on the gravel path behind her. She did not turn to face him until he stood directly behind her and asked, "You wanted to see me?"

Henning turned, slowly, taking a moment to inspect him, as if she were looking for some telltale sign. She looked different from what he remembered, a bit heavier, perhaps, and not so consciously elegant. But the eyes still betrayed a nervousness.

Michael still knew very little about her. Jimmy Legget had uncovered an old file from the Immigration and Naturalization Service that revealed that twenty-five years before, Elizabeth Henning had entered the United States from the Bahamas and later applied for a U.S. passport. It had taken months of letters and hearings and affidavits before it was verified that she indeed had been born in Georgia in March 1944. At the age of six she had left the United States with her family and moved to the island of New Providence but had never relinquished her American citizenship. INS so informed the State Department and a passport was issued. Since then she had renewed her passport whenever necessary, and sources with the IRS verified that she had filed her tax returns and reported a modest income each and every year.

Michael looked at her staring at him. "You're wondering if I'm wearing a wire?" he asked.

"It had occurred to me," she said.

Michael opened his army field jacket to the bulky oiled-wool seaman's sweater that concealed a small microphone uncomfortably taped to his chest. "You show me yours and I'll show you mine," he said.

She mimicked his gesture and opened wide her knee-length beaver coat. She smiled while Michael reflexively inspected her figure. He refused to allow himself a smile in return. It was apparent that neither was going to pat the other down.

"Let's understand each other," Michael began. "I don't expect you to trust me any more than I trust you. And be clear about that, Ms. Henning, I don't trust you. But I'm here, at your request, so until we're both sure of what we're dealing with, why don't we just keep our hands out of our pockets, so to speak, and you tell me why you wanted to see me."

"I'm afraid I can't do that," she smiled again. "What I have for you is in my pocket." She gestured with her hand the need to reach into her coat and asked, "Okay?"

Michael looked down at her as if he were peering over the top of an imaginary pair of glasses. He did not like her coquettish game but nodded his assent anyway.

She reached into her pocket and handed him a gun permit issued by the Department of Public Safety, U.S. Virgin Islands. In the lower left-hand corner was a photograph of a white male whose name was Regent Godoy, 37 Queen Cross, Christiansted, St. Croix. The man's face was puffed and discolored, with bulging eyes and very little hair on his head. It looked like an autopsy photo of a body left too long in a warm room.

Michael flipped the permit over and noted that

it was "valid only while holder is pursuing the oc-
cupation of licensed private investigator." He pon-
dered the laminated document for a few moments
and then asked, "The man Wheatley shot in the
alley?" Elizabeth Henning looked surprised and
nodded.

"Why are you doing this?" Michael asked.

"Does it really make any difference?"

"Yes, Ms. Henning, it makes a great deal of difference."

"Is that one of your rules? Everyone has to give
you a reason for their actions before you'll deal with
them?"

"There are no more rules," he said, his voice cold.
"They were thrown out yesterday."

"What do you mean? What about yesterday?"

"I was followed yesterday and I assume by your
phone call it was by your people. That makes it
personal. And in this business it's always a mistake
to make it personal."

"I don't know what you're talking about. I don't
know anything about your being followed. What I
said to you over the phone was only to convince
you to meet me." She looked nervous, and Michael
concentrated on her eyes.

"How did you know where to call me?"

"There's a file on you dating back to the investigation two years ago. Milton Higgs keeps a file on
practically everybody. We went over it with Victor
Stearman before we came down to be interviewed.
I remembered your girlfriend's name and that her
family lived out in Ijamsville. It's a strange name,
Ijamsville," she said, dragging out the pronunciation. *I'ms-ville.* "Not hard to remember. I called
your number and when you weren't home I called
information. Their number's listed. It was a shot
in the dark." She hesitated and again offered,

"The phone call, it was just a way of convincing you."

"Someone *did* follow me," he said coldly.

Henning frowned. "I have no idea why they would. But if you want, I'll try to find out and let you know. It won't be easy for me, but I'll try. It's in both our interests that we find out quickly whether we can trust each other."

Michael distrusted sincerity in a snitch. But he appreciated her reference to self-interest and asked, "Again, why are you doing this?"

She did not argue with him this time. "I'm a bookkeeper in over my head. It's time to get out and I don't want to spend the rest of my life looking over my shoulder."

"Why now?"

She lowered her eyes and spoke hesitantly. "I've been thinking about it and wondering whether I had the nerve for what all this could mean. I don't know. Christmas, I guess. And it seemed a good way to get your attention."

"How far are you willing to go?"

"As far as I have to, short of testifying at a trial or before the grand jury."

"That may not be far enough."

"How can you say until you know what I have to offer?" He did not respond, not even by his expression. "Look," she said, "you and I both know that if I ever testified, I'd be running the rest of my life, even with your so-called witness protection programs. I can be of help to you, maybe even give you what you need without it ever being known that I cooperated. Yes, I want immunity, but I know I have to give you something worthwhile in exchange. That's why I'm here. I'm ready to prove to you that immunity and confidentiality are a small price to pay for what I can do for you."

"Tell me about the governor."

Her eyes widened slightly and she hesitated before saying, "Are you prepared now to offer me immunity and the assurance that I won't have to testify?"

"No," he replied.

"Then I'm not prepared to answer all your questions. I'm not making any secret of the fact that I'm bargaining and I'm not here out of charity. You and I both know that subpoenaing me won't do you any good. I'll claim the Fifth and you'll give me immunity. I'll refuse to testify and spend a few months in jail for contempt. I'll end up being the trusted and well-compensated slave of Milton Higgs, and you'll end up with nothing but another headline and every informant you've got wondering if you'd do the same thing to them and put their business out on the street. Isn't that about how it would work? We'd both lose."

"Fair enough," Michael said, impressed but cautious, "but I'm not going to buy a pig in a poke and I'm not inclined to waste time trying to find out what's in the poke."

"Understood. And that's what that's about," she said, nodding to the permit Michael still held in his hand. "I suggest that if you look into that carefully you will find some very interesting connections, connections perhaps that that man was looking for himself. It should also prove that I am not sending you on any wild-goose chase, and we can then get on with what we have to do. But I must tell you that you can't sit on this. Things are in motion and you need to determine quickly if we are to deal or not."

"What things?"

"When we conclude an agreement, you'll know

everything I know. Check out that man Godoy. You'll learn that I'm serious."

"I need a hint. I'm not going to waste time chasing shadows."

"I don't know the details. Not yet. The way these things work, even Higgs won't know the details until the last minute. But we're talking about heroin, Mr. Holden. More than anyone in this city has ever seen at one time."

"How quickly is this happening?"

"Six weeks, two months at the most. But if we're going to help each other we need to come to some agreement long before that."

"How do I reach you?"

She reached into her coat pocket once more and pulled out a slip of paper with a telephone number written in pencil. "It's a twenty-four-hour answering service. Ask for Alethea. I'll get the message."

"You obviously know how to get in touch with me," he smiled. "I'll be in touch."

"Do you want me to find out if you were followed, if I can?"

Michael showed the first sign of emotion. "Yes, as much as you would want to know if someone was following your son, Christian, around Newport."

Elizabeth Henning's back stiffened visibly, and he could hear her breathing quicken as she controlled her own anger at what almost sounded like a threat. She held herself to a simple "I understand."

"One more thing, Ms. Henning. I think we both understand our weak spots, yours and mine. What's Higgs's weakness?"

Elizabeth Henning looked him straight in the eye. "Me," she said confidently, and turned and walked away.

Good answer, Michael thought to himself. He stood alone among the sculptured trees, suddenly very tired.

≫ ≪

Michael was not sure of Katy's mood as she dressed for dinner. She acted as if she were in high spirits, but there was an edge to her voice. "Is something bothering you?" he asked finally.

"Bothering me? Of course not, Prince Charming. You sneak out of my bed at the crack of dawn, decide you're going to restructure the social order around here, and then blow town and leave me to deal with it."

"What are you talking about?" he asked.

"This little dinner party you cooked up to cover yourself for whatever you were up to today."

"Is there something wrong with inviting everyone to dinner?"

"Sweetheart," she said with condescension, "Momma's lived on this farm all her life, and if you'd ask her, she'd probably tell you the Civil Rights Act was a bunch of jugglers she saw on 'The Ed Sullivan Show.'" Michael let out a belly laugh. "I'm serious, Michael," she continued, trying not to laugh along with him. "You know Momma has a hard time keeping track of what decade she's in. I mean, one minute she knows exactly what's going on, and the next thing you know she's trying to find 'The Coon Sanders Show' on the radio."

"Coon Sanders?"

"It was some radio show from back in the twenties or thirties that she used to listen to. And Grammy. Grammy's family and Lord help anyone who'd hurt her. But off the farm, she's hired help and it's not easy for Momma or Grammy to deal with that after all these years. And to go to a restaurant? Jesus! I have a hard enough time getting Momma to leave this farm just to go to the grocery. And I don't know that Grammy's been out to dinner except for church socials and such since Uncle Willy died.

"I have been up to my eyeballs with them all day. They've been like a couple of virgins getting ready for their wedding night. I had to drive Momma into Frederick to get her hair done and, while she was in the beauty parlor, take Grammy to buy a new dress. Do you know Momma made me go to the barn three times to make sure that old Cadillac would start while she fussed over herself to make sure she looked good enough to go to the beauty parlor? But you know what Momma said to me when she got back from the hairdresser? She said that it was high time that they got out of this old house and that she knew Grammy was her best friend and if Zaina Lowe didn't like it she could just go to the devil." Katy laughed out loud. "That's what she said, 'Zaina Lowe can just go to the devil!' "

"Who's Zaina Lowe?"

"She was the town gossip who was packed off to a nursing home fifteen years ago. I don't even know if she's still alive."

The dinner went well and both Miss Evelyn and Vera Lee sat erect at the table, the grande dames of New Market surveying the inn's guests for the latest fashions. Their posture slackened a bit with the brandy and coffee, and Miss Evelyn announced that she felt so good she just might sit up and listen to Coon Sanders. "You know," she said to Michael, "that show comes all the way from Chicago."

"No, I didn't know that," Michael said politely, and Vera Lee giggled a bit.

By nine-thirty they were home, and Miss Evelyn and Vera Lee had retired. Katy sat up in bed and asked Michael, "Are you going to tell me now what that phone call last night was all about and what you were up to today?"

Michael just shook his head in resignation. "So much for my poker face." He spent the next twenty minutes detailing the day and all the events leading up to it. Katy's silent stare grew more intense as his story unraveled, her hand clutching and twisting her flannel nightshirt, tightening the material about her full breasts, and tears began to well. "I'm sorry, Kate. I really am. I never thought anyone would be following me or that they would be keeping that kind of information in a file. We still don't know that anyone actually followed us. Maybe the car your brother saw was nothing. Just some poor guy having a bad Christmas. But I really don't think this lady calling me here means that your mother or Vera Lee would be in any danger. I really don't."

"You sonofabitch!" Katy erupted, her eyes now reddened and overflowing, and she punched him in the chest, hard. "This is my family. How could you not tell me? How can you play these games with me . . . with us? But I guess you're the only one who understands, right? Damn you, Michael!" she hissed. "Goddamn you!" She tried to punch him again, but he grabbed her and held her in a tight hug, her squirming aggravating the pain in his chest. "Let me go!" she cried. "Just let me go!"

He did and Katy turned her back to him. "I'm sorry," was all he could think to say as the night promised to be longer and darker than the one before.

Sixteen

"Well, whaddaya think?" Eddie Nickles asked, as he switched off the tape player.

Jimmy Legget was slouched in the corner of Michael Holden's office, a cup of coffee resting on one knee draped over the arm of the worn leather chair. It was midmorning and the prosecutors' offices were Sunday-quiet on this last day of the year. As far as Kitty Legget knew, her husband was out doing errands in preparation for their party that evening. Jimmy did not look at either man but stared out the window. He took his time before he asked, not moving his eyes from some distant target, "What difference does it make? I mean if we're closing down, what the hell difference does it make?"

"Man, we're not closing down," Eddie said irritably. "They are. Not us, them."

Jimmy sipped his coffee. He turned and looked directly at Michael but did not say anything.

"He's right," Michael said. "We're not closing down. We're gonna have to change tactics a bit, but there's no reason why we can't continue."

Jimmy lowered his chin. "Exactly what are you talking about, 'changing tactics'?" He paused, not so much to invite an answer as to let his thoughts catch up. "You know I was never comfortable with holding back on all that stuff in the first place—

you know, playing games with the reports. It seems to me that all we accomplished was to put ourselves in a real deep hole. And I don't like the idea of trying to dig out of it by running some kind of renegade operation. I mean, what are we talking about?"

"Nothing illegal," Michael said. "We may bend a few policies, make up our own procedures, but nothing illegal."

"What about subpoenas? How're we gonna be able to do anything without subpoenas?"

"You'll have the subpoenas you'll need."

"Yeah, fine, Mike, but I'm talking about legal subpoenas. Subpoenas that'll hold up in court if we actually come up with something we can use. Nothing personal, man, but I'm not gonna shitcan my career just to chase some ghosts from another case 'cause y'all got beat once."

"Neither am I, Jimmy," Michael said, straining for patience. "Look, the only thing that's really being closed down is the investigation of Wheatley's hanging and his story about the shooting in the alley. We knew a long time ago that wasn't going anywhere without a break from the inside. And like the boss said, if something came up later we can reopen the case. Well, something's come up. We're just not ready to tell them about it. All we're doing is what we do every day. You get some information from a snitch and you look into it. If it pans out, it's a case. If not, it's nothing. Right? What the hell's the difference?"

"The difference is we're not talking about just any case. We're talking about shit that could make downtown sit up and take notice. We're talking about lying to the people we work for." He paused for a response. Michael offered none but looked to Eddie. Jimmy did not take his eyes off the prosecutor. "And you still haven't answered my question about the subpoenas."

"I told you that's covered," Michael said with the first open hint of irritation. "I asked Harry Carson to open up a case in front of one of the grand juries in district court. We're legit."

"You told Carson what we're doing?"

"No, of course not," Michael said, surprised that Jimmy would even ask. "I just told him I had a run-of-the-mill dope case based on snitch information and to open it up so we could issue subpoenas."

"Who'd he put in for a witness?" Jimmy asked.

"Jimmy," Michael began his soft lecture, "you don't need a witness to open up a case. I just wrote out a little crib sheet for Harry to read to the jury. Said we had just come upon some information regarding narcotics trafficking and were going to be issuing subpoenas and presenting witnesses when appropriate. Gave him some bullshit about connections with New York and Chicago and that we're awaiting further information about a business connection in town. It's all standard form. No different than any other dope case that they start up. Maybe a little less information than most, but nothing that will raise any eyebrows. And it's all perfectly legal. Trust me."

Jimmy's gaze returned to the window as he took another sip of coffee.

Eddie sat in one side chair with his feet propped on another. He looked uneasy and impatient but said nothing. Jimmy then turned to him. "What about us? What are we gonna say or not say to Ursay?" Before Eddie could answer, Jimmy interjected, "You know I don't like this shit. I can't help thinking that we're playing games we don't have to play. I mean, man, we've been acting like the whole fuckin' department and the U.S. Attorney's office are all one great big goddamned criminal conspiracy. I don't believe it. And like I said, seems like we're just digging ourselves in deeper. Why not take those memos we wrote up at first—you know, the ones that laid out all the stuff Wheatley said—and take them to someone high enough up to let us continue on officially? You know, without all this behind-the-scenes bullshit."

Michael leaned low and stretched his arms over his desk, pointing at Jimmy with the coffee cup he held in both hands. "Jimmy," he asked, "do you agree that if the other side found out everything we were doing and knew everything that we knew, we'd never get them?"

Jimmy nodded slowly.

"And do you agree that at least from what Eddie's snitch said, that there's a serious leak?"

Jimmy nodded again.

"And you've read all the reports and our notes from the old case, right? Would you agree that we were sandbagged from the inside there?"

He agreed by his silence.

"So who's doing it, Jimmy? Tell me who the leak is."

"Fuck, I don't know!"

"Neither do I, my man, and that's the problem. I don't believe any more than you do that the whole department's dirty or this office is all dirty. It may only be one man, maybe two, three. Who knows? Maybe all it takes is one man who's dirty, a few others who are a little too political or a little too frightened or a little too stupid. I don't know. But my point is, unless you know who's holding the knife, how do you know who you can trust your back to?"

Michael stopped but Jimmy did not answer.

"I'll make a deal with you right now. You tell me

who to trust and I'll do it. We'll go to him and lay it all out. You just tell me who to go to."

"Sounds like you trust McKeethen."

"Yeah, I do. But he can't help us here. He could help deflect the front office, keep them off my back by giving them a memo every once in a while. You know the routine. Spend three pages telling them there's nothing new to report. But the bottom line is he's a company man, and, right or wrong, he trusts the front office. If we laid it all out for him, he'd panic. He wouldn't get involved or approve anything like this unless he could include them. We just can't afford that right now."

There was a long silence before Jimmy muttered, "Jesus Christ."

"He ain't gonna help us, son." Eddie smiled. "We're on our own."

"Why do I feel like I'm being greased here?"

"Well, you're not bent over yet," Michael said. "You've still got a choice."

Jimmy looked to Eddie, who said, "Look, my man, no one's gonna say anything if you decide not to—"

"Ah, shit, man!" Jimmy blurted out. "Don't give me some John Wayne speech about how no one's gonna think the less of me if I don't ride into the valley of death with the six hundred."

Eddie looked to Michael. "What the fuck's he talking about?"

"It's from a poem."

Eddie looked at Jimmy, then back to Michael, and to Jimmy once more. "Yeah, well, you two can talk poetry later. Right now let's stick to business. Jimmy, let's make it simple. You in or out?"

"What do we tell the sergeant or Ursay we're working on to cover our time on this?"

"That fag killing on Christmas I told you about.

There's more'n enough legwork on that thing to cover us."

"No funny business, right? I mean nothing illegal, no black-bag jobs. I don't mind bending a few rules, stretching policy and all that, but no illegal shit. Right? I mean, I'm not trying to insult anybody, but I gotta be sure."

Michael shook his head, wondering if it was time to cut Jimmy out. He kept his thoughts to himself. "Nothing illegal. No funny business."

Jimmy's eyes traveled from Michael to Eddie, and he just nodded.

"Are we through with the bullshit? Can we get back to business?" Eddie asked.

"Yeah," Michael sighed. "Where were we?"

"The tape of you and Henning. So, Jimmy, whaddaya think? She for real or not?"

Jimmy slid his leg off the arm of the chair and sat up straight. "Something stinks here," he offered, pointing one finger in the air for emphasis, "but I don't know what it is. I mean, she gives up the gun license of the man in the alley, or at least that's who we think it is. And that stuff about a major load of dope fits with what your snitch said a few weeks ago. But I don't understand why she'd suddenly decide to come in. I don't buy that bullshit about being in over her head or the spirit of Christmas or whatever. I don't know what it is, but I just can't help thinking she's running a game on us."

"That's what I thought when I first heard about the meeting," Eddie said. "But not after the tape. I mean, if the lady was bullshittin' us she coulda left off with the gun license, you know? Could've just sent us on a wild-goose chase with that. But her adding in the stuff about the dope and it matching up with what my man said, I say if she's runnin' a game, it's on Higgs and not us. I say we go with her, for now at least."

"What's that mean?" Jimmy asked. "We stop running down all those bank accounts? Concentrate on the gun permit or the dope or what?"

"No, we do all of it," Michael said. He saw the skepticism in Jimmy's face and continued. "It's not gonna be as hard as it sounds. I've got a little Christmas present for you. In all the bank records I've run down in the past few weeks, I haven't seen any new accounts. We may just have reached the point where we've at least identified everything. And something interesting has shown up. It looks like the smaller accounts, you know, the eight-, ten-, twelve-thousand-dollar ones, they all seem to be pyramiding into consolidation accounts. It's like we're closing in on the big stash. I've got subpoenas and phone calls in to the last three banks I know about and should be hearing from all of them by the end of next week. That's what I'd like you to handle while I'm gone."

Jimmy looked up, surprised. "Gone? Where?"

"I'm going to the Virgin Islands to check this out," Michael said, pulling from his desk drawer the gun permit Elizabeth Henning had given him.

Jimmy laughed. "Now that's subtle, man. What, did you go up to Joslin and tell him to sign off on a travel voucher 'cause you needed a little R and R?"

Michael didn't smile. "I'm picking up the tab myself."

Jimmy turned to Eddie. "You think that's smart? The man's gonna stick out like a sore thumb nosing around in a place like that."

"It's the only way. We talked it over," Eddie said. "We called some FBI contacts who gave us an intro to their office there on St. Thomas. It's a one-man operation. The agent down there says the only thing he knows is that this guy Godoy was reported missing months ago. But he doesn't know anything more about it. He's willing to help out, but he'd be working blind. That could take a lot more time than we have."

Jimmy turned to Michael. "I don't know. I just get the feeling this lady is leading us away from whatever it is they don't want us looking into. I just don't trust this. Why not just let the FBI man track this down and let us know what he finds?"

"First, this isn't a Bureau case," Michael explained. "The man's sitting down there in a one-man office. How much of a priority would you give it if you were him? Maybe he'll get to it next week. Maybe not. Maybe he'll track it all down in the next three or four months. But that's too late. Now maybe with me down there for a week or so, together we can get some things done in a hurry.

"Second, the man doesn't know what we're looking for, and even if we could explain everything in a phone conversation, which we probably couldn't do, there's too great a chance that he'd miss something one of us wouldn't—a name that's dropped, some little connection that even we wouldn't think of unless we heard it. The bottom line is we gotta at least give it a shot.

"Third,"—he grinned—"if I can convince Katy to go along, I get a nice little vacation to boot."

"What is it you want me to do while you're gone?"

"I just want to tell Becky to relay any messages from any of these banks to you so you can follow up. Just like we've been doing. Okay?"

"Sure. When are you leaving?"

"As soon as I can get McKeethen to let me transfer that rape trial I have up on the fourteenth and make reservations. The Bureau man said he may have a contact on a condo I can rent for a week or ten days."

Jimmy shook his head slowly. "I don't know why, but this just doesn't feel right."

"Are you kidding?" Eddie said with unusual optimism. "Hell, this is the first time since we started that anything has felt right."

> <

New Year's Eve. Specks of snow hung in the air like clouds of summer gnats swirling in the wash of cars that traveled the dusted roadway. The headlights drew the flakes into their path and the car's speed was exaggerated by the galaxy of tiny comets racing toward the windshield and then, at the last instant, swooping up and to the sides.

"You mind slowing down a bit?" Katy asked. "You're making me nervous. Besides, I'm not in that big a hurry to get there."

Katy had said little since the night Michael had returned from his meeting with Elizabeth Henning. The anger had not been resolved or forgotten. It hung over them like a headache that would not go away. At best they observed an uneasy truce to span the holidays. Michael wondered if it would extend even to midnight.

"Sure," he agreed, easing his foot off the accelerator, but only slightly. "I guess I am in a hurry. The sooner we get there, the sooner we can leave." It was almost eight o'clock and they were winding quickly through Rock Creek Park toward Dan McKeethen's house on the other side of the beltway, twenty minutes away. It was the first of two parties to which they were committed, the second being at the Palisades home of Katy's boss, Barkley Talbot, where the artists, admen, and account executives were just beginning to gather.

"Why are we going, then? I don't understand why we're going to this party if you don't want to."

"I explained that. I need Dan to transfer that trial for me."

"Michael, that's crazy. I mean, why not just call him on the phone or see him in the office? I just don't understand it. Any of it. What is it? Do they inject you people with something in law school that forever prevents you from approaching someone directly? Does everything have to be a feint and dodge?"

Michael hesitated and swallowed the temptation to fight back. He had made a studied choice not to fight back. It had been a difficult week, but he had stuck to his tactic. He would not give her an excuse to escalate the quiet skirmishing to a full-blown battle, although she seemed intent on finding one. Each word seemed to challenge—a sarcastic jibe, a lightly tossed reference to an ancient slight, a comment on some habit that had never before evoked comment—and each hung in the air until replaced by the next. He could hear her irritation building with his every refusal to join the battle; his equable passivity, at first intended to mollify, in the past few days had taken on the role of offensive weapon. For a moment he indulged the notion that Katy's mounting frustration somehow signaled that his tactics were superior, that maybe even a victory or two was in the offing. He stopped himself. Even he understood the perversity of the notion that there could be a winner in such a contest. He decided to give up and fight back.

"Speaking of feints and dodges, why the hell don't you just get whatever it is off your chest and quit all this bullshit sniping! I told you I was sorry about what happened on Christmas. I didn't plan it. And I wasn't happy when it happened. Believe it or not, I don't like the idea of people following me or you on Christmas or any other day." His voice was rising to just below a shout. "And no, I don't think there's anything even remotely exciting or romantic about my name or your name or your family or even my dog being listed in some dope dealer's file. I know you think this is some kind of game everybody's playing here, and when we all get tired of it, well, shit, just turn off the TV and walk away from it. Unfortunately, it doesn't work that way. I'm sorry my job has spilled over to you, to us. But there's nothing I can do about it except to do my job. It doesn't have to infect us, not you and me. Damn it! Instead of sulking about it, I would think you'd want me to go after the bastard."

Katy began to speak, but he wasn't paying attention.

"And what would you have done if I had told you Christmas night about that phone call and that I was going to meet with this woman? You would have argued with me, right? Probably all night, as if there was a choice. . . ."

"Stop!" she yelped, holding up both hands in surrender. She looked at him in silence for a moment and then asked quietly, "Is that why we're going to this party?"

Michael shook his head slowly. "Don't be cute. Goddamn it, Katy, you just don't fight fair."

Katy nodded and turned her eyes forward. "You're right, I don't," she said. "I guess there are some things that just don't lend themselves to a fair fight." There was more silence. She stared out into the illuminated streaks of snow, the flakes beginning to grow large and heavy so that a few broke through the barrier of wind and died on the defrosted windshield. She did not look at him as she began to speak. "I know I should say I'm sorry, Michael, but I'm not. I'm not sorry, I'm just scared. When we were together before, toward the end, you know, you scared me. I never really understood what it was like. Maybe you're right. Maybe I thought it was TV cops and robbers. I don't know. The truth is, I really never thought much about it. Anyway, it wasn't your job that scared me. It was you. I told you that months ago. And it just scares me to think of it starting up again. You shouldn't have promised. I know it's not your fault, but you shouldn't have promised."

Michael looked over at Katy, whose stare drifted off. Unconsciously, his foot backed off a bit on the accelerator, and he did not say anything.

Katy cocked her head a bit, as if the weight of some thought had shifted and her voice began to creep out slowly, softly, almost detached. "You know we all tell funny stories about my father, and he could do some funny things sometimes, but the truth of it . . . he was mad. Crazy, insane—whatever you want to call it. I never knew him when he wasn't. They always said it was the war that did it to him. But I wonder sometimes. Anyway, that was before I was born. Before I was conceived, even. My aunts and uncles used to tell me all kinds of stories about him. How different he had been before. Always calm and quiet except when he'd have a joke to tell. Everyone said Momma had gotten the pick of the litter.

"But the war changed all that. Momma never said anything, of course. Just went on pretending he was the same man. But I never really saw that man, the one my aunts would tell me about, the one Momma pretended he was. One day he'd be kind and gentle, taking Jack and me fishing or into town or wherever. And then all of a sudden he'd turn mean. No warning. You never even knew what had set him off. What not to say or do so he wouldn't start talking crazy about things I never understood. I couldn't tell you today what he was saying when he got in those moods. But I knew he was crazy. And every kid I grew up with knew. Their parents wouldn't let them come over to my house because . . . I don't know, they were scared, too, I guess."

Katy fell silent for a moment. The car slowed even more as Michael turned and looked at her. She had never spoken of her father except by anecdote. Humorous and affectionate, but distant all the same. Her voice turned curious, as if she were the subject of her own curiosity.

"I remember how scared I'd get when Poppa'd start telling his war stories. Sometimes he'd be okay, like I sometimes hear you or your friends talking about your cases. Joking about murders and rapes and whatever. Actually finding something to laugh about in an autopsy report." She shook her head. "God, it always sounds just like my father." Michael made a gesture as if he wanted to explain, but Katy stopped him. "No, I understand, I really do. Or maybe I just think I do. I don't know. But I know what I saw happen to my father. I know sometimes he'd start talking about the war like he was telling a joke and then he'd start drifting off and he'd get that look in his eye and you knew it was time to get away. You knew to run to Momma so she or Uncle Willy or someone would get his medicine. Calm him down before he'd hurt himself or one of us. And I'd cry and cry and Momma would just pretend everything was all right. 'Keep the good thought,' she'd say. And Grammy and Uncle Willy'd take me over to the cottage for a while. Sometimes I'd just stay there for a day or two until Poppa would stop raving and Uncle Willy'd tell me over and over it wasn't Poppa's fault. That the war did funny things to a man's mind, and there was no telling what might have happened to make him that way. He'd say just like the war took part of his arm, it took part of Poppa's brain and we had to help Poppa just like we'd help him if he needed a second hand for something.

"I was thirteen when my father died and I never knew why. I never knew what happened. No one would talk about it. 'Keep the good thought.' "

Michael had no real sense of the car's slowing until the snow began to collect in patterned droplets on the windshield. He turned the wiper switch to intermittent. The blades jerked upward an inch or two, then stopped before sweeping the glass clean. That done, Michael looked at Katy, who turned to look at him.

"I thought your job was doing the same thing to you. I thought maybe you were just a little bit mad."

"Jesus, Kate," was all he could muster. The wipers jerked upward again and Michael quickly cut them off as if they were interfering.

"I don't believe that anymore. I really don't. You're not mad. But you're dangerous. For me, anyhow. You go off on your own and no one knows where you are or what you're doing. And the more you keep to yourself, the more that makes me nervous. So I wanted to know everything. Or I thought I did. I thought that's all I'd need. Just to know what's going on. Then I'd understand. Then I could handle it."

Katy looked away as her eyes began to swell with tears, but her voice betrayed her.

"But when you told me about this creature who

incinerates bodies and with a telephone call can just as easily have someone killed in his jail cell as steer a city contract to a friend, when someone like that is having us followed and has you and me and Momma and Grammy in some file somewhere . . . Jesus, Michael, I don't like your job. I don't like any part of it, and I'm not sure I like you. This breezy little it's-all-part-of-the-job attitude. As if you're enjoying it all. As if you're the only one who can save this screwed-up world. As if you're the only one who understands."

A picnic area was just ahead of them, and Michael pulled in and stopped. He shook his head and a chuckle escaped, unintended and sounding sardonic. Katy's eyes turned angrily on him, and he lifted his hand to ward off the storm.

"Kate, I'm not your father. And, no, I don't think I'm the only one who understands. In fact, sometimes I think I'm the only one who doesn't. I don't think I ever have. The crusades ended for me a long time ago. I don't know, I guess I never quite got used to the idea that all the things that I thought were aberrations—the politics, the back-stabbing, even the petty little corruptions—weren't aberrations at all. They're part of the system. Hell, they *are* the system. And it's the system that's important, not what it was set up to do. In the end no one really cares about some body found in an alley or who put it there or why. All that's just an excuse to begin the games. The body's just the football. What's important is how well you toss it around. No, I don't claim to understand it. I just do it."

"Then why? Why do you do it?"

"You want me to quit?"

She let out a long, plaintive sigh. "I want you and me to be together without all this insanity between us, without all this meanness around us." Michael reached over for her hand but Katy pulled back and her eyes flared. "Yes, I want you to quit. I want you to be a poet or a farmer or a sailmaker, but you're not. So what? I'd rather have been sitting in front of the fire on Christmas Eve. But I wasn't. I was flying back from Chicago because some cretin just couldn't wait to see our snappy new ad campaign for panty shields. It's what I do. It's what you do. What's the point of arguing about it?"

He asked again, more slowly than before, "Do you want me to quit? Because if that's what you truly want, I will. Right now. Tonight."

She stared at him for a moment, trying to gauge how serious he was. Her eyes narrowed. "I want you to get that sonofabitch who has a file on us and then quit. That's what I want."

≫ ≪

By ten o'clock they were again on the road heading back to the city and Barkley Talbot's party. "Mission accomplished?" Katy asked.

"Yeah. I just told him I was going to mix a little business with pleasure and that we needed some time together. He looked at me a little squirrelly but said he'd take care of it. Incidentally, your timing was perfect. He was starting to press me again about taking a supervisor's job when you and Rachel came back."

"It was a mutual save. I like Rachel but I could only listen to so many stories about their kids' IQ and the aerobic marathon bake-off or whatever she was talking about. I don't know, she always seems starved for conversation but just doesn't have much of anything to talk about."

Michael didn't seem to hear, his thoughts quickly distancing him from Dan and Rachel McKeethen. He turned to Katy with a questioning smile.

"So—are you or are you not going to take me up on my offer for a free, all-expense-paid holiday in the Caribbean? You already admitted that this is a good time for you at work."

"There's not going to be any craziness, right? I mean, you're not going down there to single-handedly capture a band of armed dope dealers, right?"

"No, Kate, I am not crazy. I am not looking for trouble. All I want to do is try and find someone who knew this man Godoy—the man Wheatley said he killed in the alley. A wife, a girlfriend, maybe someone who worked with him. See if they have any idea what he was doing in Washington. That's all."

Katy leaned over and kissed his cheek, running her fingers down the folds of his tuxedo shirt. "I can't wait," she said. And she kissed him again before adding, "Look, I'm . . . I'm sorry about this week. I just—"

He stopped her with a squeeze of her hand. "Me, too," he smiled. "Don't worry, this will all be over soon."

Seventeen

The midday sun was smoothing the hard edge of winter, and thin rivers reached out from the banked snow to lace the otherwise dry pavement. Jimmy Legget was droning on, something about a hot tip on a mutual fund, but Eddie Nickles was not listening. His ears were tuned to the sounds from the street as the police cruiser splashed through the intermittent streams. It reminded him of bacon frying, which in turn reminded him that he was hungry. He was always hungry after visiting the morgue, an associative reaction he had never bothered to analyze.

Eddie was disappointed, but he had expected to be. The autopsy protocol, now rolled like a bat in his beefy fist, offered nothing new about the life or death of the young man murdered on Christmas night. As expected, the death was ruled a homicide: severe blunt-force injury to the left forehead. Several tiny chips of glass had been found embedded in the pulp that had once been the young man's eye socket and brow. A laboratory technician buried somewhere deep inside the fortress of the J. Edgar Hoover Building was now trying to determine if those chips could be associated with the heavy crystal ashtray found in the bathroom of apartment 4C, the ashtray washed clean of any fingerprints or particles of blood or bone or skin or hair.

But still there was no hint of who the victim was. Fifteen days had passed and still he was known only by the cryptic descriptors in the Homicide files: "B/M, 18-22, 5′9″, 140 lbs, complex. brn, eyes brn, hair blk, rt ear pierced, 3″ scar left forearm, deceased." The only thing missing, Eddie thought, was "smoked Kools." No name, no address, no driver's license or Social Security card, no one claiming his body at the morgue, no one calling to report him missing.

"Take a left up here," Eddie said, and pointed to the next cross street as a pool of slush thudded suddenly against the car's undercarriage. "I hate this shit."

"What?"

"This lousy weather."

Jimmy took his eyes from the road, exaggerating his incredulity. "What're you talking about? The sun's out, it's warming up."

"There's a connection here, you know that? I keep thinking there's a connection here. It's the bugs."

Jimmy shook his head slowly. "Man, people kept telling me but I wouldn't listen. Does anybody ever know what the fuck you're talking about?"

"You don't think there's a connection here?"

"I don't know what you're talkin' about."

"This case. The fag killing. I'm saying there may be a connection here."

"To what?"

"Look, think about it. The place is a high-class trick pad but no one's standing at the door collecting for the room, y'know? The old lady, Dalton, she says the customers are all middle-aged suits. No street garbage. The whores and fags all look cleaned up to her. And the kid. Young. Nice-lookin' kid, I guess. Kinda hard to tell with his face caved in. But nice clothes. Clean. No signs of any serious dope habit. A little coke in his blood, but that's all. A pretty little fag making a livin' lettin' some middle-aged suit give him a blow job."

Eddie reflected a moment.

Then, almost as an aside, he said, "Probably how he got killed. Refused to do the old man after the old man did him. The suit goes nuts, grabs the first heavy thing nearby, and whacks him."

"How do you come up with that?"

"No semen in the kid's mouth or anus. Anyway, the whole place is bugged. Top-of-the-line equipment. Technical people from the Bureau came over and took a look at the stuff. They say it's a class-A job. Real professional. What does that tell you?"

"Someone's spent a lot of money to set up a trick pad and take pictures. Blackmail. Maybe someone just likes to watch others do it. So what? What connection are you talking about?"

"And what the landlord said. A man comes to rent the apartment three months ago. Signs a lease. Gives him six months' rent in advance, in cash. Gives him a bank reference. The bank account turns out to be opened just a few days before the apartment's rented. The address on the account turns out to be a phony, and I'll bet you a lunch at the Chili Bowl the Social Security number comes back phony. Sound familiar?"

"You're not talking about Higgs, are you?"

"Does it sound like the same stuff Wheatley said he did for Higgs? Does it sound like the same setup that the people in the old case described to us? You read our notes. And remember what Wheatley said. Even after they got word that we had someone talking about the party houses, they didn't close down. They just moved the location. Been doing the same thing for years. Why not Higgs?"

"It's not exactly a unique setup. I mean, it's not the first time someone thought of taking pictures."

"True. But see, this is different. See, it's not like a onetime setup, like someone gets targeted and they set him up. This is an ongoing trick pad and it's moved every so often. Now the man is spending a lot of money to run that kind of operation. Am I right?"

Jimmy nodded.

"And he's not doing it just because he likes to watch people doing it. Hell, a few bucks at a video store takes care of that. So they've got to be recording folks that are worth more than a few laughs over a case of beer. Insurance, extortion, whichever. Now, who does that sound like? Take a left at the next street and find a place to park. It's the building on the corner."

"I know it sounds like Higgs," Jimmy said. "But so what? I mean, in the past few months, somebody takes a leak in the park and I'm ready to say Higgs ordered him to do it. But I don't understand the connection. And even if it is Higgs, aren't we running up the same blind alley? The lease is a dead end; the bank account's a dead end. No leads on the short, fat man, and if we do find him, what's he gonna do for us? We'd never let go of a murder just so's the man'd say Higgs set him up with a piece of ass. So what's the big connection?"

"The man in black. That's our connection. This guy's out in the truck running all the recording equipment, right? I mean, that's what the Bureau people say, right? And he's a pro. Means Higgs, say, is paying him big money over and over again. Probably an independent. Probably doing a lot of business with Higgs. Maybe been doing it for a long time. We find him and we find someone we can use. Am I right?"

"Why should he talk?" Jimmy argued. "What have we got on him even if we do turn him up? Can't charge him with the murder. What—conspiracy to solicit a blow job? Maybe possession of intercept equipment? He's not gonna do any time over that. Why would he bargain?"

"We'll think of something. . . . Over there, a space."

Jimmy stopped and backed into a space a half block before the front entrance of Ella Dalton's building. He turned off the ignition but neither man opened his door. "I don't know, maybe," Jimmy said without enthusiasm. "But the man in black looks like a dead end, too. The license number the old lady gave you was no good. Right?" Eddie nodded. "Maryland and Virginia, too?"

"The number's good in both but doesn't match the lady's description of the truck. I even tried a few different combinations, like maybe she switched a number or something, but nothing so far."

"Another dead end."

"Patience, Jimmy. It takes patience. We spend a little time with her, maybe she remembers how she wrote down the number wrong. Maybe she remembers something else. You never know what could turn up."

It was plain that Ella Dalton was glad for the company. Cookies and sandwiches awaited them on the butler's table, and a bottle of Old Grand Dad sat ready on the kitchen counter next to liter bottles of soda water and ginger ale and three tall glasses. It was barely one o'clock.

"You won't tell on us if we have a little?" she asked Jimmy quite seriously after he declined her offer of bourbon. He was on duty, he explained, almost apologized, and thanked her for the plain ginger ale. He assured the old woman that their secret was safe with him as Eddie helped fix their drinks.

Mrs. Dalton felt much better, thank you, since learning that her landlord was going to pay a one-hundred-dollar reward to the tenant who had called the police. "Mr. Vincent called me himself to thank me and to say I could stay here as long as I pleased," she said, beaming. Eddie thought Mr. Vincent had carried it off well. The man even seemed pleased to play the role of benevolent landlord, particularly with monies appropriated from the police department's snitch fund.

Her fear seemed to have dissipated, and the old woman was animated in answering all of their questions. Her voice tripped with a certain excitement in retelling the smallest of details, except, of course, when she mentioned the young man who died, at which time her voice would trail off respectfully. Again and again they asked their questions and again and again she answered, neither tiring nor becoming impatient. She was, however, perplexed about that license number. "Now I can't be for sure that it was a D.C. plate. I guess I just assumed it was. Tell the truth, I wasn't paying much attention to that, but I was sure of those numbers. Wouldn't've written them down otherwise."

"Do you have binoculars or something like that you were looking through?" Jimmy asked.

"Don't need any such thing," she said proudly. "Course, sometimes I get the round ones mixed up."

"Round ones?"

"You know, threes and eights and sixes and such."

Jimmy nodded to Eddie, as if to signal that they were wasting their time. The number she had written down was 268–933. The old woman seemed to sense Jimmy's skepticism and she struggled up from her chair without putting her glass down. A few drops of bourbon and soda spilled on the floor. She paid them no attention and moved toward the side window.

"See? This is where I saw him mostly. Parked right along this little side street or over to that parking lot. The truck looked a lot like that one there, 'cept it was all black and had no writing all over it. Come over here, Mr. Highsmith, and look and see if you can't read a license number yourself."

"It's Legget, ma'am. Detective Legget." Jimmy looked back at Eddie and rolled his eyes as he strolled to the window. It was the second time the woman had called him Highsmith.

Eddie's brow furrowed. "Mrs. Dalton," he asked, "why is it that you think this is Detective Highsmith?"

The old woman looked suddenly embarrassed and put her hand gently on Jimmy's arm. "Oh, I'm sorry, young man. Is Mr. Highsmith coming later?" A short, self-conscious giggle escaped and she said, "I'm sorry, I just thought you were Detective Highsmith."

"Which Detective Highsmith are you talking about?" Eddie asked, not wanting to alarm the old woman with the fact that he knew of no one by that name.

Ella Dalton looked a little confused, as if she might have mixed something up. Her answer was laced with hesitation. "Why, the one who called a little while after you did. He said you were busy and that's why he was calling. I told him to come along if he wanted. Wasn't that all right?"

The two detectives looked at each other and Eddie stood up and went to the window. He took the woman by her elbow and moved her gently back to her chair. Her look of confusion gave way to concern as Eddie handed her the drink and squatted down directly in front of the chair. His voice was serious. "Tell me what Detective Highsmith said. Exactly."

"Well, he called about a half hour or so after you did, like I said. And he said he was a Homicide detective working on the case with you and he wondered if he could come by to ask me a few more questions about what happened upstairs. He said you were busy and you asked him to call. Did I do something wrong?"

"No, ma'am. Now I don't want to alarm you, 'cause Jimmy—Detective Legget—and me are right here. But, see, we don't have a Detective Highsmith in Homicide."

"Oh, Lordy." She took a big swallow of her drink.

"Did he say anything about us, Jimmy and me, coming over here? Think carefully. It's real important." Eddie stopped a moment and then added, "It'll be okay. Nothing's gonna happen. But it's real important, what you said to this Highsmith."

Jimmy, too, looked concerned and had moved to the edge of the window. He was watching the street as the old woman mined her memory in silence. When she started to speak, she did so deliberately, giving voice to the conversation that replayed in her mind.

"He said he was Detective Highsmith with the Homicide squad. 'I'm working with Detective Nickles on the case of the young man who died in 4C. Did I remember Detective Nickles?' 'Oh, yes,' I said.

Well, Detective Nickles was real busy and he wanted him to call and see if he could come over and ask some more questions about what I saw. Would that be okay? Would he be disturbing anything? 'Oh, no,' I said. Was I expecting any company? And I guess I laughed a little. I guess I shouldn't have, but I did and I said of course not 'cause I had already told you that it was all right to come over and I thought what nice young men you all are. You're all so worried about disturbing an old lady who never has no company except for Lisa across the hall. She's so sweet to me, Lisa is. And he said would two o'clock be all right, and I said that'd be fine, but after I hung up I thought you had said around one, so I didn't know if he was mixed up or what, so I just got everything ready for one o'clock and said to myself I could wait if it was two and just put a little cellophane over the sandwiches. And he said that two o'clock would be fine for him and you, you know, Detective Nickles would be grateful and he asked again, you know, was I sure I wasn't expecting anyone and that he wouldn't be disturbing me and I just laughed again and said no. I guess I was acting silly, wasn't I?"

"No, ma'am. You weren't acting silly at all. But you're certain you never said to him anything about me and Jimmy coming over here?"

"No, I guess I didn't. I just thought he already knew that."

Jimmy looked back and said to Eddie, in a voice that alarmed by its obvious intent not to, "C'mere a minute." Eddie stood up and walked to the window. "Look at the truck again," Jimmy said. "Can you read the license plate?"

Eddie squinted at the light-gray van that sat parked facing away from them. He studied the plates for a few moments, then said, "I'm not sure."

"It's hard to see from this angle," Jimmy said, "but it's a Maryland plate and it looks like 266–339. The round ones could be mixed up," he joked in a whisper.

Eddie looked at his watch. It was 1:40 P.M. "Doesn't match the color or anything."

"Paint job? Switched plates?" Jimmy offered, as he pulled out his notebook and jotted down the red and yellow lettering on the van's side panel—SENTRY ELECTRONICS, BLADENSBURG—and a telephone number.

Eddie turned to the old woman, whose eyes stared at him as she took another long sip of her drink. "Was that truck here before we came? The gray one with all the writing on it?" Ella Dalton shook her head. "Do you mind if I use your phone? You have a Maryland phone book?"

"It's in the cabinet next to the phone. Right there in the kitchen. Is everything all right?" she asked nervously.

"Everything's fine," Eddie said with an enormous grin to emphasize his confidence.

The grin evaporated as he turned his back to the old woman and moved into the kitchen, where he found the phone book and began flipping the pages. The hurried snap and rustle of the pages filled the quiet apartment as Eddie searched. He stopped for an instant, then turned some more. His forefinger slid down one column and then another. The page was turned and the finger slid down another column. Shaking his head, he flipped back to the previous page and again ran his forefinger up and down the listings. "Not there," he said to no one in particular, then called out to Jimmy. "What's the number on the side of the truck?" Jimmy called it out as Eddie dialed. A few seconds passed. "Not in service," Eddie mumbled, then dialed again.

"Yeah, Harry, how ya doin'? George around?" In a moment: "George? Yeah, it's me, Eddie. . . . Yeah, yeah, later. Look, I need a big favor in a big hurry. Can you trace a Maryland tag for me—I mean ASAP? . . . Yeah, it's on a truck. Two-six-six, three-three-nine. . . . No, no—three-three-nine. . . . Yeah, right. I really need it in a hurry. Let me give you the number here." And he did. "It's important, okay? . . . Yeah, and George? Can we keep this between us right now? Thanks, I owe you."

Eddie looked at his watch again. 1:44.

Jimmy spoke without turning his head, looking through the thin space he created between the edge of the curtain and the window frame. "Ma'am, you say this man in black was a tall, thin white man?"

Eddie stopped dialing the next number, slowly replaced the receiver on its hook, and stepped away from the kitchen counter and into the living room.

Ella Dalton's eyes were expanding as she answered, "Uh-huh."

"Dark hair and a beard, though?"

"Sometimes," she said, anxiously watching Jimmy, who spoke to her without taking his eyes off whatever he was looking at. "But not always. Sometimes he's not wearing anything on his face and sometimes his hair looks lighter than others, except at night. He's always in black at night. Lord, is that him you're watching?"

Eddie saw the old woman begin to shake as she tried to put her drink down. He moved over to her and took the glass from her hand. "Mrs. Dalton, look me right in the eye." She did, but then reflexively looked back at Jimmy, next to the window. "Mrs. Dalton," Eddie repeated, and the old woman turned back to him. "We're right here and we're not going anywhere. We're not going to let anything happen to you. There's nothing to be frightened of. Okay?"

"Give me my drink," she demanded, and Eddie did so with a wink.

Jimmy motioned silently for Eddie to join him, and when Eddie was behind him at the window, he half whispered, "White dude in coveralls just walked out of the alley carrying a toolbox. Walked up to the corner and then back to the truck. Seemed real interested in looking around before he opened the back and got in. No facial hair. Wearing a cap so it's hard to tell hair color. Short sideburns, looks brown."

"He still in the truck?" Eddie asked, and Jimmy nodded. "How long?"

"About a minute. Whaddaya think?"

"Fuck," Eddie whispered, and tapped his finger lightly on Jimmy's chest. "It's the reports!" Jimmy frowned that he did not understand. "The reports, Jimmy. I put it all in the reports. That she could identify the man in black. How she said she saw him a whole buncha times. How—" And he stopped himself. "Goddamn it! How she was the only one in the building during the day. Everyone else worked. What if the man in black got access to the reports? What if there really is a connection here?"

Jimmy began an answer, but stopped and pointed out the window. "There he goes."

They watched as the truck pulled slowly out of its space and then turned right into the alley across the street. The two detectives looked at each other but did not say anything. The phone rang and Eddie looked at his watch. 1:48. "That'll be for me," he said, and hurried to the kitchen while Jimmy stayed by the window. He stopped himself next to the phone. "Ma'am, you mind answering this? And if it's Detective Highsmith, well, you just tell him to c'mon over. Okay?"

"Oh, Lordy," she said as she struggled to hurry for the phone. "Hello?" She sighed in relief. "It's for you. George somebody."

The conversation was brief and after he hung up Eddie said to his partner, "It's registered to an eighty-four Dodge van. Black."

"Oh, Lordy," Mrs. Dalton repeated, and slumped back into her chair.

"It'll be all right, ma'am," Eddie said. Then to Jimmy: "It's leased from a dealer. George is runnin' down to who. Ma'am, this may be nothing at all, you know, but if this Detective Highsmith fella wants to see you, then we want to see him. Okay? So if this man comes to the door, would you mind answering the buzzer and lettin' him in?"

The old woman looked as if she wasn't sure whether she was frightened or excited, but after a pause she nodded briskly, just once.

Eddie smiled. "If we get this guy, I'll buy you a case of Old Grand Dad."

"If you're buying, it'll be Jack Daniel's," she said without a smile. Eddie laughed anyway.

Eddie deliberately slowed the pace of things as he walked over to a corner and turned on the television. He was talking the whole time but paused between what seemed like random thoughts. "There's no other way up here but the stairs, is there? I don't see any fire escape." She shook her head. "No back staircase?" Again she shook her head. "Same for the fourth floor? He'd have to pass by here so we could see him through the peephole?"

"Yep," she said simply.

"Okay. Now if he rings the bell, you just answer and let him in downstairs. Okay?" She nodded.

"And then I want you to go into the bedroom and close the door and stay there until we say to come out. Okay?"

The old woman nodded and drained her glass.

Several minutes passed in silence before Jimmy looked back at Eddie and said quietly, "Here he comes. At least I think it's him. Just walked out of the alley and is heading for the front. He's wearing a suit. No hat. Dark brown hair. Mustache."

2:01.

Jimmy moved over to the front door while Eddie helped Mrs. Dalton out of her chair once more and held her elbow as they moved slowly across the living room to stand by the speaker and the button beside it. The three of them stood there too long, it seemed to Eddie, waiting for the buzzer. Each of them fidgeted a bit in silence.

2:03. The buzzer sounded.

"Oh, Lordy," Mrs. Dalton said as she reached for the speaker button. Eddie put his arm around her shoulder and shook his head slowly.

"Give it a little bit. You're just walking over here from your chair. It's just a bit of acting." He smiled. "How'd you like to do this for a living?"

She took a deep breath. "Jack Daniel's, remember!"

"Okay," Eddie said, and nodded to the speaker button.

"Yes? Who is it?"

A deep, pleasant voice echoed through the room. "Mrs. Dalton, it's Detective Highsmith. I work with Detective Nickles. I called you earlier to say I'd be coming over."

"Yes, all right," the old woman said, and buzzed open the security door at the first-floor entrance.

"That's good," Eddie winked at her as he helped to hurry her to the bedroom, while Jimmy moved to his position against the wall behind the front door.

Just before closing the door to her bedroom, the old woman looked up at Eddie and said, "Don't you all go shootin' him in here. You take him outside for any of that."

"Yes, ma'am," Eddie said, then quickly moved back to the front door and peered out the peephole. "You ready?" he asked Jimmy, as he slowly lifted his service revolver from its holster. Jimmy moved his revolver up in a casual salute and signaled with a nod that he was. "Here he comes," Eddie whispered, watching a peephole distortion of a tall, thin man stopping on the landing and looking at both ends of the hall. He then moved toward Mrs. Dalton's door and, as he passed the staircase, looked up to the fourth-floor landing. There was nothing in his hands, and he did not hesitate before knocking lightly.

Eddie paused before making a bit of a production of rattling open the chain lock, unsnapping the dead bolt, and clicking open the lock in the doorknob. He moved to the side and in one swift motion swung open the door.

"Mrs. Dal———" the man began, just before his knees buckled slightly.

Eddie Nickles actually grinned as the barrel of his gun moved quickly and pressed firmly to the man's forehead. "What section of the department did you say you were with, Detective?"

"Oh, fuck," Aaron Yozkowitz murmured, knowing he was the Wizard no more.

Eighteen

Aaron Yozkowitz remained on the third floor just long enough for Ella Dalton to nod her confirmation that he was indeed the man in black and to express her hope that he forever burn in hell for killing the young man. It made no difference to her who had struck the blow.

Yozkowitz did not utter a word, neither in response to Ella Dalton's identification of him nor to her viperous oath. Neither he nor the detectives spoke as he was taken to apartment 4C and seated in one of two kitchen chairs, his hands behind him and cuffed to the chair's back, his feet uncomfortably contorted and cuffed to the crossrail between the chair's legs. His only words were muttered to himself when the two detectives retired to the hallway, leaving him alone with the scars that remained of Christmas night: the bloodstained carpet and the unrepaired evidence of the removal of his microphones and cameras.

In the hallway and alone with his young partner, Eddie Nickles spoke first. "It's time, Jimmy. No more let's wait and see. You're gonna have to decide right now. The rules have to be bent and you have to make up your mind."

Detective Legget did not look away and spoke with equal calm. "Lay it out for me."

Eddie reached into his pocket and pulled out two sandwich bags from Ella Dalton's kitchen. One held an empty hypodermic needle and the second a small vial of white powder. Both items had been recovered from Aaron Yozkowitz's side coat pocket. He stared at the two clear plastic bags held by hands whose shake was barely perceptible. "Okay," he said, "this is how I see it. The man came to kill her. This," he said, referring to the vial of powder, "I'll bet is some kind of Mickey Finn. Seconal or Nembutal or something."

Jimmy shrugged that he had no idea.

"So, I figure maybe this guy thought he could schmooze the old lady into a drink of soda or tea or something and slip her a little sleeping powder. She nods off and then he shoots her with this," he said, holding up the hypodermic needle. "A big fat air bubble in her vein. Straight to the heart. It'd do an old lady like her easily."

Jimmy shrugged again.

"Anyway, she dies. Maybe they find a trace of barbiturate in the system, but who's gonna doubt that an old lady might take a sleeping pill once in a while? Maybe they don't even look for anything. She's old. She's expected to die. Maybe no one finds her for a few days or more. Anyway, that's what I figure he's here for."

"No argument so far."

"Now, the only reason he's here to kill her is that one of our brothers in blue has told this creep or whoever he works for what's in the file, that this old lady is the only witness, and that she can ID him. The truck and the license plate's no big worry. The numbers and the state are wrong. So a new paint job and he's back in business. The only loose end—the old lady. And it had to be a cop that tells him that. It never hit the papers and nothing's been presented to the DA's office. It had to be a fuckin' cop."

Jimmy remained silent and expressionless.

"But we don't know which one." Eddie stopped again, this time for himself, to let his thoughts settle into some order as he watched the toe of his shoe work the carpet. He then looked up.

"The whole thing spells Higgs. The setup with the apartment, the information out of our files going to the other side—everything. I know you think I'm stretching here, but I'm tellin' ya this is Higgs's work. And I'm gonna take a chance that I'm right. Y'know, the man's got to be wondering if it was more than just bad luck our being here. Like if he's got a snitch, maybe we've got one, too. Anyway, that's how I'm going to approach him. Just like I already know he works for Higgs and we planned to be here to catch him in the act. If I'm wrong and there's no connection to Higgs, he'll let us know quick enough. We read him his rights and call for a transport."

"And if there is a connection?"

"Then we bend the rules." Eddie did not allow a response. "Jimmy, it was pure fucking luck that old lady isn't dead right now. And in a few days she'd be found and we'd be sitting around sayin' 'Ah, shit, wonder what happened.' No leads, no nothing. But the old lady'd still be dead. Because of a cop, Jimmy. And we'll probably never know, but we both suspect the same thing about Wheatley's hanging. What do we do? Go by the manual? What do we book him on? Burglary? Attempt murder? Whatever he ends up being charged with, we'll never find out who the dirty cop is. And in the end he'll walk."

"Man, what are you talking about? We've got him cold."

Eddie took a deep breath, about to tell a child some bad news. "Jimmy, you only think we have him cold because you think like a cop. Cops don't matter in the courthouse. You gotta start thinking like the lawyers and the judges. The handwriting's on the wall in fuckin' neon here. First, the man never says a word. His lawyers say everything. What we've got is a theory that he was here to kill the old lady. A theory, that's all. No evidence. We can't really tie him to the kid's murder. Don't have a truck that matches, no match on the license plate, and I'll bet that this guy probably has an electrician's license as a cover. Okay, we got a positive ID from the old lady. How long you think that'll stand up in a courtroom? She's got the license numbers screwed up, sometimes the man has a beard, sometimes not, et cetera, et cetera. Hell, we'll probably have a hard time getting a DA to charge him and you'll never get it past a preliminary hearing.

"Next, let's assume he gets indicted for burglary and attempt murder. Just assume. Attempt murder's a misdemeanor. No felony assault here. Burglary's not gonna look all that great either, since we were the ones who told her to let the man in. The man denies he ever claimed to be a detective. Says he was on a call to do some electrical work and got the address screwed up. Who ya gonna believe? This guy or a dotty old lady who thinks he's the headless horseman? That's a wash. The sleeping powder's for his own use. The needle's 'cause he's a diabetic. Or his wife or his kid or someone. Hell, the defense attorney'll go out and rent a fuckin' diabetic to come in and vouch for the needle. Bottom line? Even if we get a conviction the man walks on probation. No time. You can hear the judge now, can't you? 'Well, after all, nobody was actually hurt, and this is his first offense.' See, my man, judges think it doesn't matter what the defendant was trying to do. They only get upset when they actually kill someone, and even then you have to listen to all that horseshit about how putting this man in jail won't bring the victim back. The man'll walk, Jimmy. I promise you. And you'll spend the rest of your days in the department looking around and wondering who it was. Who dropped the dime on Ella Dalton. You're gonna have a new partner one of these days. You want to be worrying about whether the man's bought? You want one of Higgs's men watching your back if things get hairy?"

"What's your solution?"

"The woman's got a grandson somewhere down in Virginia, Carolina—somewhere. You go back down and talk her into a vacation from the city for a while. Get ahold of whoever will take her in for a month or so and arrange it. Tell her someone will stay with her until they come to pick her up. If it can't be done any other way, I'll drive her to wherever. You just arrange all that. Okay?"

"And you?"

"And me? I'll be taking care of business."

"Eddie, c'mon, man."

"Jimmy, unless you want to be there, I'm going back in to talk to the prisoner. See if he wants to talk to me. As far as you're concerned, it's according to the book. I'll advise the man of his constitutional rights and call for a transport. I'll come get you when the transport arrives. Okay?"

"Why do I get the feeling I'll be retired and drawing Social Security before this transport gets here?"

Eddie didn't smile. "Make sure the old lady's taken care of. Okay?"

"Sure."

"And, Jimmy, have a drink with her. Relax."

>> <<

Aaron Yozkowitz was squirming in his chair when Eddie walked in and locked the door behind him.

"I don't want any trouble, Detective, and I'm not going to give you any," Yozkowitz said. "It's just that I have real bad knees. Arthritis, real bad arthritis. I'd appreciate if you just let me move my legs. That's all."

Eddie looked at the man for several moments without giving any hint of his mood. He then nodded slowly and said, "I think the first thing we're gonna do is advise you of your rights. As long as you're with me, you don't have any. Do you understand that?"

Yozkowitz stopped squirming.

"The second thing is the rules. As long as we're together the only rules are my rules. Understand?"

Yozkowitz stared at the detective without expression and did not respond.

Eddie walked up to him and stood very close. "Understand?" he asked again.

Yozkowitz leaned as far back in his chair as possible, still without answering. Eddie made no attempt to disguise what he was about to do. In a motion slow enough to emphasize the effort he was putting into it, he drew back his right arm and then slammed his fist into Yozkowitz's face, sending the man and the chair to which he was manacled tumbling to the floor. It took a few seconds before Yozkowitz tried to move from his twisted position, face down, his arms pulled back and his legs curled under the chair lying on top of him. Eddie walked over and looked down on Yozkowitz's face, the right side pressed into the carpet, the left beginning to show the redness that would soon close his eye.

"When you tell me that you understand the rules, I'll help you up," Eddie said calmly.

"I understand," Aaron Yozkowitz coughed.

It was an hour or more before Jimmy was summoned to apartment 4C and saw Aaron Yozkowitz lying back on the living room sofa, ice cubes wrapped in a towel pressed to his left eye and cheek.

"What happened?" Jimmy asked softly, and with the hesitancy of someone not certain he wanted to know.

"Tell Detective Legget what happened to your eye," Eddie instructed casually.

Aaron Yozkowitz did not move his head from the arm of the sofa. His voice sounded rehearsed and hollow emanating from beneath the towel, which covered most of his face. "I bumped into the door when Detective Nickles kindly allowed me to use the bathroom."

"These FBI types," Eddie sneered. "Can't even go to the head without falling all over themselves."

"FBI?" Jimmy started in panic.

Eddie smiled. "Yeah, it seems our man Mr. Wizard . . . What is it they call you? Mr. Wizard?"

Yozkowitz murmured self-consciously, "The Wizard of Yoz."

"Yeah, it seems Mr. Wizard, here, used to work for the Bureau. That's where he learned how to bug places. Isn't that right, Mr. Wizard?"

There was no answer.

"Anyway, our friend Mr. Wizard . . ." Eddie stopped and checked his notebook. "Aaron Yozkowitz, actually. But anyway, our friend, here, understands that it's time to switch sides. I guess it wasn't too hard for him to figure out we must've had someone to let us know that the Wizard here was coming by to do the old lady. He won't admit it, but I don't think he's really figured out who our snitch is. But he agrees we can work this problem out. He says he was only going to test Mrs. Dalton. Y'know, see if she really could recognize him. And only if she did was he gonna do her. That's reasonable, don't you think, Jimmy? We can deal with someone as reasonable as that, don't you think?"

Jimmy sat down and took a moment before he asked stiffly, "What's the story?"

"Like we already knew, he says he's independent. Free-lances for Higgs. Been doing it off and on for about seven years. Someone else gets the place, he bugs it. He gets a call a day in advance if they want a tape of someone and he takes it from there. They get the tapes. Says he doesn't keep any copies but he and I are gonna take a ride to see his shop just to make sure. Aren't we, Mr. Wizard?" Aaron Yozkowitz did not answer. He knew it wasn't necessary.

Eddie's grin was infectious and Jimmy's nerves began to settle. "Does he know the man who killed the kid?"

"He's never told who the targets are. He's recognized a few—local honchos and the like, but not this one. Not the fat man. Doesn't even know who the kid was."

"Who calls him with the instructions?"

"A lady," Eddie said with a nod, and Jimmy responded with a rise of his eyebrows. They were thinking of the same suspect. Aaron Yozkowitz was oblivious to their signals, remaining still under the makeshift ice pack.

"No name?" Jimmy asked.

Yozkowitz volunteered. "No, I never deal in names really. She'll just call and say there's a problem with the Southeast apartment or the P. G.

County apartment or whatever one we're dealing with at the time. She'll just say that there's a problem with the wiring or whatever."

"How are you paid?" Jimmy followed.

"You're gonna like this," Eddie interjected. "Tell 'im, Mr. Wizard."

"I'll get a check a few days after each job drawn on some business account with a plain slip of paper clipped to it. On the paper will be typed an address, which, if I'm ever questioned, will be the address I'm to say I did electrical work for. Some of them I know, some of them I don't."

"Give him a few examples," Eddie instructed.

Yozkowitz took in a deep breath and sighed as he sat up and took the ice pack from his face. Jimmy winced at the red and purple swelling on the left side of Yozkowitz's face, the eye completely closed. "Okay, sometimes I'll get a check from one of Higgs's funeral homes. Sometimes from New Horizons."

"Ora Fisher?" Jimmy asked, looking at Eddie. Eddie nodded.

"Yeah," Yozkowitz said. "They run a lot of real estate in town and my company actually does do electrical work for them. I've got three men working for me, but I'm the only one doing the spook work. The company's more a cover. Hell, I make three or four times the money doing spook work than all my electrical business together," he said proudly, then stopped himself. "Anyway, I get checks from businesses I never heard of."

"Tell him about some of the others," Eddie said.

Yozkowitz recited a list of a half dozen or more businesses from which he received checks. "I mean, once in a while my men'll do a small job for one of the companies, but for the most part the checks are for spook work. Like I say, most of the companies I've never heard of. I couldn't tell you if they're real or just names on bank accounts."

Jimmy looked as if something had piqued his interest but he said nothing.

There was a long silence before Eddie said, "My man here says he doesn't know who Higgs's source is in our office or the department. We had a long talk about that." Jimmy looked at the crease that was once Yozkowitz's left eye and allowed himself a smile. "He says he got a call from this lady saying to expect a note that day or maybe . . . what was it, a coupla days after Christmas?"

Yozkowitz nodded.

"That afternoon a copy of our reports on the kid killing shows up. Hand-delivered, but he doesn't know by who. The envelope just gets dropped off at his office. That about right?"

Yozkowitz nodded again.

"There's a note attached." Eddie turned to Yozkowitz. "What'd the note say?"

"I don't remember the exact words, but it said that I was to be sure that this didn't create any problems—the fact that the woman said she could ID me and all. And if I needed any help to let them know. I have a number to call if there are any problems."

The two detectives just stood staring at each other as Aaron Yozkowitz settled his head on the back of the couch, and again put the ice pack to his eye.

Eddie was looking straight into Jimmy's eyes when he said, "And the best for last." Jimmy's expression looked dulled by an overload of information, but Eddie continued. "Back a coupla years ago, during the old investigation, we were bugged. Remember Mike and I saying that we had thought we had been bugged—even had his office swept by the Bureau? Well, this sonofabitch," he said, flipping a thumb toward Yozkowitz, "was the one who bugged Mike's office. His old office in the courthouse. He even has a tape of the Bureau sweeping the place." Eddie nodded admiringly. "No shit."

"What about now?" Jimmy asked.

"Tell him," Eddie directed Yozkowitz, without taking his eyes off Jimmy, waiting to enjoy the reaction.

Yozkowitz sat up again. "I guess Higgs is worried about something. I got a call to meet with him. It's pretty rare that I ever talked to the man directly. So I went to his office the night after Christmas. Late, like eleven-thirty. I guess it was a few days later I got the copies of the police reports. Anyway, he never mentioned anything about this. He wanted to know if I would take on a special job for him and bug this guy Holden's office again. Only this time he wanted me to report only to him. Not to mention anything to the lady who he has call me or to any of the other people I call messages through if something goes wrong. Y'know, the number I gave you," he said in a nod to Eddie. "Anyway, he said he'd give me a number to reach him when I had something to report and we'd arrange a drop for the tapes."

"Tell him how you're going to get into Holden's office," Eddie directed with a hint of impatience for the bottom line.

"Yeah, well, I'm supposed to deal with the same man who took care of it the last time. But we haven't worked anything out yet. Seems, the guy's getting nervous or something and a few days ago Higgs said the man finally had been convinced to cooperate. Apparently this guy Holden's out of town?"

Both detectives nodded, more to themselves than to Yozkowitz.

"So," Yozkowitz continued, "Higgs's man is supposed to call me tonight or tomorrow and we'll set up a time to get me in when I'll have lots of privacy and time to do the job."

"Tell him who Higgs's man is," Eddie said, still not having moved his eyes from Jimmy's face.

"His name's McKeethen. Dan McKeethen."

≫ ≪

It was almost eight-thirty that night before they had left Yozkowitz's office and were driving south along Route One toward the city. Neither man had said much in the past few minutes, each quieted by the implications of their day's work.

"You hungry?" Eddie asked.

Jimmy spoke as if he had not heard the question. "You think we better let Mike know about this? Y'know, about McKeethen?"

Eddie looked over sharply. "Shit," he said softly, and looked to his watch. They drove a bit farther before Eddie asked, "You got one of those telephone credit cards?"

"Yeah," Jimmy said with a chuckle.

"I thought you might. Pull over to the first phone booth you see. I got a deal for you. You pay for the call to Mike and I'll spring for dinner."

"You got his number?"

"Yeah, no problem."

A few minutes later, as they pulled up to a phone booth at the edge of a gas station, Jimmy asked, "He wouldn't've told McKeethen why he was going down there, would he?"

Eddie shook his head slowly, but said nothing.

Part III

Nineteen

Alton Kimbough recognized the signs, and the urgent efficiency of this morning alarmed him. The phone call had come not from Ishmael Dubard but from one of his minions, and early enough for Kimbough to catch the first seaplane out of Christiansted for the island of St. Thomas, thirty-five miles to the north. A chauffeur was waiting with the Mercedes's engine running as the seaplane lumbered out of St. Thomas Harbor and came to rest on the cement apron of the tiny airport near the center of town. Kimbough deplaned, walked directly to the open door of the car, and settled in the backseat where fresh coffee awaited him. The car sped through the arid patches of commercial development that pocked the island's southern shore, then slowed as the road rose sharply, twisting toward the top of the mountain where Dubard's house perched on a crag nearly fifteen hundred feet above the ocean.

When he arrived, Kimbough was told that it would be a few minutes and so he walked through an atrium to a wide stone porch facing east toward St. John and the British Virgins, Tortola and Jost Van Dyke. He stood at the railing, watching a sea whose swells were stalled in long, feathered ridges by the force of the Christmas winds. He kept his hands in his pockets and his shoulders hunched forward against the chill. It was ten, maybe fifteen, degrees cooler there than on the beaches or on the streets of Charlotte Amalie, where the tourists and the people who served them would soon crowd. Kimbough thought little of the tourists, who he imagined thought only of duty-free gifts and suntans. But now, close to the edge and waiting for Dubard, he envied them their shallow concerns.

"Good morning, my friend," Ishmael Dubard's voice called. "I'm sorry to have called you up here this early."

Kimbough turned and smiled solicitously. Tall and thin with thick, white hair combed straight back from a ruddy brown complexion, Dubard was often mistaken for a man a decade or more younger than his sixty-three years. This morning he looked his age.

"Morning, Governor," Kimbough said, maintaining the genteel formality that had marked their relationship since the time nearly twenty years before when Dubard had been one of the last appointed governors of the United States Virgin Islands.

"Come inside," Dubard invited with a slow sweep of his hand. "We need to talk."

Kimbough walked ahead and through the bulletproof glass and wood door to Dubard's study. Inside, fresh coffee, pastries, and sliced fruits were set out on a table and Dubard gestured for Kimbough to sit. Neither spoke while Dubard poured two cups of coffee to which each man carefully added cream and sugar.

After each had gathered a sample of fruit and pastry on his plate, Dubard said, "Alton, we have a problem which needs our immediate attention." Kimbough did not respond but took a sip of coffee. "It seems this man Holden, the prosecutor from

Washington, is here on business." Dubard's voice was measured but his eyes showed the impatience that often worried Kimbough. "Here," Dubard emphasized, stabbing the table with his finger. "On St. Thomas."

Kimbough slowly lowered his cup to its saucer. "I don't understand. Higgs told us that the investigation was ordered closed. What business could this Holden have here?"

"Yes, well, according to Higgs's source, Holden is working on his own, without the knowledge of his superiors. Ostensibly he is on holiday, but Higgs is certain he is here to investigate us."

Kimbough frowned. *Caution*, he reminded himself. "I wonder about the reliability of Higgs's information. Don't you think he may be jumping to too many conclusions? With all due respect to your friend, he seems to have a habit of acting before he thinks."

"Whether he is or not, we cannot afford to take any chances. We have to deal with this as if his information were accurate."

"What do you suggest?" Kimbough asked, afraid that he already knew the answer.

"Holden is not staying in a hotel. Regis has already checked. He's checking now with the rental-car agencies and taxis to find out where he is. When we find him I want him watched. Use whatever resources it takes. I want to know everything he does and everywhere he goes. And I particularly want to know about everyone he talks to. I'm also assuming that he'll get in contact with the local FBI man. I want his movements tracked as well. If either of them meet with the wrong people, then we must deal with it. You understand?"

Kimbough took his time with a bite of danish. "Forgive me, Governor, but I wonder if that is wise.

Dealing, as you say, with a federal prosecutor or an FBI agent may cause more trouble than we can handle. It is not something that will be overlooked or forgiven. Everything has been quiet here. I don't think it wise to do anything to call attention to ourselves."

Dubard shook his head slowly. "Alton, I agree with what you say and I hope nothing comes of this. But we may not have any choice. We are too close to our objective. We have talked about this before. Right now we cannot afford to have this man bumbling around and asking the wrong people the wrong questions. If just a hint of how we've structured the casino deal gets out, the legislation will die and we lose everything. No, we cannot take that chance."

"But again," Kimbough insisted, "I wonder about the reliability of Higgs's information. I find it hard to believe that Holden is down here investigating on his own. He works for the government, after all. What motive could he possibly have? It's entirely possible that he's just here for a vacation. Correct?"

"Yes, it's possible. But that is no reason not to watch him like a hawk and to deal with him if necessary."

"My concern is that we not make the same mistakes Higgs and his people made. Let's not do something rash." Kimbough stopped for a moment and then said, "Perhaps Bertini was right. Perhaps this deal with Higgs was not meant to be. I know he has been your friend for many years, but I wonder whether he has become too reckless. It was his mishandling of the situation in Washington that caused all our problems in the first place. Perhaps there is too much interest in him right now. We might be wise to distance ourselves. Higgs is not the only one with a network to distribute our product. There may be delays but there are others with whom we could make arrangements."

"No!" Dubard insisted, bringing his fist down on the table and rattling the Wedgwood before catching himself. "We don't have the time to make other arrangements. The bill comes up this session and we must pick up our options on the hotels and have our licenses filed before it's passed. We'll only have one shot at this, and I'm not gonna let some renegade prosecutor ruin it for us."

"But Holden is just one man, Governor. Even if he is here to investigate us, what can he do? He is out of his jurisdiction. And even from what Higgs says, he doesn't have the backing of his own people. People have been carrying tales to the prosecutors here for years and they have done nothing. And the same is true with the FBI. It's all window dressing. Always has been and no one's ever complained. What could Holden do on his own that our own prosecutors have never been able to do?"

"Do you forget your own advice? You said yourself that our only concern was that no one piece together our business here with our people in the States. Wasn't that just what that vermin Godoy was trying to do? What if this man Holden is on the same track? What if our dealings with the mayor and with Otis Ottley and the rest come to light? This man Holden certainly has more resources and could be far more dangerous than some alcoholic private detective, wouldn't you agree? And whether he could ever prove anything or not is beside the point. All it would take would be one subpoena, one official inquiry leaked to the press, and the legislation will die. Think of it, my friend. The casinos, gone. All our plans, gone."

Kimbough drew in a deep breath and let it out

slowly. "I will have him watched. But we must be cautious. We can't afford to make the same mistakes as your friend Higgs."

"Agreed. But my friend, if this prosecutor makes contact with Ian Desmond or any of that group, he must be dealt with, and quickly. You understand that." Kimbough said nothing. "Vacationers have accidents. They forget to drive on the left, or they have too much to drink and go for a swim at night. Accidents happen. You understand?"

It took a moment for Kimbough to signal his agreement with a reluctant nod.

$$\gg \ll$$

Two days after their arrival on St. Thomas, and while Katy wandered through the duty-free shops of Charlotte Amalie, Michael flew to St. Croix with the local FBI agent, Tony Manion, looking for some trace of Regent Godoy, the man believed murdered by Adrian Wheatley.

On the western edge of Christiansted, in a small, tin-roofed house whose cement floor was only partially covered by a few braided mats, they found Regent Godoy's consort, a bulbous and sullen Barbadian reluctant to speak with anyone even remotely associated with the federal government. Ultimately convinced that her cooperation could stave off a visit from the Immigration and Naturalization Service, Stella Marlen told what she knew, which was very little.

Stella had lived with Godoy for nearly three years and she rarely listened to what he had to say. His speech so often slurred with rum, it was hardly worth the effort. He worked alone, she said, and if he had any close friends, other than the local bartenders, she didn't know who they might be. Six or eight months before, he had come into some money, began shaving regularly and limited his drinking to not much more than a pint each night. She had no idea what he was doing except that he said he was working. But he had always said that. It didn't mean a thing to her, not even when he said he was leaving for the States and would be back in a few days. By the end of November, when she had not heard from Godoy for more than a month, she reported him missing. She asked if Godoy was dead and Michael replied that he had no proof that he was. Without emotion, she offered the opinion that he must be and asked if there was anything else they required of her.

They asked if Godoy had any papers in the house. She said no, but they were free to look. They found nothing. They asked about Godoy's office. A few weeks before, sometime before Christmas, she said, Godoy's landlord had called to say that if the back rent on the office was not paid immediately, Godoy would be evicted and his possessions held until the debt was satisfied. She just shrugged. It was clear without her saying that the rent was not paid, and she neither knew nor cared what had become of Godoy's office or papers.

"Jesus," Michael commented as they left the house, "you wonder why she even bothered to report the guy missing."

Tony Manion shrugged. "Like I said, Godoy wouldn't've won many popularity contests even when he was sober."

"How'd he ever make it as a detective?"

"Well, drunk or not, the man knew what he was doing. Ex-DEA. Got fired about ten years ago and ended up here. Managed to get hooked into the local grapevine and a few of the local lawyers kept him busy doing off-island work. Anyway, what's next?"

"How 'bout the landlord? Think we could find him?"

Manion looked at his watch. It was almost noon. "No problem," he said, and led Michael to the Second Sister, where they found the landlord hunched over a sandwich and beer.

"He in some kinda trouble?" the landlord asked.

"He's been reported missing," Manion said. "We're just looking for any information that'll help us find him."

"Well, when you do find the sonofabitch, he owes me two months' rent."

"Is that why you evicted him? The back rent?"

"You didn't know Godoy, did you? I carried him for two years always being three, four, even five months behind. When I finally told him I was throwing him out, the bastard all of a sudden comes up with the money. You know, like he had it all the time."

"When was that?"

"I don't remember. Last May. June, maybe. Anyway, I told him if he ever got behind again I'd throw him out. Then he misses November and December's rent. What was I supposed to do? Even called that surly bitch he lives with. Gave him plenty of time to come up with the money before the first. But nothing. I had someone who wanted the place, so what the hell? I boxed his stuff and rented it out."

Michael asked, "Did you take his files? Were they part of what you boxed?"

The landlord laughed. "Yeah, if you can call them files. Mostly jumbled scraps of paper. But I've got 'em."

The landlord was right. The three cardboard boxes stacked in his broom closet were filled with papers and files arranged in no discernible order.

File folders were only occasionally labeled. Utility bills were interspersed with surveillance notes from four- and five-year-old divorce cases, and odd bits of correspondence were found in totally unrelated files. The disarray was so complete that Holden suspected it was purposeful. Not wanting to rush through the search, and becoming irritated at the landlord's constant complaints about the amount of his time that was being wasted, Michael took out a federal grand jury subpoena, filled it out in front of the landlord, and handed it to him.

"What's this?"

"It's a subpoena for you to deliver these documents intact and in person in Washington one week from today."

"Is this a joke?"

"Why don't you just go ahead and ignore that subpoena and find out how much of a joke it is."

The issue was settled with the agreement that Holden and Agent Manion would take the documents with them to the FBI office in St. Thomas. They gave the landlord a receipt and left.

≫ ≪

By three o'clock they were back in St. Thomas, where they met Katy at a café overlooking the harbor. At her suggestion, the three returned to the east end of the island and the beachfront condominium Michael had rented. They prepared a blender of piña coladas, and while Katy went for a swim, the two men sat on the balcony overlooking Cowpet Bay, sipped their drinks, and slowly picked through the boxes of paper. Katy returned midway through the second blender to find the two men convinced that the papers contained no clues, although by that time they were a little unsure of just what they had seen or were looking for.

Michael suggested dinner and Tony Manion was invited to join them. He accepted gladly, suggesting a small beachfront restaurant only a few minutes' drive away.

Tony Manion was hungry for conversation. He had been on the island almost twenty-one months of his two-year tour. A twenty-nine-year-old bachelor from Omaha, he had come to understand that it had been more than just luck that had led to an agent of his youth and lack of seniority being selected for assignment to "America's paradise." Being the only agent to cover all three of the American Virgin Islands was difficult enough. But in a territory where the regional and ethnic prejudices extended even to the natives of other islands in the same group, to be a white FBI agent from the States only exaggerated the problems.

"You sound like you'll be glad when your tour's up," Katy sympathized.

"The feelings are mixed," he smiled. "The place has its charms, actually, and once you stop expecting things to work like they do back in the States it's not so bad. But working for the Bureau doesn't exactly do a hell of a lot for your social life, and it doesn't take long before everyone knows who you are and what you do."

"Is that a problem?" Michael asked.

"Not usually. Depends on how serious your opposition is." He looked at Michael and smiled. "And after today, I guarantee that half the island know who you are and why you're here."

Katy looked to Michael, who shrugged off the comment, steering the conversation away from business as they finished their meals and drank rum until the restaurant closed.

Late the next morning, Agent Manion returned and found Michael and Katy on the beach. He was as excited as his hangover would allow. Earlier that morning he had been reached by a source he had not spoken to in months. The source wondered why the two men had been asking questions about Regent Godoy the day before.

"Jesus!" Michael exclaimed. "You weren't kidding about living in a fishbowl."

"No," Manion said, "but this time it may have worked in our favor."

"What's that mean?"

"Two things. First, you've hit a nerve, which means we've really got to lower our profile here. Second, there's a real interesting connection that I hadn't thought of. For a coupla years now there's been talk about trying to legalize casino gambling on the island. Word is that there's a few senators ready to introduce legislation and they may have enough support to push it through unless the opposition can whip up some public outcry. That's where my man comes in. He says there's a group here convinced that the whole gambling idea is being backed and financed by some mob types. You know, paying off legislators and all that. This group, whoever they are, got together and hired Godoy to find out what he could. Anyway, the informant said that this group might be willing to talk with you if it could be arranged quietly. They're impressed that someone from Washington is interested."

"Who's supposed to be the black hats in all this?"

"Hard to say, except whenever rumors fly, Ishmael Dubard's name ends up being mentioned."

Michael sat up. "Ishmael?" he repeated slowly, trying to remember. "Who is Ishmael Dubard?"

"Don't know much," Manion said. "For a short time back in the sixties he was an appointed governor. Before the islands got the right to elect their own. Anyway, he pretty much stays to himself, except that he's always rumored to have an unrecorded piece of the action on almost anything that's making money here. Everything from liquor distributorships to government construction projects to real estate. Whatever. It's hard to tell truth from fiction. Just like everything else, people here never let the truth stand in the way of a good rumor, and they say he's been into everything from gunrunning to dope. No one's ever come up with any evidence, though. At least not that I've ever seen."

"Governor?" Michael asked softly, more of himself. Then: "Of course. The governor. Ish, the man Wheatley—you remember? The man I was telling you who killed the cop?" Manion nodded. "He was talking about someone who Higgs called Ish and who everybody else called Governor."

Tony Manion asked for details and Michael repeated what little Wheatley had told and some history on Milton Higgs.

"Sounds like a match made in heaven," Manion cracked. "Aside from being a big moneymaker, having your own casino would sure make the laundering of dope money a whole lot easier. This may be getting interesting."

"What's next?" Michael asked. "How do we get ahold of these people?"

Manion smiled. "We don't. They'll contact us. Maybe. Sorry, but that's the way things work here. You gotta remember this is a very small town and these people can't afford to go after the king unless they're sure they can kill him—at least not publicly. The man you want to talk to is Ian Desmond. My guess is they'll get in touch with us. There'd be no other reason for them to call. Until then, relax, enjoy the sun."

There was nothing to do but wait.

> <

It was the seventh day and the sun had passed its peak, heading toward the crest of hills behind the beach. Michael sat lazing just beyond the long shade of the palms, listening to the fronds clack in the wind, just one of many who freckled the bright white face of the beach. Each day the people would gather at about the same time and arrange themselves in about the same places. Within the confines of their territories, they would move about and change positions in response to the path of the sun, either seeking or avoiding its intensity. Occasionally they swam or wandered over to a bar and hamburger stand set back among the pines. But mostly they remained in their spots and kept to themselves until it was time to leave, about the time they had left the day before and would leave the day after.

Michael had come to know them, but only by Katy's descriptions. In the short time they had been here, she somehow had collected the names and assorted bits of history of those who settled routinely at their end of the strand. He never saw the approach or introduction, just a casual wave or a chirped hello, and if he bothered to ask, she would report what she knew in a casual, offhanded voice, as if referring to an old friend. "Oh, that's Gregory. He has a gallery in town. Gave me the name of a good restaurant we should try."

Michael glanced at Gregory, crowding fifty, and his much younger lover, Hal, each reclined on his elbows at the edge of the water, their fashion-covered eyes synchronously circumnavigating the near horizons of beach and bay. Midbeach, Estelle Aron-something, a widow from Cohasset, sat as she always sat, full face to the sun, shading her eyes with a raised and heavily ringed hand, chatting with Anthony Higgins, a retired plastics manufacturer, and his wife, who were already looking forward to next week's departure of their three teenaged grandchildren. At the water's edge, Ursula, the late-twenties wife of a Dutch engineer preparing bids on several local construction projects, fussed over her twin toddlers, who refused to keep the inverted sailor caps on their heads, which were so blond as to look bald.

And there was Katy, swimming toward the shore with an easy, athletic motion that made Michael feel awkward just sitting. Emerging from the surf, she stopped to speak with Ursula, her hands suddenly animated with conversation—the Taliafero genes—and her laughter rising above and then dying in the wind. Ursula, ten years Katy's junior and by comparison pale and dimpled, laughed, too, a laughter that Michael could see but not hear. He watched Katy as she stood in the last bright sun of the day, her body erect and glossed with a wet tan, and he smiled. It was the smile that would come to him at times she often thought inappropriate, when she spoke seriously, or at least not humorously, or when she sat quietly reading, not saying anything. She'd furrow her brow and look or feel for something out of place. "What?" she'd ask. "What's wrong?" But nothing was ever wrong or out of place or even remotely humorous. She simply made him smile as he did now, watching her return the children's wave as they did, fingers only.

Michael looked down at himself. Perspiration and suntan lotion had pooled on the top of his belly, which tended to balloon when he sat. He tightened his stomach to let the pool drain as Katy turned and saw him staring. She folded her arms loosely in front of her, suddenly self-conscious, and she moved quickly toward him. She did not stop or hesitate but in a single motion straddled his lap and sat down.

"I told Ursula to gather up her kids and hide," she said. "I am about to perform some unspeakable acts upon your lean"—she stopped and looked down at the stomach he was trying to hold in—"well, almost lean body."

"Sure, but will you respect me a week from now?"

"Don't flatter yourself. It won't take that long."

"I don't know, Kate. I've been making a list of all the unspeakable possibilities, and it's gonna take at least another week."

She cocked her head and smiled. "Are we staying?"

He nodded. "I called the agent. We can keep the apartment for another week. Okay?"

She took his face in her hands and kissed him. "I could get real used to this, Holden. You see? All you had to do was tell me in the beginning what this cops-and-robbers stuff was all about. If I had known your job was lounging around on exotic beaches waiting for someone to talk to you, I would have been a fan a long time ago. Let's go check your list."

Later, he lay beside her, waiting, watching her nap, studying her until the phone rang and he rushed to the living room to answer it before she awoke.

"Mike? It's Tony Manion. Hate to spoil your evening, but they just called. They want to meet tonight. The drill is, they'll call for a Dennis Bolling at the Fallen Parrot some time around eight. If you can meet, you answer the call and they'll tell you where. If not, they'll try again in a few days."

"What about you?"

"They want to meet with you alone."

"Do you trust them?"

"Yeah. These guys are your basic church-and-family crowd. They're just a little nervous about being seen talking with the Bureau."

"Where is this place—the Drunken Parrot or whatever?"

"The Fallen Parrot. It's a restaurant down in Red Hook, about five minutes from your place. It's got a dock attached to it. You can't miss it. It's just before the ferry to St. John. On the right. I thought I'd meet you there around seven or so and we can talk it over."

"Okay, that's fine." Michael then lowered his voice. "Listen, Tony, how about if I bring Katy and you and she can have dinner and drinks or whatever until I finish? Would that be okay?"

"Sure, that'd be great."

Two hours later they were sitting at a table next to the railing of the open-walled restaurant overlooking a dock, which reached beyond the marsh grasses to the dark waters of Vessup Bay. Katy reached over and put her hand on Michael's, stilling his nervous twisting of a plastic straw. "You're starting to make me nervous," she said gently. "Either he'll get here or you don't take the phone call. Right?" It was nearly a quarter to eight, and Tony Manion had not appeared.

Michael nodded. "Yeah, I guess I am getting a little jumpy. But I think I should take the call even if Tony doesn't get here. I mean, there's no risk in taking the call. Right?"

Katy started to argue but stopped herself, looking over Michael's shoulder. "Here he is," she smiled.

"Jesus, I'm sorry I'm so late," Manion said, half

out of breath. "I stopped to pick up a few things at the market and somehow lost my car keys. Kept retracing my steps back and forth but I never did find them. I ended up taking a cab over here. Any word?"

"No, nothing yet," Michael said.

Manion signaled for the waitress, who came over and took his order for a beer. When she left the table he turned to Michael.

"I called San Juan to check their files on Ian Desmond. Like I thought, he's listed among the white hats. He's given the Bureau information before and has never asked a favor in return. Just remember that you gotta take a lot of what these people say with a grain of salt. They'll pass on rumor as if it were gospel. But Desmond's different. If you get to talk to him directly you can probably trust what he's got to say."

The waitress returned with Manion's beer and asked if they were ready to order dinner just as the bartender called out, "Is there a Dennis Bolling here?"

"In a few minutes," Michael answered the waitress.

He stood and walked to the end of the bar, where he was handed the phone. After a few seconds of conversation he turned and nodded to Manion, still seated with Katy at the table. Manion returned the nod and Michael returned to his low conversation. Holding the phone to his ear, he looked to the end of the dock and the crowd of boats anchored beyond. He nodded his understanding of what was being said and noticed that a man at the far end of the bar was following his gaze out to the water. Suspicions flipped through his mind but he dismissed them as nerves.

"All set," Michael said when he returned to the

table. "I'm supposed to walk to the end of the dock in a few minutes and someone in a dingy is going to take me out to Desmond's boat."

Katy furrowed her brow and looked to Manion. "I don't know if that sounds like such a good idea," she said.

"No, I think it's okay," Michael assured her. "The guy said he was Ian Desmond and apologized for all the cloak-and-dagger stuff. Said it's just that he really can't afford to be seen in public talking with the FBI. He sounded all right to me."

Michael saw the man at the end of the bar get up and disappear down the hallway leading to a public phone. His eyes followed the man and for a second he wondered if he should say anything to Manion. Again he dismissed the thought, inwardly embarrassed by his nervousness.

"It's gonna be a little nippy for a boat ride to-night," he joked, and feigned a shiver in the sharp breeze blowing in from the water.

"Wanna borrow this?" Manion asked, opening his blue windbreaker to a white, short-sleeved shirt beneath.

"No, that's okay," Michael said halfheartedly.

Manion insisted. "Really, we'll just be sitting around here, or, if you don't mind," he said to Katy, "maybe you could give me a lift back to my house to pick up my other set of keys. Then I could pick up my car and we'll come right back here for dinner and wait for Mike."

"That's fine," Katy said, and Michael agreed to the loan of the windbreaker, which he slipped over his own white, short-sleeved shirt.

"See you guys in a little while," Michael said, touching Katy lightly on the shoulder as he rose, then walked to the end of the dock.

≫ ≪

From Tony Manion's house in Louisenhoj, the road edged the Skyline along the north slope until it met the Mandal road and curved south and east down the mountain toward Smith Bay. It wasn't driving on the left that made Katy uneasy, but traveling this moonless night on the outer lane of a narrow, twisting road bordered only by a few brambles at the edge of a precipitous drop. She was glad for the diversion of Manion's light chatter about life in the islands and took no notice of the headlights closing in behind her until the road's descent steepened and curved close to the edge. For a short distance the road straightened and widened and Katy relaxed as the headlights behind dropped back.

At the end of the straight, the road bent sharply to the right and edged even closer to the side. The car behind closed in and suddenly the night was filled with its high-beamed light and Tony Manion twisted around. "What the hell's his problem?" The trailing car swung to the right and pulled quickly alongside of them.

Katy's foot stabbed for the brake but it was too late. There was the sudden sound of collapsing metal as the car lurched violently to the left and into the abyss. Everything went silent and she could only sense their falling, there being nothing to see but blackness and nothing to feel but fear for what seemed an eternity.

Twenty

The squeak of crepe-soled shoes annoyed the otherwise silent corridor as puddled footprints trailed Eddie Nickles toward a small sitting room where Michael Holden slumped in a vinyl armchair. The detective barely broke stride as he walked up and not so gently shook Michael awake.

"How is she?" he asked as Michael strained to recognize the thick, whiskered face leaning into him. "Wake up, man," the detective ordered. "How is she?"

Michael's puffed and heavily veined eyes closed lazily as his head settled on the back of the chair. Even with the help of the FBI, it had taken two days to arrange the special medical flights that delivered Katy's broken and only occasionally conscious body from St. Thomas to the Washington Hospital Center. In that time Michael had not showered, shaved, or slept for more than an hour or two at a time. Eddie had to ask the question a third time before Michael drew the energy to sit up a bit and take a deep breath. He ran his fingers through his matted hair and mumbled, "It's bad. Real bad." His expression contorted with the effort of recalling the inventory. "A broken back. Fractured skull and cheekbone. Both wrists, a forearm, and one leg broken. Ribs. God knows what internal injuries."

"Jesus Christ, I'm sorry," Eddie moaned. "But she's gonna be okay, right? I mean, she's gonna make it, right?"

"I don't know." Michael suddenly sat up straight. "What time is it?"

"It's almost two-thirty . . . in the morning. Why?"

"They're supposed to operate soon." He then looked up and asked, "Got a cigarette?" Eddie looked surprised but handed him a flattened Camel and matches without comment. Michael coughed at the first puff and then took another, deeper drag. "Whatever they did in the hospital down there was just to patch her up enough to get her here." He leaned back and closed his eyes. "I don't know how she lived. They say it was almost a hundred feet to the bottom of that ravine." A chill shook him and his eyes teared.

"I'm sorry," Eddie said quietly. "Is her family here?"

"Yeah." Michael sighed, his eyes blinking open. "Her brother took her mother and Vera Lee to a hotel. They'll be back in the morning. I didn't know what to say to them. I . . . uh . . . I just . . ." His voice trailed off and he looked away.

"I'll be right back," Eddie said, then rushed off down the hallway. In a few minutes he returned. "C'mon, man, you're coming with me. They're not gonna let you or anyone else near her. She's completely knocked out and surgery's not scheduled for another four or five hours. There's nothing you can do. You need some food and coffee and we need to talk." Michael looked up, as if trying to decide what to do. "Look," Eddie said, "I promise to have you back here long before she wakes up. I've got a cruiser so they can raise us if anything comes up. But right now you're coming with me."

• • • •

Michael was quiet and Eddie didn't press him until they were settled in a booth at an all-night diner and the steak and eggs and coffee had been set in front of them.

"Were you ever able to talk to her about what happened?"

"Not really," Michael sighed. "She was all doped up. But she kept fighting it, trying to tell me it wasn't her fault."

"What about the agent? Did you ever speak to him?"

He shook his head. "No. He was dead at the scene."

Eddie thought for a moment and then said, "Katy's right. It wasn't her fault. And it wasn't an accident. I talked to the Bureau earlier tonight. There were paint scrapings from another car found on the right front door and fender of your rental. And from the scrape marks, it looks like the cars were going in the same direction. It wasn't an accident, Mike. Someone forced her over the side."

Michael looked up and his hands started shaking. "What are you talking about?"

Eddie took a deep breath. "I don't know if this is the time to be telling you all this, but you've got to know before people start asking questions."

"What are you talking about?" Michael asked more urgently.

"First of all, McKeethen's the one who's been feeding information to Higgs."

It didn't register. Michael just shook his head, confused. "I don't understand. What's McKeethen got to do with anything?"

Eddie spoke slowly. "Dan McKeethen has been in Higgs's pocket the whole time. We were right.

Your old office in the courthouse was bugged a coupla years ago. McKeethen was the one who set it up. And everything you've ever said to him about our investigation has gone straight to Higgs—including, no doubt, that you weren't really in St. Thomas for a vacation."

It took a moment for Michael to catch his breath, and when he did it was labored. He took deep gulps of air to stifle the nausea until he became dizzy and his eyes watered. He fought it off, his whole body tensing until it shook. The knuckles of his right hand turned white as his grip tightened around his water glass. Suddenly the glass snapped and he let out a low, sharp cry.

"Jesus Christ!" Eddie barked, and grabbed Michael's wrist and saw the shards of glass in his palm and the blood flowing onto the table, mixing with the spilled water.

A waitress lounging in another booth reading the paper looked over. "God! What happened?" she asked.

"You mind getting us some clean cloths?" Eddie said, and she quickly gathered a supply of laundered towels and a first-aid kit.

Michael covered his face with a cool, wet cloth to absorb the tearing, while Eddie pulled the glass from his palm and tried to staunch the bleeding by tying several cloths tightly around the hand.

"C'mon," Eddie said, "I'm taking you the emergency room. You're gonna need stitches."

Michael shook his head, but said nothing for more than a minute, waiting for the emotion to drain from him. When it had, he took a quick, deep breath and dropped the cloth from his face. He didn't look at Eddie right away but took a long sip of his coffee and a bite of toast. "We're not going anywhere until you tell me everything," he said in a voice so cold as to stop the protest Eddie was about to offer.

The detective spoke deliberately, providing every detail of his encounter with Aaron Yozkowitz. He ended by telling Michael, "Tonight, maybe even right now, Mr. Wizard is bugging your office."

"That's good," Michael said, nodding appreciatively at Eddie's choice of tactics. He fell silent, thinking, his eyes darting about while he remained otherwise motionless. Eddie, too, remained silent until Michael finally spoke.

"The jacket. It was the fucking jacket."

"Jacket?"

"There was a guy at the bar where I got the call from the snitch. He was watching me—the guy at the bar—and looking out toward the dock when I did. I didn't say anything about it. Thought I was just being paranoid. But then I saw him get up and leave and that's when Tony Manion, you know, the agent, that's when he loaned me his jacket. He was wearing a white shirt just like I was. They thought it was me, didn't they? It was dark and they saw a guy in a white shirt leave with Katy and they thought it was me. . . . God, you should have seen her."

"Easy," Eddie cautioned. Then he added, "Good chance you're right. They probably did think it was you. Tell me about your meeting with the snitch. What'd he have to say?"

It took some time for Michael to get the image of the man at the bar out of his head while Eddie waited patiently. "Well, first, he really doesn't have any hard information. Just a lot of suspicions and whatever Godoy was able to dig up. Basically what's happening is that for a few years now there's been talk back and forth about legalizing casino gambling in the islands. There's a lot of local opposition from church groups and people claiming that it'll draw the mob and whatever. So the pro-gambling lobby's come up with a plan to overcome the opposition. They'll put a provision in the legislation that'll prohibit any business from ever getting a gambling permit, except those owned by residents and already incorporated and actively doing business before the passage of the gambling act. That way they can argue that the casinos will be owned and controlled by locals, which is really their biggest gripe. You know, the idea of outsiders coming down and skimming all the money for themselves.

"This guy Ian Desmond and a bunch of his friends lead the opposition. Completely against the idea of casinos. Corrupting the locals and all that. They got together and found out that a number of people they knew who hadn't had two nickels to rub together suddenly were opening small businesses around the island. That's when they hired Godoy. Godoy figures out that a lot of these small businesses were just fronts being financed by off-island money.

"Then sometime last August, Godoy finds out that a group of these small-time fronts have gotten together and purchased options to buy three hotels, two on St. Thomas and one on St. Croix. Guess who turns out to be doing all the negotiating for these local islanders?"

Eddie shrugged.

"None other than your good friend Victor Stearman."

"Motherfucker," Eddie enunciated carefully.

"No shit," Michael agreed. "And these hotels turn

out to be the only ones around big enough to accommodate a good-sized casino operation that won't be owned almost entirely by off-island corporations. Not bad, huh?"

"How'd Stearman manage to hook into that nice piece of business?"

"Remember Wheatley talking about the 'governor'? The guy called Ish?" Eddie nodded. "Turns out he really was a governor, back in the early sixties sometime. Name's Ishmael Dubard. He's the local don, except no one's ever been able to do anything more than spread rumors about him. He's been using Stearman as his lawyer for years. This guy Desmond says that if anyone ever came up with proof that Dubard was connected with the casinos—and particularly if he's setting up fronts for off-island money—there'd be enough of a stink to kill the legislation no matter how many people he paid off." Michael stopped suddenly.

Eddie looked him in the eye and nodded twice. "No wonder they were so upset about your nosing around."

Michael spoke quietly. "He said that's what Godoy was doing in Washington. Following Dubard, because he said he thought he had tracked some of the fronts' investors back to D.C."

"The Friday-night meeting," Eddie said, completing Michael's thought. Then he asked, "This man know anything about dope?"

Michael answered but his voice was distant, as if he were talking about something other than what he was thinking. "No, not really. He said that there's a lot of coke in the islands but very little heroin. No big-time trafficking like we think of. There's always some rumors about Dubard, you know, dealing. But he thinks that if Dubard is involved in some major load of dope, it's probably to finance the casinos. But he's just guessing." Michael looked down at the table and at the dozen or more little wads of paper Eddie had torn off from his napkin, rolled into tight BBs and piled in a small pyramid. Eddie kept his head down, and there was a long period of silence before Michael asked, "What is it?"

"Look, man," Eddie said without looking up, "I can't tell you how bad I feel that I didn't call you as soon as Yozkowitz told me about McKeethen. It was eight or nine o'clock before Jimmy 'n' me finished with him back at his shop and I called. I guess you were already at the restaurant. I should've known to call you earlier—as soon as I heard, you know, about McKeethen."

Michael shook his head. "I probably wouldn't have done anything differently if you had called. I just assumed she'd be all right with the agent. Even if I had known about Dan, I would never have thought they'd pull something like this."

Eddie nodded, still without looking up.

Michael asked, "What's Jimmy up to?"

"He's real upset 'bout all this. Kinda confused. Hasn't been getting any sleep, either. Staying up all hours going over the bank records. He says he's on to something after talking with Yozkowitz. I really don't know what he's doing, but we can talk to him later."

For some time Michael sat quietly, staring down at his hand and the blood seeping through the makeshift bandage, his thoughts his own until a slight chuckle escaped and he said, "McKeethen."

Eddie reached over and took Michael's other wrist in his grip. "Mike, listen to me. We'll get them, I promise you. But we can't do anything crazy. We

can't blow it on revenge right now. Give us a chance
to do it right, the way it should be done."

"Whatever it takes," Michael hissed, then stopped
and sat back, his eyes rolling upward. "Man, maybe
you'd better get me outta here. I think I'm gonna
be sick."

Twenty-one

Michael was not prepared for his own reaction. Every muscle tensed and a sharp dizziness rolled over him at the sight of the bottles of fluid and tubing and the white plaster casts covering Katy's trunk, both arms, and her right leg, and the bandaging of the face and skull, which accentuated her deeply blackened eyes. She seemed less alive now than when he had seen her bloodied and battered on the gurney, being rushed toward the operating room of the hospital in St. Thomas. Even less was he prepared for her reaction to him.

Katy's mother was fussing over the flowers he had brought and talking to Katy as if she weren't heavily drugged and barely conscious. Vera Lee sat next to the bed, her hand patting the heavy plaster that encased Katy's left arm from midbicep to fingertips. Michael leaned over and began to speak. Katy's eyes blinked and began to fill with tears. She let out a low, awful moan as he tried to tell her that he was there, that everything would be all right. As he spoke her eyes widened, and suddenly she was twisting at the casts and bandages and restraints and tubes. He reached out a hand to calm her, which only caused a more violent reaction, and her slurred speech could not mask the urgency of her pleas that he not hurt her anymore. A nurse rushed in and, while Katy's mother chattered on for everyone to keep the good thought, Vera Lee leaned close to Katy's ear and whispered the panic down. Michael quickly backed out of the room, feeling his own panic.

Minutes later he was standing stiffly at the end of the hall staring out the window when he felt Vera Lee's hand on his forearm.

"It's the pain medicine, son. She don't know where she is or what she's saying. You know that." Michael looked at the old woman but did not answer her. "It's just all that medicine making her crazy with nightmares. That child's had more heartaches than you'll ever know. It may not be you she's afraid of, so you best not worry about anything she might say until she can speak for herself without all that pain and drugs running through her head."

"I hope you're right."

"I am right!" she snapped. "I know that little girl like she were my own flesh and blood. Now she's the one we've got to worry about, so you just stop feeling sorry for yourself and be ready to do whatever it takes to get her through this. Are you listening to me?"

Michael barely smiled. "Yes, ma'am. I'm sorry."

"No need being sorry. Plenty a need to be helpful. Right now, you best just stay away. When she's ready she'll be needing you."

He nodded and squeezed her hand. "Thanks. You'll let me know?"

"And you be here when I do," she said, then turned to walk back to Katy's room.

Michael turned toward the elevator and saw Dan and Rachel McKeethen walking toward him carrying another arrangement of flowers to go with the half dozen or more already crowding Katy's room and confusing Miss Evelyn, who couldn't decide how best to position the vases.

"Oh, God, Michael, I'm so sorry," Rachel said and hugged him. "How is she?"

Dan McKeethen looked solemn and saw Michael's bandaged right hand. He took Michael's left hand in both of his, like a minister at a funeral. "Are you all right? I didn't know you were injured, too."

Michael stiffened with the effort of not reacting and said to Rachel, "She's going to be okay. It's gonna take some time and another operation or two, but she'll be okay." More to keep his mind off the fact that McKeethen had not released his hand, Michael went slowly through the list of Katy's injuries, ending with, "Anyway, the bottom line is that it's bad, but there's no spinal-cord injury or paralysis. The orthopedics are the main worry."

"My God! What happened?" Rachel asked, while her husband remained silent, shaking a sympathetic head and now putting his hand on Michael's shoulder.

Michael wondered if McKeethen could feel him tense, could sense the fragile facade of calm that masked his thoughts. "We don't really know, except it looks like another car might have forced her off the road. They were coming back from the agent's house. He had lost his car keys and she had driven him home to pick up another set. I was . . . uh . . . going to meet them later at a restaurant. Anyway, the road was up on the side of a mountain with no guardrail and"—he hesitated and looked Dan McKeethen in the eye—"she ended up going over the side."

Both McKeethens shook their heads slowly, and Rachel asked, "Can we see her? Is she awake?"

"Not really. She's heavily sedated. I think it's going to be a while before she'll be able to see anyone but her family." Rachel nodded and Michael anticipated her question. "But I'm sure it'd be all right to just step in and leave the flowers. It's the last room on the left."

Rachel squeezed Michael's unbandaged hand and Dan McKeethen told her, "Honey, why don't you take those down and let me talk to Mike for a minute." McKeethen removed his hand from Michael's shoulder and the two men watched Rachel walk down the hall before he spoke. "Do you think the accident was in any way connected to what you were doing down there?"

"I don't know. I find it kinda hard to believe, but maybe. I don't know anymore."

"What were you doing? You never really said."

Michael took a deep breath. "We had a lead on the guy who we think might have been the one killed in the alley behind Higgs's house. He was a private detective from St. Croix."

"How'd that come up?"

"Pure luck," Michael deadpanned, then frowned. "Guess it didn't turn out so lucky. In any event, this detective's wife or live-in or whatever she was had reported him missing to the local FBI months ago and said he was last known to have been traveling to D.C. The agent knew a report was forwarded to the police here. But when he called up to check on it, you know, just making a routine check, he was told there was no report on file. A week or so later the agent, Tony Manion—" Michael stopped and again looked McKeethen in the eye. "I liked him. If it wasn't an accident, he died over bullshit. . . . Anyway, Manion just happened to be talking to Billy Colquit in Tampa. Remember Billy? He worked the city hall case with me?"

McKeethen nodded.

"Well, Manion's just bullshitting with him and mentions this problem he's having with the D.C. police, 'cause he knows Billy used to work here, and Billy tells him to call me. That's it."

"Did you find anything down there? I mean, anything that might have caused someone to run your car off the road?"

"Nothing, really. This detective, Godoy, was trying to dig up evidence about some connections with businessmen in the States backing legislation to legalize gambling in the islands. He was hired by some locals who are opposed to gambling and they knew he was supposed to go to Washington, but they never heard from him after he left St. Croix. The guy was a drunk and didn't bother phoning in reports of what he was doing. Anyway, no one really knows what he found out or whether he ever made it to D.C. Maybe he's the guy in the alley. Maybe not. Either way, it's a dead end."

"Does this have anything to do with the bank accounts you said you were looking into?"

"No, not at all. Like I told you before Christmas, we can't trace anything back. Higgs is careful. I'll say that for him."

McKeethen shifted his weight to his other foot, looking a bit uncomfortable. "What's next?"

Michael did not hesitate with his answer. "I'm through with it. I'd appreciate it if you didn't say anything to anybody right now, but I'm going to start looking for another job."

"Mike, I know this is a bad time, but don't you think you might—"

"No," Michael interrupted, "I've thought about it. It's time. The only reason I'm telling you this is to let you know I still have almost two months' leave built up, and I'm going to be taking a lot of it while

Katy's laid up to look for a job. I haven't got any trials scheduled right now so you might as well start figuring out who you want to transfer my cases to."

"What about the Higgs matter? Have you talked to the detectives about this?"

"No, but I will today. I told you it's going nowhere."

"Mike, you know there's a supervisor's job available. All you have to do is say so. It'd get you out of trial work and investigations for a while. Give you a chance to cut down on your hours. You ought to think about this. Give some priority to the fact that you've got all those years in the retirement system."

Michael could not help but smile. "Thanks, but I have thought about it. Priorities change, you know?"

Rachel McKeethen approached the two men, dabbing her eyes and wiping her nose with a large white handkerchief. She walked directly to Michael and embraced him.

"Oh, Michael, it's just awful," she said.

Twenty-two

"Goddamn it! You can't give up on this now."

"How many times have we got to go over this?" Michael argued, sweeping his hand over the top of his desk and knocking a file folder to the floor. "There's nothing to give up on. We've got no evidence. Every lead has dead-ended. That's it."

"You talk to him, Jimmy. I'm gettin' nowhere."

"Look, Mike, I think Eddie's right. How can we give up on this? I mean, we know the sonofabitch is dirty and, proof or no proof, we all know he probably had something to do with what happened to Katy—and Wheatley, and God knows what else. I mean, we just can't say what-the-hell and walk away."

"For the last time," Michael said with exasperation, "what do you suggest we do?"

"Do what Jimmy said," Eddie barked. "Flood Higgs with subpoenas for all his records. Subpoena his businesses and every fucking bank in town. Roust some more people and throw 'em in the grand jury. No one's gonna crack unless we put pressure on 'em."

"I already told you. That just isn't gonna work. First, it'd raise such a stink, the front office would be all over us. Just like I'd be if I were them. And we've got nothing to tell them that'd justify reopening. The Virgin Island lead didn't pan out. It's just like everything else. It makes a good story but we've got no evidence and nothing to follow up on."

"What about his bank accounts?"

"Look, even if we had Higgs's bank records, you think we could trace the few thousand dollars in cash they spent on rent and deposits for those trick pads or to pay off a few cops? No way. What's Higgs have—five, six funeral homes in the area? And a major real estate business? Hell, three, four, five thousand a week coming out of petty cash wouldn't prove a thing. And you can bet they've got a file cabinet filled with dummied receipts to cover them. You'd never be able to trace it." Jimmy started to speak but Michael held up his hand. "Before you say it, I know if we got his records there's no telling what we'd find. But we can't just go fishing like that without some justification, and we haven't got any."

"So you just give up?"

"No, I just start looking for another job. I told you that's all I'm talking about. And if you guys come up with anything—another lead, anything worth following—I'll stick it out to the end. But right now, even you can't think of anything but to paper the city with subpoenas. And in the long run you know all that'll do is make everyone nervous and clam up."

Eddie spoke in a very low voice. "Mike, look, I know you're real upset about Katy, but—"

"Don't say it, man. This has nothing to do with her. . . . Okay, maybe it does. But I'd be looking for another job anyway. It's time, that's all. But that's got nothing to do with this case. This is the last time I'm going to say it. You come up with some legitimate evidence and I'll stick it out. But until then, I'm going to start looking." There was a long silence, which Michael finally interrupted. "How 'bout I treat you guys to a coupla drinks and a steak?"

> <

An hour later, the three men sat in a booth at the rear of the restaurant looking serious but not somber.

"Think they'll buy it?" Jimmy asked.

Michael smiled. "Shit, I was starting to buy it myself. That was a nice little touch bringing up Katy," he said, shaking his head.

Jimmy lowered his eyes sheepishly, but Eddie just shrugged, drained his glass, and signaled for the waiter. "I'll get ahold of Yozkowitz tomorrow. Have him arrange a little electrical problem to blow out the bugs. Between McKeethen and that little performance, Higgs should be satisfied. And if not, Mr. Wizard'll let us know."

"You trust him, right?" Michael asked.

Eddie smiled. "We have an understanding, so to speak."

"I won't even ask," Michael said, and even Jimmy smiled. "But listen, why don't we wait a day or two for him to disable the bugs? I want to meet with Henning, and it'd be interesting to see if she says anything about it." Eddie nodded his assent. "Which reminds me, Jimmy. You said you came across something in the accounts?"

Jimmy perked up and pushed away the glasses and plates and silverware which sat in front of him and the prosecutor. "It's beautiful," he said, as he pulled from his briefcase and spread on the table a large sheet of columned accounting paper filled with numbers and notations. The waiter arrived and Jimmy looked up and said, "Another round."

Eddie smiled appreciatively, and all three men looked down at the spread sheet.

"Look at this," Jimmy said to Michael. "You were right. Every one of those accounts Wheatley had listed, and all the others we tracked, have been feeding into these second-level accounts. All, that is, except one trust account for Henning's kid. Anyway, there are twenty-seven accounts down here at the first level. Now the only place money is going out of those accounts is to one of the second-level accounts, and there are . . . uh"—Jimmy ran his finger down one column, counting—"there are eight of those. It doesn't look like anything is going out of those. Like you said, it looks more like they're just consolidating money that's moved out of the first level."

"Okay," Michael said with interest, and Jimmy took a sip of his Glenlivet.

"Now, when we were talking with Yozkowitz about how he was getting paid, you know, through company accounts he never heard of, something rang a bell. I went back through the list of these first-level accounts, and damn if there weren't three or four accounts in the same names Yozkowitz had mentioned." Michael looked up with real interest in his eyes, and Jimmy said with a smile, "Yeah, it's getting good."

"What? I don't understand," Eddie complained.

"Go on," Michael encouraged.

"Anyway, so Eddie and I go back to Yozkowitz and I get as many copies of checks or receipts or whatever he's got, and guess what. All but one or two of the companies that Yozkowitz is paid through match the names on these first-level accounts, *but*," he emphasized, "the account numbers are different. Even the banks are different."

Michael started a smile of recognition. "And?" he asked.

"And I go back to a couple of the local banks

we've been dealing with, on the QT, you understand, and I look through the signature cards to see who's listed. They're all different."

"What's different?" Eddie demanded as the second round of drinks was delivered.

Michael waited for the waiter to leave. "Let him explain, man." And Jimmy did.

"The names and signatures on the accounts used to pay off Yozkowitz are completely different than the names and signatures on the accounts Henning's running. But the company names are the same."

"Goddamn!" Michael said slowly, a smile lighting his face.

Eddie banged his glass impatiently on the table. "What the fuck are you guys talking about?"

Michael spoke slowly, not taking his eyes off Jimmy. "Henning's skimming from Higgs."

"I'm sure of it," Jimmy said triumphantly, and he offered his palm, which Michael slapped softly.

"Nice work." Michael grinned and held up his hand to Eddie, who looked as if he were going to get violent if someone did not explain what his partner and the prosecutor were talking about. "Explain it to my friend here."

"Look," Jimmy said, "Henning's the bookkeeper, and she's the one who takes care of making all of Higgs's payoffs and setting up these little wash accounts. So she figures why not take a little for herself. But to cover her ass, she sets up a whole bunch of new accounts using the same business names as Higgs is used to seeing. The same business names they use to run the payoffs through. That's what she was using Wheatley for, is my guess. To open these accounts for her. And that's why Wheatley didn't want to say anything about Henning. Probably promised him part of the action. Maybe she

just led him on, let him think they'd run away together. Who knows? Anyway, with the accounts set
up in duplicate names, if Higgs decides to take a
quick look at expenditures or walks in and surprises
her with a request to look at the bank statements,
even the bill-payer statements which list the payee
names, the only expenditures he's gonna see are to
company names he's familiar with. He's never
going to remember account numbers, so everything's gonna look okay to him. She can nickel and
dime him to death. And with the money that
Higgs's operation is generating, legally and ille-
gally, the nickels and dimes can amount to big
bucks."

Eddie nodded his understanding and asked,
"How many bucks you figure?"

Jimmy tilted his head and took another sip of
Scotch, clearly enjoying himself. "In the eight consolidation accounts, you know, the second level,
there's a little over nine hundred fifty thousand. I
don't have a total in the first level, the twenty-seven
accounts, but I'd say maybe another two hundred
fifty, three hundred thousand, maybe more."

Eddie jabbed a thick forefinger toward Michael.
"That's why she had to come in. Her tit was about
to get pulled into the wringer."

Both Michael and Jimmy cocked their heads as
if not quite sure of Eddie's meaning.

"Sure," Eddie said, and gestured to Michael.
"Don't you see? You tell McKeethen just before
Christmas that you've come across a couple of accounts involving Wheatley. McKeethen passes it on
to Higgs. Higgs wants to know what's going on, so
who does he call in but his fuckin' bookkeeper, and
she panics. For sure she panics. If Higgs starts looking into those accounts and finds her skimming,

she knows she's got a one-way ticket to the ovens. Am I right?"

Michael and Jimmy looked at each other in agreement.

"Sure. So she's got to get us away from looking into those accounts 'cause she knows Higgs has got a snitch and maybe even knows it's McKeethen. She can't afford for us to keep looking at all that. She comes in with something else for us to look into. Something to divert our attention." Eddie stopped and then waved the same forefinger in the air. "Gentlemen, we've got the lady by the short hairs." He smiled. "She's gotta do what we tell her now."

"I don't know about that," Jimmy said. "After that little act we put on for Yozkowitz's bugs, she's gonna think she's home free. I mean, we made it sound like we're closing down. What do we do? Go tell her it's all a big joke? That Yozkowitz is working for us now?"

Michael held his double Wild Turkey over ice just under his nose as if testing its bouquet. "What do you think?" he asked Eddie.

"You're forgetting one thing. The bugs. If she's listening to the tapes or even Higgs telling her what's on them, her asshole is going to be real tight just waiting for us to start talking about her. If she knows about the bugs, she's got to let us know about them. If she doesn't, we can always drop a small dime to get her attention by bringing up the accounts again, maybe even mention a snitch—anything that'll make Higgs start asking more questions."

"Makes sense," Michael agreed.

"But you know," Eddie continued, "there's something else. She's a smart lady. She's got to know that if she's skimmed big bucks from Higgs, she's got to have a way out before too long. And it ain't easy walking away from a man like Higgs. I'll bet she sees us as the perfect way out.

"Remember what she said at the arboretum? If she testified she'd be on the run the rest of her life. Same thing if she walks out and later Higgs figures she scammed him. She's using us, man. It plays. See, she gives us Higgs on a silver platter. Higgs and Roscoe and this governor or whoever all go down on a major dope beef and she walks away with her money. Nobody's left to follow her or really know enough to figure where her little piece of change went. No, my bet's she's not gonna be happy to hear we're backing off." He looked at Michael. "My bet's you don't need to worry about contacting her. She's probably trying to raise you right now."

They were silent for a moment and then Eddie began to grin. He flipped his thumb toward Jimmy as he said to Michael, "Not bad, huh? I taught the kid everything he knows."

Michael laughed. "Another round?"

> <

The call came at two in the morning on Michael's unlisted phone. At three o'clock that afternoon, he once again stood among the dwarfed and sculptured trees of the bonsai exhibit waiting for Elizabeth Henning. She arrived a few minutes after three.

Michael's feet had begun to feel the pinch of cold that pierced his thin black socks and worn loafers. His breath caught on the collar of the topcoat pulled around his face, leaving a faint odor of moistened wool. "I've got to tell you that this is a lousy place to meet," he greeted her, his hands stuffed in his coat pockets and his feet shuffling back and forth on the gravel walk.

"It's better to be cold than to be seen," Henning said in her long beaver coat and boots whose lamb's-wool lining fluffed over their tops.

"I'm talking about being seen," Michael said. "This is a terrible place. I figure you keep picking it because no one's around here in the winter and it's open all around the entrances so you can check if anyone is watching. Right?"

She looked at him curiously and said, "Is there something wrong with that?"

"Yeah, there is. If someone does follow you, you're never going to be able to explain our being here together, even if all they see is us entering or leaving the park at about the same time. Next time we'll pick a place downtown in a crowd, something like that."

"I see your point. I'm new at this. You should have suggested another place."

"Ms. Henning, it was two in the morning. You're lucky I even answered the phone." He shrugged. "Well, this is your meeting."

Henning looked down at her feet as she began to speak. "I'm awfully sorry about what happened to your girlfriend. Is she going to be all right?"

Michael was offended by this woman's offer of concern but gave no hint of it. "The injuries were very serious. *Very* serious," he emphasized. "I don't know yet how she's going to be."

"I'm sorry," Henning said, then hesitated. "You know it wasn't an accident," she said a little more directly than he expected. For an instant he imagined that he saw a hint of sympathy in her eyes. "If I had known anything like that was going to happen, I would have warned you. I understand that you have every reason to suspect my involvement. But still, I called you and came here alone and I'm telling you it was no accident. My point is that we haven't got time for any more cat-and-mouse games. They've proven too dangerous for both of us. I'm going to tell you what I think you need to know, and if you give me the immunity I want, I'll answer any questions you have. All right?"

"Agreed. You first."

"The first thing you need to know is that your office is bugged."

Michael reacted visibly. "Jesus Christ!" he exclaimed, then paused. "How long have you been doing that?"

"Not me. Higgs. I just found out last night. Believe me, if I had known before I would have told you. Do you mind if we sit down?" Michael shook his head and they moved to a small bench a few feet away. "I'll tell you, Mr. Holden, last night I thought I was just a few minutes away from death."

"What happened?"

"Higgs called me to his house around eleven or so. A man named Roscoe Barbosa was there. He's—"

"I know Roscoe. He was there the morning Wheatley shot Godoy. It was his gun that killed the police officer."

Henning looked shocked. "I don't understand. If you know all about this, why—"

"Just go on with what happened last night. We can talk about that later."

"All right. As I said, this Barbosa was there and Higgs said he had something he wanted me to hear. He turned on the tape recorder. When I heard you talking to the detectives I honestly thought I was going to throw up."

"Jesus Christ!" Michael said even more emphatically. "What were we talking about? When were we taped?"

"I don't know when. You were arguing about whether you were giving up on the investigation. I just knew at some point you were going to mention me. I've never been so scared in my life."

Michael stood up and started pacing. "But we did mention you, didn't we? I remember talking about what to do with you—unless that was earlier, before we got back to my office."

Henning sighed audibly. "It had to be, thank God. Believe me, if you had said anything about me on that tape, I wouldn't be here now."

"What was on the tape? What'd you hear?"

Henning repeated with remarkable detail the investigators' conversation staged for Aaron Yozkowitz's recorders. Michael continued to pace as he listened without interruption.

When she finished, he said simply, "Tell me what you know about St. Thomas."

"I'm going to tell you, but first I've got to know something. You seem to know a lot more than I thought, and certainly more than Higgs thinks you know. And I've told you about this narcotics deal. Why are you giving up?"

"If you give me something solid to work on, that's one thing. But I told you right from the beginning that I wasn't going to waste time chasing shadows."

"But even on your own you know about the apartments we've used to rent to tape the sessions to, you know, blackmail people." Henning seemed almost embarrassed to be speaking on that subject.

"Who does the taping and who has the tapes?"

"I don't know anything about that. I just set up the accounts and pay the bills. It's not for money, by the way. It's much more to hold over people that Higgs can use. Government types. Police. I think

Higgs even had a DA for a while. Anyway, you know about this madman Barbosa. I heard you mention some bank accounts you know about. So why are you giving up?"

"You sound like the detectives."

She looked him in the eye. "Well?"

"Like I told them, knowing and proving are two different things. You heard what I said. Aren't I right? All those apartment expenses have long since been covered with phony receipts we could never disprove. And the bank accounts? We know they exist, but that's about all. Did you set those up?"

Henning nodded. "We just set up a separate account for every apartment we used. Higgs insisted we change locations every six months or so and I'd set up a new account for each one."

"Through Wheatley and with cash deposits?"

"Yes. Wheatley and a few others. Did he tell you about them—Adrian, that is?"

Michael hesitated, as if reluctant to share such information, but then sighed with resignation. "He told us that's what was done, but claimed he didn't know who did it. But in his wallet were a few scraps of paper and he had written down a couple of numbers. It took us a long time just to figure out it was an account number and then find the right bank. But as you know, it led nowhere. I hate to admit it, but you've done a good job of camouflage." Henning did not change expression. "Sure, we could subpoena every record you've got, and by the time all the lawyers finished haggling over the subpoenas, you would have dummied up enough and destroyed enough to make it impossible to prove anything."

Henning smiled her agreement and then offered, "I could get you a list of all the accounts used for each apartment."

"And prove what? That Higgs likes to have an apartment available for whatever? Who's going to testify about the reasons? I need a witness and the only way I could link the apartments to the cash deposits in accounts under phony names is with one witness. You."

"I can't."

"I know."

"What about all the other things you know about? The drugs, and I suspect now you have some idea of Higgs's dealings down in the islands. What about all that?"

"Look, to do what you're talking about I need manpower and an active grand jury. I was hoping to turn up enough on my own to convince my front office to reopen. But right now I couldn't convince them of anything without telling them about you. I can't do that. You said yourself you think Higgs has an informant in my office."

"Had. I'm not sure if he still does."

"The point is, unless I know for sure, I can't tell anyone about you—except the detectives, of course."

"You trust them?"

"You're still alive, aren't you?"

She nodded and looked carefully at Michael, as if she saw something she had not expected.

"Do you know who the mole was? Or is?" he asked.

"No. I really don't. I wash Higgs's money and keep an eye on the business's books, but he doesn't tell me things like that."

"What about in the police department?"

"Same thing, except it's a certainty he has people there. He even brags about it. But he's never said who. You've got to understand, even though I know what he's doing, last night was the first time he ever let me listen to a tape or a bug or whatever you call it. I guess he just wanted to put me at ease. Lately I haven't been as calm as I should have been. Things have been a little strained and he thought your investigation was bothering me. If he only knew."

"Tell me what you heard about St. Thomas."

"What's our deal here, Mr. Holden? What happens with me if I cooperate?"

"A complete pass. You walk away."

"No testimony? My name never comes up? I'm never listed as one of your sources or whatever?"

"If we can really work together, there won't be a need for any of that."

"Will you be able to get Higgs without it?"

Michael sat down on the bench next to her and spoke in a low, even voice. "Look, I suspect you've figured out that sooner or later the house of cards is going to cave in. If not now, then sometime. If not me, then some other DA. You're not here out of civic duty. You want out. Am I right? Maybe you've got your own little nest egg built up and it's time to leave. I don't care."

Henning gave no hint of a response.

"The problem is you just don't decide to walk away from an organization like that. When you leave you want to leave clean, without having to look over your shoulder for the rest of your life. Enter the feds. You want immunity from us and some reasonable insurance that Higgs or his people will never come looking for you. I've got no problem with that. It's the same deal that I'd want.

"But the only way to really do that is to catch the man with his hand in the till, so to speak. If you cooperate completely, we can do that. If not, you'll just have to settle back and keep working for Higgs—and wait for the day when someone else decides to come after you. You know it'll happen. It's just a matter of playing the odds. Maybe you'll win, maybe you won't. With me, the deal is simple. But it's now or never. No testimony. No listing your name as an informant. Just cooperate fully, help us catch him in the act, and you walk away. From us and, maybe more importantly, from Higgs."

Henning stood up and started pacing slowly in front of Michael. "Okay," she said finally and began her story.

She confirmed that Ishmael Dubard was the "governor" at Higgs's dinner party the Friday night before Wheatley's death. The meeting involved some but not all of the investors who were financing the business fronts being set up to secure the casino licenses in the Virgin Islands. She could provide a list of all the investors if he wanted. He said that he did. She said that Higgs knew that the investigation was being officially closed almost a week before the announcement from the police department appeared in the papers. When Higgs learned that Michael had gone to the Virgin Islands and was asking questions about Godoy he was very upset. She knew that he had called Dubard about it.

"Somehow, he got the idea that you learned about Godoy through some missing-persons report. What made him think that?" she asked. Michael smiled but said nothing. Higgs was even more upset, she said, when he learned that it was the FBI agent and not Holden who had died in the car. She actually stopped and stared at Michael as if to apologize for her boss. "You can draw your own conclusions."

Michael sat in silence while Henning stood looking at him. She grew impatient and started once more to pace until Michael asked, "And now?"

"You mean after hearing the tape?"

"Yeah. What's he think now?"

"He's pretty confident. Thinks the worst has blown over. He told Barbosa to keep a real low profile. He doesn't want anybody doing anything to draw attention to themselves until after this narcotics deal goes through."

"When is that scheduled?"

"There's no date yet, but soon."

"Okay, tell me how it works. Is it a straight exchange? Dope for money? Cash, wire transfers? What?"

"Wire transfers. What they've done in the past four or five deals is to negotiate a price for an amount well ahead of time. Then they're notified of a potential target date for the delivery a few weeks in advance. Monies are transferred into some foreign accounts. Then a day or two before the delivery they're told where to be."

Michael interrupted her. "You keep saying 'they.' Who exactly are we talking about? Does Dubard work for Higgs, or Higgs for Dubard? I mean, who's doing all this?"

"You may not believe this, but I'm not quite sure. I know it's Dubard or his people who deal directly with the supplier. But Higgs takes care of the money and the distribution. As far as I can tell, it's a partnership."

Michael nodded and said, "Okay, go on."

"Anyway, when the narcotics are delivered . . . What are you smiling at?"

"Sorry," Michael said. "It's just that you make it sound like soybeans when you say 'narcotics.' I'm just used to cops and junkies—you know, 'dope,' 'smack,' 'horse,' whatever."

Henning smiled herself, a little self-consciously. "Well, when the dope is delivered, Higgs will have someone there with a chemist. They'll test it for purity, and if it's satisfactory they'll call back to Higgs. Higgs will then notify the bank where the money is on deposit to transfer it to whatever bank or account the seller has designated. It's all done with prearranged identifier codes. When the seller's people are notified that the transfer is complete, which doesn't take but a few minutes, they turn over the narcotics—or heroin or dope or smack or whatever you want to call it."

"What's your part in all this?"

"I'm told when and how much to start transferring to Stearman's accounts."

"Stearman?"

"Yes, Victor Stearman. He takes care of moving the money to offshore accounts. I take care of washing the money through a series of domestic accounts before they go to Stearman. He takes it from there."

"You know all of Stearman's accounts?"

"No, but I suspect he does what I do, just on a bigger scale. When I'm ready to transfer funds, I call Victor and within a day he'll call back and tell me which bank and which account to wire funds to."

"You have a list of all those?"

She smiled. "Of course. But for the exchange of funds for the narcotics, Victor arranges for all the special instructions to the banks and gets the code numbers. Higgs actually takes care of the calls himself. The past few times he has wanted me to be there just in case there's any mix-up."

"What banks do you use to wash his money?"

"Have you got an hour or so for the list?"

"Let's put it this way—do you know what banks they're going to use for the transfer this time?"

"No, I don't. Look, Higgs doesn't keep any

money in U.S. accounts for very long, except for what he needs to keep the legitimate businesses going and enough to satisfy the IRS that he's not evading taxes." She laughed at this and shook her head. "Sorry, sometimes it just seems so funny. Anyway, I spend three-quarters of my time moving money around from bank to bank in the States until I'm told to transfer whatever amounts he says to Stearman's account. Stearman takes care of moving it offshore. The Bahamas, I suspect, the Caymans, Anguilla. Places like that."

"Is that what you do with your money?"

She looked harshly at him. "Higgs pays me well, but not nearly as well as you might suspect. I can't go off for more than a half day without having to leave a number where I'm going to be. And he'll call just to check. He's paranoid about someone stealing from him. I know my phones in the office and in my house are bugged. He'd never let me go to the Bahamas or the Caymans or someplace like that where I could set up an account."

"Why does he trust Stearman so much?"

"I'm not sure he trusts him any more than he does me. He just figures that by splitting the duties between domestic and foreign accounts there are two people keeping records on each other and it makes it harder for people like you to trace the money."

"Are you moving money to Stearman now?"

"I will be. Last night Higgs told me to start moving funds to get ready."

"How much are we talking about? What's this deal worth?"

Henning took her time before announcing with some pride in her voice, "A little over thirty-eight million."

Michael did not even try to hide his reaction.

"Jesus, I'm impressed. Higgs has that much cash on hand?"

"No. He has about half of it, and it's going to take just about all he has on hand—give or take a million or so." She smiled again. "The rest is coming from Dubard and some other investors. And the buyers, those Higgs has already made deals with."

"He's collecting before he delivers?"

"He's worked out a system. It gives him some front money and a real quick turnover. I don't know anything about how the narcotics are cut, but I know that he isn't reselling to major wholesalers. What he's been able to do through people like Barbosa is to deal fairly large amounts to individuals who are actually selling it day to day. Higgs cuts the heroin he gets two or three to one, I'm not exactly sure. Then he turns around and sells it to these people at proportionate rates. He requires them to buy in fairly large quantities. Five, ten kilograms at a time. And they have to put up some good-faith money. The buyers are happy to get a good price and Higgs can unload what he has very quickly. It will only take him a week or two, but he will have unloaded everything and at least tripled his money, maybe more."

"And if he doesn't deliver?"

"He's got some very unhappy people at his door."

"Do you know how much heroin he's buying for that thirty-eight million?"

"Around two hundred kilograms, I think. I know that it's supposed to be guaranteed to be at least ninety or maybe ninety-five percent pure. I assume that that's good quality, correct? You're smiling again, Mr. Holden. I'm a bookkeeper, not a dope dealer. I don't involve myself in such things. Really, I don't."

Michael held up his hand. "You don't have to

convince me. I really don't care. You understand that you're going to have to keep me informed at every step—the banks you're transferring monies to and from and in what amounts. You're going to have to let me know as soon as you know when something is about to happen. I'm going to want to know what phones you or Higgs will be using." She frowned for a second. "Listen, I don't care about you, but if we can tap the phone that Higgs uses to okay the transfers and receive word that the dope is delivered, we'll have him without anyone ever needing to know about you or hearing your voice."

"I understand," she nodded. "You just need to explain these things to me. How am I going to reach you? I don't know whether your home phones are tapped as well. That's why I never said who I was last night and just told you to meet me at the same place."

"I can take care of that. Don't call for a day or two unless it's an emergency. If you have to reach me, just say that you're my sister Sally, and I'll tell you where to meet me. Then we'll meet one hour before whatever time I say. All right?"

Henning nodded hesitantly. "Do you have a sister named Sally?"

Michael frowned. "What difference does that make?"

"I don't know how complete Higgs's file may be on you. He could have the names of your family."

"You're not serious?"

"Remember, Mr. Holden, in addition to being very careful, this man has an almost childlike fascination with being what he is. It's a big game to him. A dangerous and very profitable game, but it's still a game. He has people followed just for the excitement of knowing things about them. That's how this whole business of the apartments started. Years ago he set someone up for a reason. He needed some stock or something. And when it worked out so well he just kept doing it. Probably fewer than ten percent of the people he has on tapes even know it. They may never know it. He just likes having it. Don't underestimate how dangerous he can be."

"Sarah," Michael said very quietly. "My sister's name is Sarah."

Michael started to add something but Henning interrupted him. "You don't have to say anything. I understand."

"Do we have a deal, Ms. Henning?" Michael asked as he held out his hand.

Her eyes were clear, as if she had resolved whatever questions might have been on her mind, and she said, "Yes, we do, Mr. Holden." She shook his hand lightly, avoiding the bandage. "And I really am sorry about what happened to your friend. I hope she'll be all right."

Michael nodded slowly, his eyes narrowing just a bit. "I hope this turns out all right for all of us. I'm sure it will as long as no one does anything precipitous . . . jumps the gun too soon."

"What do you mean?"

"Just make sure you maintain the status quo until this is over. Don't get greedy. You just never know who's watching what."

"What are you trying to say?"

"I'm not trying—I'm telling you not to get too greedy too soon. You make any unusual moves and the whole thing could fall apart. Understand?"

Henning's eyes grew curious and she drew in a deep breath and started to say something.

But Michael interrupted. "You go on ahead. I'll give you four or five minutes before I leave."

>> <<

Michael slid into the backseat of Jimmy Legget's Lincoln and immediately started to complain.

"Goddamn it, Eddie, this tape feels like it's gonna pull my skin off. Why do you have to put so much tape on?"

"Yeah, yeah, just give me the recorder."

Michael opened his coat, unbuttoned his shirt and pants, and unfastened the elastic cloth belt that held a tape recorder smaller than a pack of cigarettes in the small of his back. He pulled out the thin wire to the microphone and handed the recorder to Detective Nickles. Eddie looked at the recorder and tossed it in Jimmy's lap, shaking his head.

"See, Jimmy, what do I keep sayin'? Lawyers're nothing but fuck-ups."

Jimmy picked up the recorder and was pushing its buttons as Michael asked, "What's wrong? What'd I do?"

Jimmy turned toward the backseat and held up the small gray box. "You forgot to turn it on, man."

"Fuckin' lawyers," Eddie grumbled.

"Shit!" Michael mumbled. "Well, I told you we should've used a transmitter instead of this stupid recorder. Didn't I tell him, Jimmy?" Jimmy just chuckled. "Doesn't matter. It went like clockwork. Let's get a drink, and I'll tell you all about it."

Twenty-three

The first sound was a loud pop that Stan Rubinow thought came from Michael Holden's office next door. He started to get up from his desk when there followed another muffled pop and then the spitting, fizzing sounds and the acrid smell of an electrical fire. The southern wing of the Felony Trial Division suddenly went dark. People poked their heads out of their offices while Rubinow looked in vain for a fire extinguisher and then searched in vain for a fire alarm. Others debated with Becky, Holden's secretary, the wisdom of her using a passkey to open Holden's office. It was shortly after one o'clock in the afternoon, and Michael was in Omaha for the funeral of Special Agent Tony Manion.

A fire extinguisher was finally produced, and Holden's office was opened by an impatient Rubinow, who was scheduled to begin a first-degree murder trial the next day. He did not have the time for this crap. Rubinow yelled down the hall for his witnesses to go back into his office before turning his attention to the smoke seeping from an electrical outlet in the corner of Holden's office. Over Becky's objections, Rubinow picked up a souvenir nightstick from behind Holden's desk and bashed a hole in the thin plasterboard where the first sign of blistering paint had appeared. Smoke billowed out as

Rubinow emptied the fire extinguisher into the hole in the wall and then, without further comment, returned to the witnesses sitting in his office. It was after the fire had been extinguished that the alarm was sounded and all work in the office came to a halt—except in Rubinow's office, where the witnesses were told, fire or no fire, they were not leaving until they had straightened out the inconsistencies between their photographic and lineup identifications of the two men accused of stabbing the decedent.

By the time all but the odor of smoke had been cleared and the power restored, there was a new cause for congregating in small huddles of hushed conversation. Searching for the cause of the electrical fire, the inspectors had found what they suspected, and what several officers had confirmed, was a listening device and transmitter mounted inside the wall next to the electrical outlet behind Holden's desk. The Technical Services personnel from the FBI were called in and a thorough search of the adjacent offices was carried out. When no other bugs were found, Tom Joslin demanded a sweep of the entire office, beginning with his. At nine-fifteen the next morning, Michael arrived at his office and was greeted with a stack of messages urging him to call the front office. He did so and was asked to report upstairs immediately.

There was an air of seriousness about all three men who sat in opposite corners of Joslin's office, each attached to a phone, each apparently carrying on the same conversation.

Tom Joslin sat at his desk. "Harry, this has got to be given top priority."

Hyskal Gaelen nodded into his phone. "Absolutely, Harry. Absolutely."

Both men ignored Michael.

FBI Special Agent Dennis Curran, holding the office's third extension to his ear, smiled and silently offered his hand to Michael. They were old friends. Curran had been the supervisor of the squad assigned to the city hall investigation two years before and was one of the few FBI agents with whom Eddie Nickles actually got along.

"I can take care of that," Curran said.

Joslin and Gaelen chimed in with, "Good, good. That's fine. Good. We'll get back on that."

All three men simultaneously hung up their phones, and Joslin and Gaelen turned on Michael while Dennis Curran sat quietly. There was a minute or two of questions about Katy's health and instructions to give her their best wishes. Another minute was spent shaking heads with somber expressions of regret over the death of Special Agent Tony Manion. Joslin asked Gaelen if he had remembered to tell Vivian to send flowers and a note of sympathy to the agent's family, and Gaelen said that he had. That settled, Joslin asked Michael, "What the hell do you make of this listening device we found in your office? By the way," he added cautiously, "we're safe in talking here. This office has been thoroughly swept and cleared."

"I don't know what to make of it," Michael said, "except that I suspect Higgs or his people. But we'll never be able to prove it. The investigation is closed down anyway, so I don't see that there's much of anything to do."

Joslin looked disappointed. "But this is serious. We can't have people bugging our offices. We have to do something about this."

For fifteen minutes Michael listened to Tom Joslin and Hyskal Gaelen express their concern for the "implications" of the bug that had been found. Unable either to assuage their concern or defuse their zeal for capturing the culprit, Michael offered, "Tom, I understand your concern, and although I'm not optimistic that we'll be able to track down whoever did this, I'll be more than happy to give the Bureau whatever grand jury support they need."

Dennis Curran sat expressionless and deadpanned, "I'm sure with Mike's help we'll be able to conclude this matter quickly."

"That's what I want to hear," Joslin beamed. "There'll be no Watergate on my watch."

There was a round of pleasantries, and as Agent Curran and Michael Holden began their exit, Joslin took Michael aside, indicating to the others that he wanted a moment in private. Joslin put his hand on Michael's shoulder and guided him back to the sofa, where they both sat.

"Mike, we got a call from Olivia, down in personnel. She thought she was supposed to report that one of her people saw you in the personnel files. Apparently, somebody once wrote a policy memo saying that no one but supervisors and personnel people are supposed to be in there."

Michael smiled pleasantly and said, "I didn't realize that my file was such a carefully guarded secret."

"It's not, you can see it anytime you want. It's just, well, you know these admin types. They get real uptight about policy and all that. Anyway, that's not what I wanted to talk to you about, although you're supposed to consider this a slap on the wrist." Joslin smiled broadly at his little joke, and Michael nodded in return. "No, I was concerned that you might be considering leaving us and that's why you wanted to get your files."

"I am, Tom. I really didn't want to say anything

until I had found something, but I might as well tell you that I have decided to start looking around."

Joslin shook his head. "I know this is a difficult time for you, as it would be for anybody, and I just want you to know how much we appreciate the job you're doing. I hope our decision to close that Wheatley thing didn't precipitate your decision."

Michael looked surprised. "Oh, no, not at all. I understand your position completely. I just think that it's time for me to try something a little different. Something outside the government. You understand, I'm sure."

"Absolutely, I do. And let me say if there's anything I can do to help, I want you to just give me a call. In fact, why don't we have lunch one day and kick it around? Check with Viv to see what day might be good."

"Thanks." Michael smiled. "I appreciate it."

>> <<

Dennis Curran was waiting for Michael by the elevators. " 'There'll be no Watergate on my watch'? What the hell is he talking about?"

Michael laughed. "Don't ask me. Maybe he thinks we were bugging ourselves and are trying to cover it up."

Curran shook his head. "Well, now that I've got you alone, what *is* going on? Has this got anything to do with that business down in St. Thomas?"

Several other people were approaching the elevators and Michael said, "C'mon down to my office."

Detectives Nickles and Legget were waiting for Michael when he and Dennis Curran arrived. After some uneasiness surrounding Michael's excusing himself to speak to the two detectives alone for a few minutes, Dennis Curran was invited into the office. Over a cup of coffee and in the presence of the two silent detectives, Michael explained that they were sure that the bug had been set by one of Higgs's people, but they had nothing more than suspicions. Michael also explained that they had reliable information that there was a mole inside the prosecutor's office, but again, they did not know who. Finally Michael held up his hands in a gesture to the two detectives that asked if they were all in agreement.

Jimmy looked to Eddie, who simply growled, "Yeah, Jimmy, it's okay," and Michael turned to Dennis Curran.

"Dennis, I was going to be calling on you anyway, but things are suddenly moving quicker than I had expected. I'm about to ask you for some big favors and a lotta trust. We're going to need DEA or the Bureau, but we can't get into a lot of meetings and have memos and airtels flying around. Basically, the story is that within the next week or two or three—we don't know yet—we've got a shot at Higgs and as much as two hundred keys of heroin. Ninety to ninety-five percent pure. But we're probably not going to know the details until the last minute, which means somebody has to be ready to set up a lot of manpower in a hurry. The main problem, obviously, is that Higgs seems to have snitches everywhere, including, as I said, in this office and probably in the police department. For all I know, even in the Bureau. So whatever is done to get ready has to be done very quietly with little or no backup information. And when I say quiet, I mean all this nonsense about calling in the marines over this bug. We need to let that slide until this dope deal goes down. Can you do it?"

"Jesus! Two hundred keys?" He laughed. "Is this a cash transaction?"

"Wire transfers. I'll have all the warrants ready for wiretaps, but we can't submit them to a judge until the last minute. I just wouldn't trust them sitting in the clerk's office somewhere, even under seal."

"This is all supposed to happen in D.C.?"

"To tell the truth, we can't be sure. But probably it'll be in this area. Maryland or Virginia maybe."

Curran sat for a moment in thought. "I know the people in headquarters who can get you the manpower on a phone call. But you understand that whatever you tell me, I'll have to pass on to them. And they'll want to be briefed by you on the details."

"Fair enough," Michael said, and looked to the two detectives. "Any problem, gentlemen?" Both detectives shook their heads.

Michael proceeded to detail the highlights of their investigation, including its connection with the events in the Virgin Islands. Curran was well aware of Milton Higgs and his organization and thus did not need to be impressed with whom they were dealing. Michael made no secret that he would not identify the snitch or its position with Higgs. Eddie divulged the information imparted by the Peeper with the same understanding. Only the vaguest references were made to the bank accounts. There was no mention of Aaron Yozkowitz.

"So the bottom line is," Curran said, "you've got one snitch who works for Higgs and a second who's an independent dealing with Higgs who both say he's about to bring in a major load of ninety-percent-or-better dope. But your snitches also tell you that you're surrounded by moles, which means you can't sneeze around here without taking a chance of blowing the whole thing and being left empty-handed. Again!" Curran shook his head.

"That's about it," Michael said. "Can you handle it?"

"I'll see what I can do. I wouldn't worry about it. Once they hear Tony Manion's death is connected to this, they'll want to jump on board." Curran stood up and moved slowly toward the door. "You're confident of your snitches?"

"The information's good," Michael assured him, and the agent reached for the door.

"I'll let you know."

> <

Jimmy had reassumed his position of New Year's Eve, slumped in the large leather chair, staring out the window.

"What's wrong, Jimmy?" Michael asked.

Jimmy quickly sat up straight, looking angry. "Man, I don't know what the hell's going on here. I mean, if we trust this guy Curran and we need the Bureau to help us out, then why are we lying to him? Why didn't you tell him about Yozkowitz and McKeethen and all the accounts? I mean, what's going on here? Why the games?"

Michael looked to Eddie Nickles, who sat still and said nothing. "Look," he said slowly, "it's a very simple game. If I had told him about McKeethen and Yozkowitz, he would have to tell his people. I'd expect him to. And the prospect of nailing a dirty DA might be too much for someone at FBI headquarters. They just might start nosing around, maybe looking into those accounts. Yozkowitz would be an even greater temptation. I mean, an ex-Bureau agent gone bad? We're just too close to take the chance that someone might get ambitious or overanxious and blow everything by jumping too soon. The point is, you tell them enough to let them know you're serious and on to something, but not enough that they can work anything alone. They've got to wait for us. Dennis understands that. He's not going to say it, but he knows there are things we're not telling him, just like he'd do if he were in our shoes. Am I right, Eddie?"

Eddie nodded.

Jimmy pulled a number of subpoena forms from his pocket. "I guess you don't want me tracking any more of those accounts right now?"

"Jesus Christ, no!" Michael exclaimed. "We don't go anywhere near those accounts until after this dope deal goes down. Not Higgs's, not Henning's. We're too close, Jimmy. Why take chances? Henning's confident we don't know anything about her money. It's not going anywhere."

Eddie spoke up. "And so what if it does? You've traced it this far. You can trace it some more if you have to. Besides, my man, what's the worst that can happen? The bitch ends up walking away with a million of Higgs's cash. So fuckin' what? She's gonna give us the man up to his ass in ninety percent smack and with that much less money to buy some smart-ass lawyer." Jimmy started to speak, but Eddie cut him off. "Let it go, man. Mike knows what he's doing."

"What's next? What do we do now?" Jimmy asked.

"Nothing," Michael said. "We sit and wait for the word from Henning or Eddie's snitch. I'll take care of the paperwork, but other than that we just keep our mouths shut and do nothing."

Jimmy pressed his palms to the side of his head and groaned, "Man, it's all getting too confusing. Seems like we've got so many games going I'm hav-

ing trouble keeping track of what I can say to who.
I feel like when this is all over I'm gonna wake up
with my wallet gone and a deed to some swampland
in Florida. You know what I'm sayin'?"

Michael smiled. "Trust me, Jimmy. The check's
in the mail."

Twenty-four

On the fifth floor of the huge concrete bunker known as the J. Edgar Hoover Building, the FBI's Assistant Director-in-Charge of the Criminal Investigations Division sat with his feet propped on his desk gazing out into the frozen, oily drizzle that filled the night. Dennis Curran had not bothered trying to snake his way through the intermediate supervisors, the Assistant Special Agent and Special Agent-in-Charge of the Washington Field Office, but had gone directly to headquarters and to Clark Baylen, gambling on Baylen's unique and admirable reputation as one who had made it to the top without forgetting the friends who had helped him get there.

Baylen studied the burning tip of a very short cigar, physically relaxed but mentally bothered by Curran's proposal. "You're asking us to put a lotta faith in this guy Holden," he said quietly, "and he doesn't seem willing to share much detail with you." He turned to the short, balding man seated to Curran's left. "Whaddaya think, Riley?"

Riley Cotman, the Assistant Director-in-Charge of the Technical Services Division, looked equally disturbed. Cotman did not answer the question but turned toward Curran. "Dennis, I understand why you came directly to Clark, but there's no way to

avoid the field offices. The SAC and ASACs have
got to be included."

Curran sat forward and tugged at his pants,
which were crimping the knees of his excessively
long legs. He swept an errant lock of thin gray hair
from his forehead and answered politely, "I understand that. I didn't mean to imply that they
shouldn't be. It's just that I didn't feel like I had
the time to go through channels. This thing could
come down any day. Obviously, I came here because you've got the swak to cut through the
bullsh—— . . . the normal administrative delays."
Baylen smiled and Curran went on. "And let me
make it clear that no one is saying that there're any
security problems with the SAC or ASAC. But you
just never know. It's not like we haven't had problems with secretaries and messengers before. But
forgetting any security problems, we just don't have
the luxury of time. And I don't think this is an
opportunity we can afford to blow."

Baylen gave a sympathetic nod and asked, "Any
possibility Holden's exaggerating the security risks
for effect? I mean, I don't know the guy except by
reputation." Baylen's tone implied some skepticism.

"I trust him on this," Curran answered without
hesitation. "Look, I'm not harboring any delusions
here. If this thing all turns to garbage, I know I'm
gonna take a lotta heat, but I'm ready to take that
chance on his word. Sure, the guy rubs some people
the wrong way. But they're usually the ones who
can't think of doing anything unless they find it in
a manual. Mike may not always follow the manual,
but he's no cowboy. He knows what he's doing. He
deals with the reality of how things get done, and
he's willing to take a few chances. That's all. Like
I said, I trust him and I know him well enough to

tell you that he wouldn't have brought it to me unless he was sure of it."

Riley Cotman's eyebrows raised a bit as he asked, "When you say he's willing to take chances, what are you talking about? This has all the odor of a renegade operation, and I'll be honest, it makes me nervous. You think he could be stretching things a bit? Maybe going over the line because he's after a piece of flesh over what happened to his girl-friend?"

"He may be after a piece of flesh, and I wouldn't blame him. But if anything, that'd make him even more careful about what he's doing. He doesn't want any screw-ups. He's not gonna take the chance that someone'll walk away from this on a bad bust."

"How is his girlfriend?" Baylen asked.

Curran frowned. "Mike hasn't said. Won't talk about it. But I know it's bad. They still won't let anyone but her family in to see her, and Eddie Nickles told me she's gotta go through at least one, maybe two more operations."

Baylen shook his head and quickly changed the subject. "What about this mole in the DA's office. Do you really think Holden doesn't know who it is?"

Curran smiled. "No, I'm sure he knows or at least has a pretty good idea who it is. And he knows that I know that he knows. He just doesn't want us get-ting sidetracked and wants to be sure we keep the information as close as possible. Same as we'd do if we were in his shoes. No one's fooling anybody here."

Riley Cotman sat back, pushing his glasses up on his forehead and rubbing his eyes. "You're confi-dent these snitches exist, right? I mean, you've got no question he's not bullshitting you on this?"

"Yeah, I'm confident. I mean, he's not gonna give us enough that we might be able to identify who they are, but he's not gonna make up phantom sources either. I can press him if you think we need it."

"Press him," Baylen said. Then he asked, "What about these MPD detectives? We don't exactly have a great track record working with those guys. And there'll be a lot of bent noses over our letting them work with us without their people knowing about it. Jesus, the politics!"

"Well, to be honest, I don't know the young guy Legget, but I know Eddie Nickles." Curran could not suppress a grin. "And Eddie makes Holden look like a bean-counting bureaucrat. But no one knows the street and can work snitches better, and if things get down and dirty he's the one man I'd want covering my back. He won't screw up. As far as the politics with MPD, I figure that's their problem. The detectives, I mean. If they're willing to take the heat, so be it."

Curran watched the two men glance back and forth in their uneasy silence and once again emphasized his strongest argument.

"Look, again, the bottom line here is that aside from nailing a major load of dope and a guy like Higgs, these guys killed one of our own. And Holden's offering us a chance to do something about it. I'll say it again. I know the man and I trust him. And I think we owe it to Tony Manion to give it a shot."

Baylen turned back toward the window. "And you'll get Holden in here to talk to us directly?"

"No problem. The detectives, too, if you want."

"Riley?"

The Technical Services chief nodded silently and the decision was sealed. Another half hour was spent dividing up the responsibility for gathering and putting on alert the needed manpower and equipment through direct orders and more than a few favors owed. Dennis Curran was put in charge of the actual operation and was then reminded of what he already knew.

"Dennis, you know that if we pull this off we'll all be heroes. But if we don't, you'll be the goat." Curran nodded. "And I want a stack of memos covering our ass on this. You know what we need."

"I'll take care of it."

Baylen let out a long sigh and relit the stub of his cigar. "Let's just pray we've got enough time to get ready."

Twenty-five

The Miami sun was bright, the temperature in the low seventies, and the breeze off the water just strolled across the brief patches of green that framed the condominiums along Brickell Avenue. It was hard to be anything but pleasant on such a day, and so they were; Victor Trezza, the commercial accounts manager of the Southgate Bank and Trust, and the man who had just introduced himself as Robert DiPrete, managing partner of Resource Investment Partnership of Washington, Philadelphia, and now Miami.

"Could I offer you a cup of coffee?" Trezza asked.

"Yes, thank you," DiPrete answered.

"Cuban or American?"

"Well, Cuban, I think. As our business is expanding south we should begin to adapt our tastes, don't you think?" DiPrete smiled broadly. Trezza smiled in return and stepped away from his desk.

DiPrete had already explained that Resource Investment Partnership was a relatively new venture whose general partners had decided to take advantage of certain commercial real estate investment opportunities overseas. As they were about to get involved in several Caribbean resort ventures, they were looking for a local bank with experience in the Caribbean basin.

Trezza returned with a small pot of thick, black coffee, two small espresso cups, cream, sugar, and a list of a dozen or more correspondent banks throughout Mexico, Central America, and the islands of the Caribbean. There followed a lengthy discussion of the bank's policies on overseas investments, commercial-loan policies, and the procedures by which international wire transfers could be effected over the phone or by letter through the establishment of prearranged codes used to identify both the accounts and the authorized account holders.

Satisfied that Southgate offered the services that Resource would need, DiPrete removed from his briefcase a number of documents and laid them on Trezza's desk. DiPrete laughed a bit and said that he had no idea how strong Cuban coffee was. He reached for the cream.

Trezza smiled. "It does take some getting used to, but you'll soon find it quite addictive."

DiPrete seemed awkward adding the cream to the small espresso cup and several drops fell to the desk. Trezza ignored them and reached for the papers and began to leaf through them. On top was a partnership resolution signed by all five general partners authorizing Robert DiPrete to establish the bank account in the partnership name and to act as the signatory for the account. The resolution and attendant signatures were all attested to and sealed by a notary. Trezza nodded approvingly, putting it aside.

DiPrete put down his coffee. "I've taken the liberty of including there, in addition to the names, the bank references for all the general partners. I'm certain we soon will be talking financing and lines of credit and I thought it wise that you have all that in your files. That way, if we decide to go forward on one of these projects we have in mind, you could start your credit checks after just a phone call."

"Yes, this will be helpful. Do you know yet how much these projects will entail? How much financing you may be looking for?"

"I'd rather not speculate right now, but within a few weeks I would expect that we would have on deposit here something in the neighborhood of a million dollars."

Trezza did not blink. This was Miami, after all. He simply nodded and asked how much of a deposit DiPrete would be making to open the account. DiPrete answered a thousand dollars and produced that amount in cash. Trezza did not react at all.

DiPrete asked Trezza's advice on suitable office space. "I've rented a small office over on South Miami Street but only temporarily. I'd like to find some permanent space quickly so we can list something other than a post office box for our address here."

Trezza suggested that, as it was getting close to noon, they have lunch and discuss not only office space but places to live, since DiPrete had said that he intended to move to Miami from Philadelphia as soon as the business became established. DiPrete thanked him but said that he had to catch a one o'clock flight for Chub Cay. He intended to get in a day or two of bonefishing before returning to Philadelphia.

"Then why don't I go ahead and open the account?" Trezza said. "Establish an account number and, perhaps, if you're prepared to do so now, we can establish the codes to be used for any telephone or mail orders for the transfers of funds. Of course, you'll be the only one who can draw on the account until whichever partner you designate comes in to sign the account cards."

"I understand," DiPrete said.

There followed a short discussion of some of the more desirable areas for office space and Trezza jotted down the name of his brother-in-law, who was a commercial real estate broker.

By noon, the two men had shaken hands and Robert DiPrete was hailing a cab to take him to the airport.

> <

Maureen Lambe was sorry she had ever talked Father Conlan into establishing St. Brigid's bank accounts at her branch of the First National Bank of Washington. He was becoming a real pain in the butt, quite frankly, coming in every Monday afternoon to remind her that she had missed Mass and to ask the same stupid question about how much interest God had earned in the last week. She had a bad cold and Albert, who she had been certain was going to be different from all the other men she had dated, had not called all weekend. And now this. Five minutes before closing, a customer had to walk in and insist on speaking with the manager about his account.

"Mr. Banyon," she said with more than a hint of impatience, "if all you need to do is add some payees to your bill-payer list, you can do that over the phone. Do you have our booklet of instructions on the procedures for all the transactions you can do over the phone?"

"Yes I do," Banyon said. "But in addition, I need to change the mailing address for the business and I need to see your file and the signature cards."

"The signature cards?"

"Yes. Well, to be frank, there has been some discussion within our company about signatory powers and I need to review the account file."

Miss Lambe, as she insisted upon being addressed, said, "Fine," in a tone that clearly indicated that it was not. She reached for a tissue to dab her raw nose. "What is the account number?" The man pulled a sheet of paper from the briefcase on his lap and read off a series of numbers that Miss Lambe punched into the computer terminal on her desk. "Enter your secret code to verify the account," she directed, nodding toward the small, square box of numbered buttons next to the computer. The man punched in a four-digit number code, pressed the Enter button, and the computer screen indicated that the code and the account number matched. "You're Jervis Banyon, I take it?" she asked, looking at the information on the screen.

"Yes."

"And you want to see the file?"

"Yes, the signature cards and the corporate resolutions."

"I'll have to go back to the file room. It'll take a few minutes," she said, as if this might deter him.

"Fine. I've got plenty of time."

Miss Lambe was not about to leave this man alone in her office. She did not trust him, not with the piles of correspondence, memoranda, and lists of things to do stacked in neat piles on her desk. There was also her prized brass paperweight, a souvenir of two weeks in Ireland, where she had met and loved a man who had promised to write her but never did. No, she did not trust him—Jervis Banyon, that is—although she had no reason other than his looks, which this day seemed reason enough. His hair was dark, almost black, combed straight back and divided by a severe part that reminded her of the actors in those old movies she'd watch only if Albert or someone like him insisted. Banyon's eyes were covered by dark-rimmed and tinted glasses that made him look even more suspicious, particularly on such a gray and cold day as this. Even his mustache, although full and neatly trimmed, seemed odd. Perhaps it was too neat, she thought, not a stray whisker, each side perfectly balanced.

Miss Lambe stepped out to the management trainee's desk just outside her office and directed Curtis to retrieve the account files from the storeroom behind the tellers' cages. She then returned to her desk and said simply, "It'll be a few minutes."

"Fine," Banyon said, and left it at that.

To distract herself from the uncomfortable silence, she looked again at the computer screen and noticed for the first time the blinking code for special instructions and casually accessed that code. The screen displayed the message:

Notify Branch Manager 16th St of any inquiries or changes to account.

It struck her suddenly, being the manager of the Sixteenth Street branch, who this Mr. Banyon might be. She voided the inquiry to the computer, and the display screen went blank as she looked up and saw Curtis walking across the lobby with a file folder in his hands.

"Excuse me a moment," she said quickly, then jumped up to intercept the file before it reached her office. With her back to her office, she took the file from Curtis and told him, "Just stand here a moment." She opened the file and saw the federal grand jury subpoena and her own handwritten note with the name and telephone number of the Assistant United States Attorney who had personally asked to be notified of any changes to the account or if anyone else but himself made any inquiries about it. "Take these to your desk," she said, and handed Curtis the grand jury subpoena and her note. She then took the file back to her office and sat down behind her desk.

"Is there some problem?" Banyon asked.

"No, not at all."

"Well," he said, holding out his hand for the file, "may I see it?"

"Yes, of course." She handed him the file and then said, "Will you excuse me? I have some matters to take care of. You can stay here to review the file if you like."

"Thank you," he nodded politely.

She walked out to the trainee's desk, picked up the phone, and dialed the telephone number she had written in large, felt-tipped strokes on a sheet of white note paper.

The phone rang twice before she heard, "United States Attorney's Office. May I help you?"

"Yes, is Mr. Holden in, please? This is Maureen Lambe from First National Bank. It's very important."

"I'm sorry, Mr. Holden isn't in the office today. Is there something I can help you with?"

"Uh . . . yes. Who is this?"

"I'm Rebecca Fowler, Mr. Holden's secretary."

"Ah, yes, Miss Fowler. Is there somewhere I can reach Mr. Holden? He had asked me to notify him right away if anyone made any inquiries or changes to an account he had subpoenaed, and someone is here right now. I need to speak with him right away."

"Well, I don't know. I—"

"It's very important. I'm sure he would want me to call."

"Yes, I understand. It's just that we're not allowed to give out home phone numbers without permission."

"Well, could you call him to get permission or have him call me? It's very important."

"Hold on while I try to reach him," Holden's secretary said, and the phone went silent. Miss Lambe turned slowly toward the smoked-glass partitions that defined her office. She watched Jervis Banyon turning one sheet of paper over to expose the next. Her foot tapped the carpeted floor impatiently and Curtis looked uneasy having his boss stand over him. "Hello?" The secretary's voice came over the phone.

"Yes?"

"I'm sorry, ma'am, but I can't reach Mr. Holden. Do you know which case this is? Perhaps I could reach one of the detectives."

Miss Lambe picked up the subpoena and said, "Well, it says 'In Re Possible Violation of Eighteen U.S. Code, Section three-seven-one.'" She could hear the secretary chuckle.

"Yes, well, that's what they all say," Becky said, referring to the prosecutor's habit of titling virtually all the federal cases under the code citation for conspiracy as a means of avoiding any reference to a particular target or even the specific criminal offenses about which he might be talking to the grand jury. "Is there a name of a detective or FBI agent listed on the subpoena?"

"No. It just has Mr. Holden's name at the bottom. He had subpoenaed the records of the Resource Investment Partnership. Does that help?"

"No, I'm afraid not. All I can do is keep trying to reach him and have him call you as soon as possible."

"All right." Miss Lambe sighed and gave Holden's secretary her direct-dial number, as well as the general number for the bank. She started to leave her home phone number but decided against it since the prosecutor would not allow his to be given out. She hung up and returned to her office.

Jervis Banyon held up a sheet of paper and several account signature cards. "Would it be possible to get copies of these?" he asked. "I'm afraid our copies seem to have been misplaced and that's the cause of our controversy." He smiled, and when Miss Lambe looked reluctant, he said, "I'll be happy to pay for the duplicating costs."

He had no need to be insulting, she thought to herself. "No, of course, I'll have my assistant make copies." She walked out and charged Curtis with the task. "And these?" she asked, returning to her desk and holding up the papers Banyon had given her that listed the new address and the additional payees to be added to those to which payments from the account could be made by telephone.

"No, thank you," Banyon said. "I already have copies."

Miss Lambe looked down the list of payees and said, "This last one here, you've listed the bank and account number, but you don't have a name of the payee. We need that so that the recipient bank can cross-check the account name to make sure there's no mix-up."

Banyon paused and appeared hesitant. "Yes, well, it's McKeethen. Daniel L. McKeethen." And he spelled *McKeethen* for her.

"Oh, it's an individual account?" she asked, surprised. "All the others are corporate accounts."

Banyon looked irritated at her comment and said curtly, "It's a mortgage account, actually. How soon can we start making payments to these . . . uh . . . new payees?"

"By the end of the week you'll be getting a new listing with the code numbers."

"At the new address?"

"Yes, of course."

Curtis returned with the original signature cards and the corporate resolutions and their copies. The original documents were returned to the bank file and Jervis Banyon placed the copies in his briefcase and stood to leave. Miss Lambe primly offered her hand to Banyon, and he shook it lightly, almost effeminately, only their fingers touching.

"Thank you," he said to Miss Lambe with a smile. "You've been very helpful and I'm sorry to have kept you past closing time. I hope your cold is better soon. It sounds as if it's quite painful."

She thanked him for his concern and, as he turned to leave, thought perhaps she had misjudged him.

Twenty-six

Tuesday night. The third week of February. Eddie Nickles's patience was nearly exhausted. "Look, man," he snapped at Jimmy, "how am I s'pose to know what's going through the man's mind? Besides, what difference does it make?"

They were driving north on Fourteenth Street. Jimmy was again asking about Michael Holden, whom they had barely seen in the past month. With the agreement of Tom Joslin and Dan McKeethan, Michael was not being assigned any new cases, and what little time he spent in the office was spent preparing transfer memos in the few remaining cases on his calendar. Although no one in his office really knew, since Michael never talked about his activities outside the office, it was assumed that he was dividing his time between the National Rehabilitation Hospital, to which Katy had been transferred, and plumbing the job market over lunches with old friends. Neither detective had spoken to the prosecutor in almost a week.

"It seems to me that it makes a big difference," Jimmy argued. "I mean, what if Henning is trying to let him know the deal is on and he's not around for the call? I even left a message for him at the hospital two days ago and he's never called."

Eddie turned angrily on his partner. "Goddamn it! You oughta know better'n that. You got no business botherin' Katy unless it's an emergency. Did you tell her it was an emergency?"

Jimmy's voice turned apologetic. "No, I didn't speak to her. It was some other woman. She sounded like she didn't even know who Holden was." Jimmy waited for a response but Eddie just stared straight ahead. "Okay, so maybe it was a bad idea, but it just makes me nervous that we can't get ahold of him."

"Trust me," Eddie said, "all you have to do is leave a message on his machine that it's important. He'll call. And quit worrying about Henning. They have a system worked out if she needs to get in touch with him. The man's just not in the mood to hold hands right now. So relax."

Eddie would not say so but he, too, was nervous. It had nothing to do with Michael Holden. It was the waiting that kept him on edge, and that was all there was to do. Whatever preparation they could do had been done.

There had been a long, late-night meeting at FBI headquarters, and two days later, Dennis Curran passed on the assurances that several squads of FBI and DEA agents from the Baltimore–Washington–Richmond area had been put on a twelve-hour alert and a select group of Technical Services personnel had been briefed and readied. As Curran had predicted, the fact that they were targeting people responsible for the death of an agent was enough. The prospect of interdicting two hundred kilograms of heroin was enticing but not a determining factor. Holden had prepared the affidavits in support of wiretap and search warrants, and the only information missing was the designation of specific locations. That information would have to wait on their informants.

Michael had met twice with Elizabeth Henning—

where, the detectives did not know. She had turned over handwritten lists of banks and account numbers together with brief notes describing how Higgs's money was laundered. The FBI was impressed with the comprehensiveness of Henning's information although still in the dark as to who she was. Neither Michael nor the detectives undermined their credibility or Henning's by revealing her failure to list a single bank at which she had opened her own skim accounts. Indeed, no mention of those accounts was ever made. Henning also turned over the names of the banks and the corresponding account numbers designated by Victor Stearman to which she had been directed to funnel the monies needed for the purchase of the drugs.

There had also been several telephone contacts between Henning and the prosecutor. In the last of the reported conversations, Henning had revealed the location of the latest apartment Higgs had ordered equipped with microphones and video cameras. She also suggested, although emphasizing that she could not be certain, that Higgs might well use the telephone in that apartment to conduct the final negotiations for the purchase of the heroin. That information particularly pleased Eddie since it corroborated what he had been told by Aaron Yozkowitz the same day. Those two informants, at least, were proving reliable.

The Peeper was another story. When it came to addicts, Eddie Nickles was neither surprised nor disappointed by their unreliability. No matter how long Adonis Smith had been in his stable or how many times they had exchanged favors, Smith was still a junkie. Once the immediate threat of an arrest had passed, Smith had tried to fade away, dodging Eddie's phone calls and avoiding meetings. Eddie was not so much concerned about the gathering of new information as he was worried that for any number of reasons—fear, greed, or simply for a bag of dope—Smith might decide to inform on him to Roscoe Barbosa. It would not be difficult for Smith to concoct a story that would let Barbosa know that the police were aware of the impending drug buy while maintaining that he had refused to answer any of the detective's questions. Eddie had to be sure Smith was more afraid of him than he was of Barbosa.

"Let me off at the corner and circle the block," Eddie said.

Earlier, they had parked their police cruiser and switched to Eddie's battered Oldsmobile. Jimmy drove. Eddie had not shaved that morning and wore a ragged topcoat and a knit cap pulled down over his ears. At ten-thirty on a cold February night he would look no different from any of the faceless, raceless addicts who wandered in and out of the oil joints that littered the side streets near Fourteenth. Eddie was familiar with a few of the Peeper's favorites.

Jimmy looked around as he pulled up to the corner. "Are you sure about this?"

Eddie nodded as he opened the door. "Yeah. Just circle the block and if I don't show up in a half hour start looking around Chico's. You know that place?"

"Yeah, I know it. A half hour," Jimmy said, then drove off.

It took almost fifteen minutes to find the Peeper in an alley behind a small apartment house abandoned by everyone but the addicts who huddled each night in its basement. Eddie leaned into the crook between a trash dumpster and a brick wall that moments before had served as someone's ur-

inal. The cold suppressed but could not eliminate
the stench. Eddie did not move since the spot provided a good cover from which he watched Adonis
Smith stand over another addict, waiting for a reaction. Supplies were running low, Eddie thought.

When the heroin gets scarce, dealers will add
sleeping powder or an antihistamine with sedative
side effects to the cut, enhancing the nod a user
will experience. It provides the illusion, however
temporary, that the dope is better than it is. But
the mixing process is often less than an exact sci-
ence. Too much diphenhydramine and the powder
will gum up when cooked, making it difficult or
sometimes impossible to shoot. Too little and the
dope has no kick. Either way, the customers are
dissatisfied. People like Smith were sent out to find
testers, addicts happy for a free high and willing
to shoot the experimental cut and offer an expert
opinion.

Eddie watched the ritual nod of the head and
the soft slap of palms that signaled that the tester
was satisfied. Smith turned and walked confidently
toward the corner of the alley where Eddie waited,
pressed back against the wall. When Smith came
within a few feet, Eddie struck, slipping his hand
under the open collar of Smith's coat, his thick fingers digging deep into the hollow behind the man's
collarbone. Smith's high-pitched howl echoed down
the alley and he dropped to his knees. Eddie
stopped the piercing cries with a fist to the side of
Smith's head, which bounced on the pavement. The
tester looked up and moved away quickly as Smith,
now facedown, tried to roll to his left and pull his
right hand toward his waist. Eddie dropped one
knee into Smith's back and heard the breath leave
him.

"Motherfucker, you reach for a piece and I'll tear your head off."

Eddie reached under Smith's belly and pulled a nine-millimeter automatic from the man's belt. He slid the gun into the pocket of his coat before standing back and letting Smith roll over to see his assailant. Eddie recognized the look in Smith's eyes. It was homicide, not fear, that fired his brain. In an instant Smith recognized the man standing over him and his attitude changed visibly.

"You crazy, man? What the fuck you doin'?" He started to get up and Eddie assisted by hoisting him by the collar of his ski jacket.

"I told you what would happen if you tried to duck me. Your time's up."

Smith held up both palms, submissive and backpedaling. "Man, I been tryin' to raise you. No lie. Things is happenin'. But like you ain't been 'round, you know?"

"Don't give me that horseshit, you sorry motherfucker. You've been duckin' me."

"Man, keep your voice down," Smith begged, his voice squeaking with the urgency for quiet. "People sees me talkin' with you and I'm fuckin' dead in a heartbeat. You're crazy, man."

"You're right, and you're about to find out just how crazy if you don't start talking."

The Peeper was looking all around for signs of anyone in the alley. "Man, we can't be talkin' here. No lie, man. How 'bout we meet t'morra? I got lots to tell, only this is crazy. Not here." Eddie reached slowly for the Peeper's collarbone and the man winced and held his hands up again. "Okay, okay," he pleaded.

Eddie's eyes narrowed and he leaned closer to the Peeper's face. "I haven't got time for your bullshit. See, I don't give a fuck if someone makes you as a snitch 'cause you ain't doing me any good. In fact, I'm thinkin' maybe you've been trying to run a game on me with the Dip. Am I right? Maybe you figure you'd tell Roscoe I been askin' around about this latest load of dope? Maybe be a hero, get a little more of the cut later on?"

Smith almost laughed. "Whatjou been smokin', man?" He shook his head and his whole body bounced and shuffled nervously. "What, you think I'm gonna go up to the Dip and tell 'im like, 'Hey, Roscoe, I just been talkin' with my good friend the police from Homicide about that load you're 'bout to bring in'? Yeah, man, that's what I'm tellin' Roscoe. Shit, you ain't too crazy." Eddie stood his ground while the Peeper leaned even closer and spoke into Eddie's ear. "Man, can we like move 'round the corner where my people ain't gonna walk down on us?"

Eddie nodded and they moved quickly down the alley to a cut between two apartment buildings and into a stairwell where Eddie could barely see Smith's face.

"Talk to me, Peeper, and make it fast, 'cause neither of us got much time."

"Look, like the deal's ready to go down. I don't know where or when, but soon, man. Like maybe just days."

"Tell me something I don't know."

"Man, like alls I know is the Dip wants me and another dude to drive him somewhere in the morning. Like real early. Says we're going right after we finish collectin' tonight. Like six o'clock, or five, maybe."

"Where to?"

"I dunno. Just somewhere not too far. Roscoe

said it'd only be a few hours, but I don't know where."

Eddie reached up and took ahold of the Peeper's shirt collar and twisted it tightly against his throat. "If this deal is going down tomorrow morning and you didn't tell me about it, you're in big fuckin' trouble."

"No, man, it ain't like that. He's just scoutin' the place, y'know, to make sure of what he's doing when it does happen."

"How do you know?"

" 'Cause he told me to get my cousin's fish truck and be ready to use it when he said."

"Fish truck? What are you talkin' about?"

"My cousin, Dutton, like he's got a fish market over on Benning Road. And he's got this 'frigerator truck to pick up his fish in, y'know, like to keep 'em iced down to when he gets them back to the store. So Roscoe says he wants to use the truck to, y'know, pick up the load. So I got Dutton to say okay. And Roscoe's gonna pay him for the truck."

"Did Roscoe say to get the truck tonight?"

"No. We're riding in Roscoe's car. Like I said, he's just scoutin' tonight." Adonis Smith paused and looked at Eddie Nickles and started to shake his head. "I mean, you ain't need to be comin' up here like this, hasslin' me 'n' all. I told you I'd be straight. Just like nothin' been happ'nin' till today. You check, man. See if there ain't a message from me when you get back." Eddie did not answer the man's lie and just stared at him rolling his right shoulder in response to the pain. Smith then spoke slowly. "Yeah, you want this one bad. For real."

Eddie again leaned close. "Mr. Smith, I'll tell you how bad I want this one. You do right and not only will that gun charge go away forever, but I'll owe you one. A freebie, so to speak. And afterward, I'll never come up on you again. You'll be free of me. Forever, man. Understand?"

Smith did not move or speak. He knew there was more.

"But let me tell ya, you fuck up and this deal goes sour, I will personally hunt you down and kick your ass. Then I'll bust you on that gun charge and see to it you get every fuckin' minute of your backup to boot. And once you're in jail it just might slip out that you've been snitching for me for years. Do you understand me?"

Smith stood rigid for a moment and when he spoke it was with hesitation. "Man, y'know, like, shit, I don't control nothin' here. Y'know, like I only do what the man says. I can't make this deal go or not."

"Just make sure you don't do anything to queer it. Understand? You haven't said anything, have you? I mean, I'll let you live if you tell me now, but I gotta know."

"No, I ain't said nothin'. The deal's on far as I know." He stopped and thought for a moment. "Like what happens if I'm there when y'all bust 'em? Like what happens with me?"

Eddie smiled his satisfaction that the deal was still on. The Peeper was scheduled to take part and had not blown his cover. "You walk, man. You'll get busted so no one knows you've talked, but you'll walk on some legal bullshit."

"Cool."

"Do we understand one another?"

"Yeah, I unnerstand."

"So you're gonna let me know tomorrow where you and Roscoe went and how to get there and what Roscoe had to say and when Roscoe calls for the fish truck. That right? You know the number to call?"

"Yeah, same number, right?"

Eddie nodded.

"Can I have my piece back?"

"Don't be stupid. That junkie saw me jump you. You just got robbed. You got any samples?" Smith reached in and pulled two cellophane packets of powder out of his coat pocket. Eddie took the packets and emptied the contents on the ground. Kicking dirt over the white powder, he asked, "Money?"

"Aw, man, come on."

"Give it up. You think the Dip'll believe you got taken for your gun and a coupla packs of dope but they left you your money?" Smith reached inside his shirt and pulled out a roll of twenty-dollar bills. "The Police Boys' Club thanks you." Eddie smiled. "You want me to bust your lip? Make it look bad?" Smith felt the welt on the side of his head and shook it. "Okay," Eddie said. "Give me five minutes before you tell Roscoe to call out the soldiers. Can you handle it?"

"Yeah, man. It's just my rep, y'know? Ain't nobody never took me for my piece."

"That's okay, Bo Peep, I still respect the hell outta ya."

≫ ≪

Wednesday morning. Eddie could not remember when he had felt so good; so good, in fact, that he was conscious of not wanting a drink. Shortly before eleven that morning, the Peeper had called to report that he, Roscoe Barbosa, and a third man called "Cake" had driven to Annapolis, where they had spent an hour driving up and down the streets near a place called Tilghman's Oyster Company.

Shortly after seven A.M. Roscoe had gone into Tilghman's building, while Smith and Cake were told to stay in the car. Fifteen minutes later Roscoe returned to the car and they drove back to Washington. Just before he dropped him off, Roscoe had ordered Smith to have Dutton's truck ready to go by midnight Thursday. That was all he knew.

It was enough.

When Eddie could not reach Michael by phone, he called Dennis Curran and reported what Smith had said. Curran said he would notify everyone necessary and invited Eddie to ride with him and another agent to scout the area around Tilghman's Oyster Company that afternoon. Eddie said thanks but he had some other business to take care of. They agreed to meet that night, when Curran would have gathered the supervisor from DEA and someone from their Technical Services Division who would be responsible for the wiretaps and communications between the various squads of agents during the raid. Eddie promised that he would find Holden and have him at the meeting. He did not say it but Holden was the only element of which Eddie was unsure.

Eddie's other business was Aaron Yozkowitz. As soon as he had finished his conversation with Curran, Eddie called Yozkowitz and found the man sounding nervous and complaining that Eddie's phone had been busy for more than a half hour. Yozkowitz wanted to meet, and Eddie agreed. They now sat in the rear of Yozkowitz's van, parked in a Beltsville shopping center. Eddie's calm surprised even him, and it was that calm, apparently, that was making Yozkowitz even more nervous.

"Don't you see?" Yozkowitz asked urgently. "Don't you understand the problem we have here?"

"No, friend, I really don't. Look, what's the big

deal? Higgs wants you to sweep his house for bugs and wiretaps tomorrow night. You know we'll be listening to everything. You just tell him the place is clean and walk away. What's the problem?"

Yozkowitz rubbed his knees vigorously as he took a deep breath. "Okay, let me explain this. See, I'm the best there is. Or at least one of them," he added with modesty.

Eddie smiled broadly. "I'm glad to hear that. It's nice to know I nailed the best. I was having my doubts after you nearly burned the DA's office down a few weeks back."

"Look"—Yozkowitz scowled defensively—"you're the one who wanted the bug blown in a way it would be discovered so Higgs'd understand we wouldn't be able to get back in for a while. You're the one—"

"Yeah, yeah"—Eddie stopped him—"but I didn't tell ya to fuckin' torch the place."

"Yeah, well, I was in a hurry there. You know, it was just supposed to blow out a few circuits." Yozkowitz's expression signaled that he considered that little glitch inconsequential. "Anyway, what I'm talking about is that Higgs knows I'm the best, too. That's why he pays me as much as he does. And let me tell you I don't come cheap. The point is, if I sweep his house and give him a clean bill of health and then you guys come up with tapes of his phones—"

"Wait a minute, Mr. Wizard," Eddie laughed sarcastically. "Are we talking about your rep here? Is that what you're worried about?"

"The hell with my rep. I'm talking about my ass. If you come up with tapes, which you will . . ." Yozkowitz paused. "And, man, I don't want to know what's going on. I can guess, but I don't want to know. But when you come up with tapes after I said the place was clean, Higgs isn't going to think the Bureau beat me. He's going to think I turned on him. I'm just saying this because it's true. I mean ever since he listened to my tape of the Bureau sweeping the DA's office, he thinks I'm infallible. Which also means this little business of yours could get me killed."

"You're better'n the Bureau?"

Yozkowitz hesitated. "Not when they get serious."

"What's that mean?"

"Look, that old business in the DA's office wasn't much. When the Bureau's called in for some routine check of offices like that, they don't have the time or the interest. It's easy to beat them. But when they're serious, they do good work. Maybe I could pick them up, maybe not. You know, it's not like people think—that all you have to do is put a meter on the line. They can beat that. I can beat it and have. My point is, whether I can beat them or they can beat me doesn't matter. Higgs believes I can. So if he gets popped on a wire my ass is gone."

Eddie sat back and thought for a moment, his continued calm visibly agitating Yozkowitz. "No problem," he finally said. "You go through your little dance at the house and tell him everything's clean. I'll fix up the logs to say that you were under surveillance and when we saw you enter the house we turned off the tap. When you came out the tap went back on. You're covered."

"What's the reason for the surveillance? What are you going to put in the reports?"

"We kept running license numbers until we hit yours. Put you together with an electric company. Thought of the bugs. Asked the Bureau for help and they gave us your background. Thought you were worth following."

Yozkowitz considered the story for a moment and then sighed. "Yeah, it'll play. Okay." He then asked, "And afterward?"

"Whaddaya mean, afterward?"

"I mean, what happens? You've got me in reports linking me to the killing in the apartment and, you know, the . . . uh . . . thing with the old lady."

"*Thing*? What *thing*? You talking about your planning to kill her? That *thing*?"

"Yeah, okay. What about it?"

"Depends on how good you do."

"How long are you planning to keep me on the hook?"

"As long as I need to."

Yozkowitz nodded slowly. "Tomorrow night. Are you going to keep the taps on the whole time? I need to know."

"You bet your ass we will. By the way, why's Higgs using his house? Why not this apartment you've got rigged?"

"I don't know. Maybe he doesn't want to be seen going in and out of a strange place. Maybe he just feels safer at his house. I told you all about the security systems. The place is like a vault. His only worry is wiretaps. That's where I come in."

"Okay. We straight?" Eddie asked, and Yozkowitz nodded. "You've got the number if there're any changes. If I'm not there, put it on the answering machine. Neither one of us can afford to fuck up here."

"Is this serious or just a shot in the dark? I mean, is the shit about to hit the fan?"

Eddie grinned and leaned over to pat Yozkowitz gently on his cheek. "Just be glad you're standing behind the fan this time. How's that eye, by the way?"

$\gg$ $\ll$

Wednesday afternoon. Michael pulled up and stopped in front of a door leading to the elevators on the second level of the garage beneath a shopping mall in Chevy Chase. Elizabeth Henning got in quickly, and he drove toward the ramp leading to the first level.

"Something's wrong," she said.

Michael could see that she was nervous. "What? What's wrong?"

"I don't know exactly. Victor Stearman's coming in tonight."

The tires squealed on the smooth concrete, and he wasn't sure that he had heard correctly. "Did you say that Stearman's coming in tonight?"

"Yes. The only reason I know about it is one of the secretaries called to tell me his flight reservations were confirmed. She just assumed I wanted to know since I'm the one who usually takes care of things like that. Not making the reservations but making sure it's done. I didn't know a thing about it."

Michael had not seen her like this before. Her hands moved quickly and constantly, from her lap to the door handle and back, pulling on her coat, adjusting her purse, fingering a button, brushing back an imaginary hair from her face. "What else?" he asked evenly.

"I don't know what else. That's what has me worried."

"What do you mean? Why are you worried?"

"Don't you see? I think this narcotics deal is about to happen. I told you the last of the money was transferred to Stearman's accounts last week. But I haven't heard a word from Higgs since then. Every other time he's included me. Made sure I knew to be around weeks in advance. But this time, nothing. And Stearman doesn't come here except for emergencies. He's never been around for these deals. He just sets up the money and stays in Miami. Don't you see?"

"Sounds like you're out of the loop."

"It's going to happen and you're not going to be able to get him, are you? I mean, I have no idea where the narcotics are going to be delivered. Nothing. It's all falling apart, isn't it?" Henning had abandoned all pretense of calm. Her fear was obvious.

Michael circled the first level and headed for the down ramp. He did not say anything until they had descended to the third level where he found a spot squeezed between two cars in a far corner. He pulled in and left the engine running.

"We're going to get him as long as you stay calm and don't do anything stupid."

"But how? You don't know when or where."

"Look at me," he said, and she did, her eyes signaling a sudden curiosity. Something was coming that she had not expected. "We know when and where." Her surprise was evident, and her fear more palpable than before.

"But how? I don't understand."

"And it's best that you don't. The simple fact is that we know, and it's important that you not do anything—and I mean *anything*—that could cause a problem."

"How much more do you know?"

"It doesn't matter. What you have to worry about is how much Higgs knows about what you may have been up to. He may be just testing you. But for your own sake, I would advise you to do nothing but wait and follow whatever orders he gives you. Just be aware that he might know more about you than you think."

"You're not talking about my cooperation, are you?"

"Ms. Henning, we made a deal and I intend to keep it. I don't give a damn about whatever's between you and Higgs. I really don't. I'm just telling you this for your own sake. Don't do anything stupid right now. In a few days it'll be all over, and you can do whatever you damn well please. But if you panic, you could be in serious trouble. Understand?"

"You are going to get him, aren't you?"

"As long as you don't panic. All he has to see is you acting just like you are now and he'll want to know why. If he asks questions, answer him. Don't put him off. You're smart enough to have ready explanations for anything he might question you about. Am I right?"

She hesitated without moving her eyes from Michael. "Yes, if it came to that."

"Good. It probably won't. Just give us a few days. It'll be all over by then. In the meantime, I repeat, do not do anything. Am I making myself clear?"

Henning sat silent for a time and nodded.

"Don't take this the wrong way but you understand that if this little operation of ours falls apart all we lose is a case. You stand to lose much more."

She suddenly smiled and shook her head. "You've known all along, haven't you? The . . . uh . . . special accounts, I mean. You've known about them all along, haven't you?"

Michael raised his finger like a teacher emphasizing the obvious. "Be patient for a few days. You panic and it could all go away."

"All right. I understand," she said, and the tension seemed to leave her. Resigned, she told him, "Good luck."

"To both of us," Michael said.

Elizabeth Henning looked around, and, seeing nobody in the area, she stepped out of the car and walked toward the elevator doors. Michael waited and through the rearview mirror watched her disappear.

Twenty-seven

Eastport is the other side of Annapolis, literally a bridge apart from the historic homes and historic families. The peninsula, once home to watermen and tradespeople and the neighborhood bars that served beer in cans, had long since been given over to the commuters from Washington and Baltimore who preferred taverns with live ferns and waiters in deck shoes who would not take an order without first introducing themselves. Even the sturdy wooden oyster boats, once a fixture of the city's docks, were now visitors, and only occasional ones at that, the crowded marinas now filled with polished fiber-glass yachts whose owners shopped at ship's chandlers for solid-brass hardware to hold back their Laura Ashley curtains.

Tilghman's Oyster Company survived as one of the few reminders of the old days, its low, cement-block warehouse squatting on Eastport's southern shore, just west of Horn Point where the Severn River and Back Creek met and emptied into the Chesapeake Bay. The building took up most of the street's east side, extending from the waterfront to a short alley on the other side of which sat a bankrupt and boarded-up beer distributorship occupying the inland corner of the block. On the west side, a high chain-link fence overgrown with vines and bushes separated the street from a yacht yard and marina. Immediately to the north of the yacht yard and directly across the street from the alley, a small, two-story office building sat vacant and advertised for rent. The owner maintained enough heat in the building to prevent the pipes from freezing but not enough to keep Special Agent Thurmond Saunders from complaining.

It was 3:15 A.M. Friday.

"Have some coffee and quit bitching," Dennis Curran said as he once again scanned the area with a pair of night-vision binoculars. The night was clear and full-mooned. A single, tin-hooded lamp lit the end of a long wooden pier reaching out into Back Creek from the south side of Tilghman's. Curran worried that the night was too clear, providing too little cover, unlike the dark inside of this second-floor office where he had set up his command post. The building's owner had agreed to cooperate once he had been assured that the government would reimburse him for any damage. The keys had been turned over and, by eleven-fifteen on Thursday night, Technical Services had installed the necessary telephones and communications equipment.

They had dubbed the office the "Crow's Nest," and from it Curran could watch several blocks of the street that ran straight across the peninsula from Back Creek to Spa Creek on the other side. He could also see four of the five entrances to Tilghman's building. The fifth entrance, a garage-like door opening onto Tilghman's pier, was being covered by six heavily armed and flak-jacketed DEA agents who waited in a fifty-four-foot sport fisherman seized by the government two years before. The boat had been moved down from Baltimore and was now loosely tied to the outside dock of a marina less than a hundred yards east of Tilghman's. The boat was designated "Crow One."

"Crow One. Anything?"

"Not a thing," the special agent reported, scanning the horizon from the enclosed and darkened fly bridge. The waters east and south of Back Creek glowed green in his own night-vision binoculars and the channel markers gave off intermittent and phosphorescent bursts of light.

"Crow Two?"

"Nothing here, Nest. All's quiet." Crow Two was located in one of three small cottages nestled along the shore between Tilghman's and the marina where Crow One was docked. The owner, Nelson Dorn, his wife, and two-year-old son had agreed to be the overnight guests of the FBI at a local Holiday Inn while four FBI agents sat in their kitchen watching the back of Tilghman's building, which had no doors but a half dozen windows.

"Say again, Crow Two?"

"I say all's quiet," came the still-muffled response of the agent who had discovered a batch of Mrs. Dorn's brownies and still had half of one in his mouth. "Just enjoying a little breakfast."

"Shit," Thurmond Saunders said to Curran, "Charlie's probably eaten everything in that house by now."

"Hold on, Nest. This is Crow One. We've got a boat to the south and he's running without lights."

"How far, Crow One?"

"Hard to tell. A half, three-quarters of a mile. Looks like he's headed this way. I'm guessing it's an oyster boat. Cabin like an outhouse and there's rigging in the back."

"No running lights?"

"No lights."

There was a minute of silence.

"Nest, this is Crow Six. You've got a small Chevy van, gray with Maryland plates, just turned on

Chesapeake coming toward you." Crow Six was a car with two FBI agents sitting in the side lot of a church that had been converted to a real estate sales office at the corner of Sixth Street and Chesapeake Avenue. Chesapeake was one of only two streets leading onto the peninsula from the main road. Crow Five was parked among a half dozen cars waiting to be repaired at a service station at the corner of Sixth Street and Severn Avenue, the second access road.

"Occupants?" Curran asked.

"Could only make the passenger. White male."

"Okay, Six. Five, you there?"

"Five, check."

"Three and Four. You awake?" Six blocks away, on the Spa Creek side of the peninsula, two vans with six agents each waited in the parking lot of a waterside restaurant surrounded by shops and yet another yacht yard. There had been some discussion about locating that far away the main assault teams and the vehicles needed to block the street in front of Tilghman's. But both Curran and Eddie Nickles agreed that it was highly probable that the immediate area around Tilghman's would be carefully scouted by the opposition before they committed themselves. It would be virtually impossible to keep the agents in the vans warm and at the same time keep frost on the windows. A van parked on the street in the early hours of a February morning without frosted windows would look suspicious, and so Curran had opted for the cover that the distance gave him.

"Three, check."

"Four, check."

"Nest, this is One. The boat's just turned. He's dead on the first channel marker. Definitely heading up the creek."

"Check, One." A few seconds passed. "This is the Nest. Okay, everybody keep your head down. The van's just turned our way." Curran turned toward Thurmond Saunders, who sat behind the bank of equipment that recorded the wiretaps and radio traffic. Two other agents sat leaning against the wall, their weapons braced beside them. Curran spoke to all three. "No matches or lighters until it's clear," he said, then returned the microphone to his lips. "Crow One, how far out is the boat? In time."

"He's moving slow. My guess, ten, twelve minutes to the dock if that's where he's going."

Curran turned again to Saunders. "Everything set?" he asked, referring to the wiretap and recording equipment.

"All set," Saunders said, slipping on his earphones.

For the next few minutes Dennis Curran gave a running commentary of the arrival of the small van, which slowly approached Tilghman's Oyster Company and stopped in front of a garage door facing the street almost in the middle of the building. A white male got out on the van's passenger's side, unlocked a wooden door about ten feet south of the garage, and disappeared inside. A few seconds later the garage door began to rise and the light from inside filled the street. The van moved inside and the garage door closed like a sleepy eyelid. The street and building were again dark and silent.

Several minutes passed.

Crow One picked up the chatter, detailing the progress of the oyster boat as it approached, then passed channel marker one, then three, then five. "Ahab's home," he announced as the boat slid up to Tilghman's pier and docked. "Four white males.

They're looking around. C'mon, asshole, can't you see me staring you in the face?"

"Easy, Crow One," Curran said softly. "What are they doing?"

"One's walking toward the door. One's on the dock next to the boat. The other two are still aboard."

"Weapons?"

"Not that I can—Whoa! There they are. Two men in the boat are handing them up. Look like full automatics, but it's hard to see. Could be Uzis. There's one, two, and a third. These guys are definitely serious. I'd say our wait was not in vain. Oysters are not that expensive."

Then the garage door facing the dock opened. Crow One reported two men standing just inside the doorway until the new arrivals joined them inside and the door rolled shut.

"Light's out," Crow One announced as the single tin-hooded lamp at the end of the dock was extinguished.

"What's next?" Crow One asked.

"We wait," Curran answered. 3:40 A.M.

3:50 A.M. Eddie Nickles had been unusually upbeat, several times breaking into a silent, secretive grin, since Michael Holden had told him that Victor Stearman most likely would be on the scene with Higgs. Jimmy was not quite so exuberant as they sat in the communications truck listening to the distant chatter in Annapolis and monitoring the silent phones in Milton Higgs's house, just a block away.

"I would have thought he'd want to be here, you know?"

"Jimmy, leave it alone, will ya? I mean, you been

worrying that shit to death, and hasn't it been just like I told ya? Mike got everything done that needed to be done. Right? The warrants, Henning—everything. What more do you want? You think he should strap on a gun and kick in the door, too?"

"No, I'm just surprised, that's all. I just don't understand why he wouldn't want to be here."

"Look, the man's head is somewhere else right now. But he's pulled it off. And there ain't nothin' left but for us to do our job. If we need him he'll be there. I guarantee."

"Incoming," said the FBI agent monitoring the wiretap on Milton Higgs's phone, then switched on the tape recorder.

Eddie switched his earphones from the radio traffic in Annapolis to the monitor and heard the phone ringing. Jimmy signaled that Curran simultaneously was reporting a call being placed from a telephone inside Tilghman's Oyster Company.

"Hello?"

"Is this the funeral home?"

"Yes."

"This is Mr. Streater. I had called before to make arrangements for my uncle's funeral."

"Yes."

"Well, he's just died, and I wonder if you could come to pick up the body."

"Yes, of course, I'll have someone there right away."

"You have the address and all the particulars?"

"Yes, everything is in order."

"Thank you," the voice said, then hung up.

Higgs's phone was then picked up and a number was dialed that was later determined to be a phone booth at an all-night restaurant near the intersection of Routes 301 and 50, midway between Annapolis and Washington. The caller simply directed the listener to pick up the remains of Horace Streater. There was no discussion about whether the listener knew of the late Mr. Streater or where his remains might be found.

The tail car that had followed Dutton's refrigerated truck to that restaurant had been pulled because the paucity of people and cars in the area made the chances of being spotted too great. The tail car had moved to a bridge crossing over Route 50 at Davidsonville, where it now waited. Ten minutes passed before it reported Dutton's truck traveling under the bridge on its way toward Annapolis.

"Okay, everybody, it's time," Curran said. "Check in." Each station acknowledged the call in sequence. Curran looked out and saw that an overhead light above the street-side garage door had been turned on. "Garage light just came on. They're expecting guests."

"Nest, this is Five. A black, four-door Mercedes, D.C. plates, with four passengers just turned left on Severn."

"Three and Four, this is Nest. Stay low. This may be an inspection run. The Mercedes is on your side."

"Three, check."

"Four, check."

A minute or more passed. "Okay," Curran reported, "here they come, straight toward the Nest." Curran watched as the large Mercedes pulled up to the corner and stopped. It then turned right and moved out of sight. "Five and Six, heads up. The Mercedes is headed back toward you. Did you get a number on the plate, Five?"

"Negative."

"If it's our man, he's sniffing the air."

Several more minutes passed in silence. Curran

started to ask if anyone had seen the Mercedes when Crow Five called in. "Nest, this is Five. Your Mercedes just turned off of Severn and is headed back over the Spa Creek bridge."

"Say what?"

"That's right, Nest, over the bridge. You want us to follow?"

"*No!* Stay put!" Curran snapped, concerned about the reason why the Mercedes was leaving the area entirely. "Did he make you, Five?"

"No sign of it. Just drove by."

"How 'bout you, Six? Could he have made you? Anybody?"

"This is Six. We never saw him after the first sighting. If he made us he's got night vision in the back of his head."

"*Shit!*"

Ten minutes passed with no chatter. Then Thurmond Saunders said, "We've got an incoming call." Curran slipped on his earphones and heard the phone being picked up.

"Hello."

"This is the funeral director."

"Yes, we're ready."

"Five minutes."

"Okay."

The phone went dead.

Three minutes later, Curran watched a man step out of Tilghman's doorway and stand next to the still-closed garage door. A few seconds later the radio crackled. "Nest, this is Five. Your Mercedes is back and trailing a friend. Dutton's Fish Market, it says."

"Nest, this is Six. We've got 'em. Turning left on Chesapeake."

It took less than a minute before Curran reported. "This is Crow's Nest. I've got them." He watched as the black Mercedes drove directly toward Tilghman's and the man standing next to the garage shouted something toward the door, which then rolled up slowly. Curran counted five additional men standing in the interior light of the warehouse, four of whom were holding automatic weapons. He alerted his units as the Mercedes drove inside the warehouse, followed by the truck. He could see the shadows of people moving about. One man stepped outside and the garage door again rumbled closed.

"Nest, this is Five. You want us to move up?"

"No, everyone stay put. There's one lookout outside. Repeat, one lookout outside, by the front door. Bird Dog, are you on?"

"I'm here," Eddie Nickles answered from the truck in D.C.

"Dog One?"

"Dog One's here," answered Wes Duncan, the FBI agent in charge of coordinating the six units set to sweep down on Milton Higgs's house.

"Okay, are we set on timing? We move as soon as the product's confirmed?"

"Check."

It had been agreed that once Higgs received the signal that the heroin was of an acceptable purity, all units would move in simultaneously. By then, they predicted, Higgs's voice, and they hoped Stearman's, together with the placement of both interstate and international calls, would have been recorded. That, in addition to the heroin, would provide more than sufficient evidence of the narcotics conspiracy and a plethora of federal criminal offenses that would attach. By moving at that point, it was hoped that Higgs's money would not yet have been moved to the seller's account. The possibility of freezing and recovering that money from its overseas account was an open question.

"Nest, this is Crow One. We've got two subjects on the dock moving toward the boat."

"Just two?"

"Check. They're in the boat now, in the stern. . . . They're working at something in the back." Several minutes passed in silence. "Nest, I think we have our sample. First subject's on the dock. Second subject's handing up a package, maybe the size of a shoe box. Okay, both subjects are moving back inside."

"Check, One. All units get ready." Curran stopped and thought for a moment. There were at least four automatic weapons inside the warehouse. Only a sample of the heroin had been brought inside for testing. The rest remained in the boat. He again picked up the microphone. "Okay, all units listen carefully. We're gonna seal the place. Repeat, seal the place. No one goes through a door unless I say so. Copy?"

"Check," his units responded in turn.

≫ ≪

Back in Washington, both Detectives Nickles and Legget drew in deep breaths waiting for the phones to ring. There were four lines into Tilghman's Oyster Company and three into Milton Higgs's home. All seven lines were tapped.

4:55 A.M. The first call came from Tilghman's Oyster Company to Higgs's home. The caller said simply, "The body's here. Place your call. I'll hold."

As Eddie heard the tones of Higgs's second phone being dialed, he saw the agent point to the numbers being displayed on a small screen indicating the number dialed. The agent smiled at the first six digits, 011–41–1, and quickly flipped through a list he had before him and nodded as if he had known all along. "Zurich," he said, and looked at his watch. "It's just about eleven A.M. there. Banker's hours."

Within a minute there were three active telephone lines in use, the first between the people at Tilghman's and Milton Higgs's. Jimmy was listening to that call. The second line connected a voice Eddie recognized as Victor Stearman's and a bank in Zurich. The third was an open line between a voice Special Agent Thurmond Saunders picked as Irish and a second bank in Zurich.

Dennis Curran made his first move. "Crow One, begin to move into place." The boat's engines were started and an agent let go the only line holding the stern to the dock. Without turning on its lights, the boat eased away from the dock and moved to a position less than twenty feet off Tilghman's pier, directly blocking any escape by the oyster boat but still invisible to the lookout standing by the front door around the corner.

Eddie looked to Wes Duncan. "Whaddaya think? Start moving in slowly?"

Dog One nodded and radioed the order to his men. Jimmy held up two fingers crossed for luck and Eddie nodded.

Dennis Curran radioed, "All right, Crows Three, Four, Five, and Six, start moving. No lights. Repeat, no lights."

The four units checked off.

"Crow Two, move outside. Quietly."

"Two, check."

The four agents eased out of Nelson Dorn's kitchen door and into the backyard. A portable klieg light was uncovered and one of the agents placed his finger on the switch and waited.

Jimmy Legget and both agents monitoring the wiretaps raised their hands at the same time. Each heard the voice from Tilghman's warehouse say to Milton Higgs, "It's verified at ninety-three-point-eight. Do we have a deal?"

Milton Higgs responded, "We have a deal. I'll order the transfer."

"All units, this is the Nest. The deal's done. *Go!*" Dennis Curran repeated the command with a shout. "*All units go!*"

"This is Dog One, all units move in. *Now! Move in now!*"

Eddie reached over and gave Jimmy's coat a gentle tug. His voice was even, but his eyes were wide and fixed on his partner's as he said, "It's our turn now, my friend. Let's go."

Within seconds the night had exploded with the sights and sounds of men and equipment converging on Milton Higgs's compound. Eddie was breathing hard as he ran toward his designated point of entry, his head filled with the music of sirens wailing from a black horizon now lit with blades of red and blue light, his eyes watching a ballet of cars and vans emptying themselves of men in thick jackets emblazoned with huge white letters, "FBI" and "DEA"; men with shotguns and automatic weapons, tear-gas grenades, battering rams, and bullhorns; men who instantly choked off every exit from Milton Higgs's house; men who had no need to shout but who quickly moved into position and waited for instructions—or for someone inside to do something foolish.

He felt an almost embarrassing urge to giggle as Dog One, positioned at the front door, bullhorned the announcement that they were federal agents and ordered the occupants to surrender. Duncan had barely gotten the words out when Eddie growled, "Kick it!" and a battering ram collapsed a side door leading to a hallway between the kitchen and dining room, the entrance both Aaron Yozkowitz and Elizabeth Henning had said was the least secure. Within seconds, Eddie was within the house, following the darkened hallway toward the library, where they assumed Higgs would be. He took gulps of air to chill his nerves as he approached an interior foyer, glad he had left his department-issue revolver behind in favor of his personal nine-millimeter automatic. The house was now infested with federal agents who had finally broken through the front door and were shouting over the wail of Higgs's security alarms, warning the occupants and one another of their converging presence. While they spread through the house, Eddie stopped at the edge of the foyer next to the library door as Wes Duncan and two backup agents quickly approached from the opposite side. Eddie cocked his head toward the closed door and Duncan nodded, tipping the barrel of his pump-action shotgun toward the door. The invisible hand squeezed Eddie's throat and to himself he said, "Fuck it!" and slammed his shoulder to the door and spun into the room.

"*Freeze, muthafuckas!*" he screamed as he dropped into a crouch. Suddenly his knees weakened and began to shake and he felt an almost uncontrollable need to laugh as he saw Milton Higgs and Victor Stearman on their hands and knees in front of the fireplace, shoveling papers into the roaring flames.

It took several minutes before the hard beat in his chest stopped and the cold sweat faded. Once the alarms were turned off, Eddie relaxed and enjoyed the sounds of Milton Higgs's pathetic arrogance, his whining complaints that the handcuffs hurt his wrists, that he should be allowed to make phone calls before they took him away, that he had the right to surrender voluntarily to a judge—every manner of complaint that became even more foolish as each was ignored as if never spoken at all. And it was with particular relish that Eddie listened to Victor Stearman's whispered suggestion that he contact Michael Holden, that perhaps they might have some things to talk about, to which Eddie whispered back, "Do you have an appointment?"

Later, and for years afterward, Eddie would hold on to the vision of things he never saw. Through the lens of Dennis Curran's memories, he watched the lookout in Annapolis peering down the street at some movement in the dark and recognizing too late that movement as a line of speeding vehicles that suddenly burst with loud, piercing wails and bright, flashing lights: the man's panicked shouts through the door to Tilghman's and his confused hesitation, a jerk toward the alley leading to the rear halted by a flash of white light and the shouts to "*Freeze!*" His turn toward the water suddenly flooded with light from a source he could not see. The Irishman, Tim Carmody, awkwardly trying to bail out a rear window, and Alton Kimbough doing the same, both stopped by the shouts of agents and the sharp, metallic sounds of shotguns pumped and automatic weapons snapped to the ready. The muffled sounds of a rush to the garage door leading to the dock and its being cracked only for the instant needed to see the floodlights and hear the bullhorned instructions to surrender. The short, obscene debate from within, to give or to fight. The minutes of silence and the ludicrous effort to bargain. Then silence before the garage door opened and from within, the slow, single line of men stepping out as instructed, one at a time, hands over their heads. Four-hundred-thirty-eight-point-six pounds of ninety-four-percent-pure heroin seized and not a shot fired.

But more than anything else, Eddie would remember that for weeks afterward, he could not stop grinning.

Twenty-eight

It was well after daylight before Elizabeth Henning dared leave her house and drive past the few remaining vehicles of the federal agents still inside Higgs's home conducting the warranted search. She drove to a phone booth and called Michael Holden's house. There was no answer. She left a message. She tried again an hour later. Still no answer. All day and late into the night she tried: his home, the U.S. Attorney's office, even the National Rehabilitation Hospital. She never reached him, and he never called.

Shortly after ten P.M. she drove to a small, third-floor apartment on Corcoran Street that, more than a year before, Adrian Wheatley had rented under one of the many aliases she had arranged for him. As she opened the door she could see the red light of the answering machine blinking across the sparsely furnished room. There were four recorded messages, each from an increasingly agitated and nervous Dan McKeethen, whose last message quavered with the sound of panic. "Elizabeth, for God's sake, what's going on? You've got to call me."

She sat quietly for a moment, thinking, then dialed McKeethen's home. "This is Special Agent Dolcey of the FBI," she told Rachel McKeethen.

"Is Mr. McKeethen in?" As she listened to Rachel call for her husband, Henning wondered whether "Special Agent Dolcey" was this month's code or last. It did not matter.

McKeethen answered the phone, his voice lowered like that of a child feigning maturity. He sounded foolish. Her mind wandered from their cryptic conversation and for a moment settled on Rachel McKeethen, a woman she had seen only in her mind and had heard only through clips of conversation McKeethen would repeat with a sneer, demeaning himself more than he demeaned his wife.

How could this woman not know? Henning wondered, then stopped herself. She had stopped asking herself such questions years ago. Listening to McKeethen's chopped, self-conscious half sentences, she understood that she had extracted all that she could from him, that she had sucked him dry and left him without even the pretense of substance. His voice grated, and she cut him off. "Meet me in a half hour. Same place."

"Well, I'm not sure . . . uh . . . you know, that that's necessary. You know, it's not—"

"*Do it!*" she ordered, then slammed down the receiver. She walked over to a small bedside dresser, certain that McKeethen was still mumbling into the phone, talking to himself to maintain his imagined cover. From the top drawer she removed a .38 caliber, chrome-plated Smith & Wesson Chief's Special. She opened the cylinder and confirmed that all five chambers were loaded before slipping the weapon into her purse. She returned to the phone and again dialed Michael Holden's private number. Still there was no answer. She dialed his answering machine's number but the phone just continued to ring. The answering machine had been turned off. She nodded to herself and left the apartment.

The weather had warmed since the night before and the parking lot of the church just over the District line was shrouded in a wet mist. She shook her head as she slipped into McKeethen's car and told him to turn the windshield wipers off. He did so without question.

"What the hell is going on?" he blurted out. "I can't get a straight answer from anybody. Shit! I can't even get Holden to return my calls. Do you think they know—you know, about me?"

"I'm fine, thank you for asking," she said evenly.

A moment passed in uneasy silence before McKeethen tried to speak. When finally he began, she cut him off instantly. "Why didn't you tell me that you had Holden's office bugged?" she demanded.

"What? I don't understand. What are you talking about?"

"It's a simple question. You had to be the one who arranged access to Holden's office so Higgs could have it bugged. Why didn't you tell me about it?"

"Jesus Christ, you knew what I was doing for Higgs. You were the one who dragged me into this bullshit in the first place. You know Higgs. I couldn't say anything. Besides, what difference does it make?"

Henning watched his nervous hands massage the steering wheel while his eyes scanned the darkness of the parking lot. There was nothing to see and yet his eyes never stopped moving. "You turned on me," she said. "You were supposed to let me know everything. Remember? *Everything!*"

"I didn't have a choice."

Her voice lacked all emotion and her eyes never strayed from his. "What else did Higgs tell you?"

He ignored her question. "Elizabeth, you've got to tell me what's going on. Do you think Higgs will talk? I mean, do you think he'd turn to try and get a deal? I can't believe this all happened without Mike saying a word to me. They've got to know about me, don't you think?"

She said, "You could have gotten me killed."

"What are you talking about?" McKeethen snapped with irritation.

"The bug you arranged for Holden's office. My name could have come up on one of those tapes Higgs got, and I would have been dead."

"What are you talking about?" he repeated, a little more slowly.

"I was working for Holden."

McKeethen's mouth opened, but no sound came. His hands stopped moving, as did his eyes, but his face began to show a perceptible shake.

"That's right," she said, "and when you decided to change the rules without telling me, you could very well have gotten me killed. Do you ever stop to think before doing what you're told?" She shook her head at his silent stare and laughed a bit. "It's almost funny. I trust Holden more than I do you."

"You made a deal with him?" he said between quick breaths and waited for an answer. When she offered none, he asked, "Where do I fit in this deal?"

Henning sighed and opened her purse. "I don't think you fit in at all. Not anymore."

His only movement came from the rise and fall of his labored breathing. "What's that mean?"

"It's simple. You're weak, and that makes you

dangerous. I suppose I should have known that all along."

His jaw tightened and his voice rattled. "Don't threaten me. If they come after me you'll be dragged into it no matter what kind of deal you made. And where'll that leave Christian? What do you think'll happen if—" He stopped suddenly at the sight of the short, chromed barrel that had been lifted from her purse. "My God! What are you doing?" He shrank against the driver's door, his face oddly twisting, his fear pulling him inward. "You can't!" he pleaded. "I'm his father."

Henning's eyes snapped wide and her voice seethed. "How *dare* you claim him now, like this." It took less effort than time for her to reach over and stab the barrel against his temple and to pull the trigger.

>> <<

It was after midnight when she returned to the Corcoran Street apartment. She fixed a drink and sat down at the small desk where she laid out sheets of paper and began dialing the phone.

"Thank you for calling Telecheck. Please enter your account number."

She did.

"Please enter your secret code."

She did.

"Please enter payee code or function code."

She did.

"Available balance is one hundred twelve dollars and forty-eight cents."

She looked up sharply.

"Please enter payee code or function code."

She tried again.

"Available balance is one hundred twelve dollars and forty-eight cents."

She tried again. The same. And then another account.

"Available balance is three hundred sixteen dollars and twenty-one cents."

Another account and another and another until the stunned confusion evaporated and her face flushed and her breathing became labored and she understood. There was nothing left but nickels and dimes.

The Afterbath

From an altitude of thirty-seven thousand feet few people noticed the change in the water's color, the thick, blue-gray thinning to a turquoise mist where the shallow peaks of the Bahama Bank occasionally poked through the ocean's surface to form islands with names like Green Turtle or Little Stirrup, Hard Bargain or Man O' War. Some slept, their heads tilted awkwardly into the crook of the seat and window frame, while others read—paperbacks or magazines or the slick promotional publications that told them where to shop and eat and what to see and do on the island where they would land in a little more than two hours. Most were on holiday. Some held hands, while others did not; but for the most part, they smiled at one another and at the flight attendants when they were handed their drinks.

A few, lawyers mostly, were not on holiday, and if they smiled at all when their drinks came, the smiles were perfunctory, smiles that saved them the effort of saying "thank you." The attendants were used to it, particularly on the outbound flights, when the lawyers never put the briefcases filled with the currency of their trade in the overhead compartments. They held them close, on their laps or by their feet, but never out of sight or out of reach. The attendants would see them again in a day or two, flying north, not tanned but smiling and thanking them for putting the then empty briefcases in the overhead compartments along with the tourists' souvenirs and soiled laundry.

Somewhere south of Grand Turk, where the ocean turned a deep coral blue above the canyons leading to the volcanic islands still farther to the south and east, Jimmy Legget looked to his watch for the second time in as many minutes. Others mimicked his impatience, anxious to escape the confining seats and the conditioned air for the clean heat and clear waters, the postcard sunsets and piña coladas that spiced their conversations.

Jimmy, who carried a briefcase filled only with sheets of penciled notes, was anxious only to make a connecting flight and avoided talk. When at last the jet had landed, he grudgingly excused himself and pushed through the crowds toward the far end of the converted Quonset hut, where a small, inter-island air service lazily boarded passengers.

Jimmy, and a few men he recognized from the previous flight, followed the local islanders toward a weary DC-3 that squatted like a frog at the edge of the tarmac. Once on board, they spread themselves thin so that the stifling heat would not be made worse by closeness. Everyone fiddled with the air vents that offered no relief, while the copilot twisted back from his seat with a litany of safety instructions no one could hear over the rumble of the engines. Jimmy stared straight ahead as the plane lumbered down the runway and lifted quickly into the air, struggling to rise above the red tin roofs dotting the high, green peaks of the big island. Only after the plane had cleared the island and turned south did he relax and let his attention drift outward, when there was nothing to see but ocean.

The winds were steady from the east, and it took

less than the scheduled hour before the plane began to lose altitude and banked right, circling west until it reached a point two miles north of Tarpum Head. There it swung south again and passed the Hog Cays before turning eastward into the trades and diving toward the short runway.

To the east and a mile or more away, Michael Holden lay in a hammock watching the sun flush a deep red as it sank into the thick, humid haze of late afternoon. He saw the plane as a distant speck whose sounds he heard clearly only after it had descended behind a stand of casuarinas whose long, soft fingers waved lazily from the far side of the bay.

It meant nothing to him, and the day passed.

The next morning, lying suspended on the surface, Michael heard only the sounds of his snorkeled breathing and felt nothing but the slight chill of the waters of the Bight, a nearly symmetrical horseshoe bay whose entrance was guarded by a long reef. A school of blue tang mingled in the dappled sunlight around the branches of an elkhorn formation and then, in unison, darted away as he drifted too close. A small trunkfish awkwardly maneuvered its fat, wedge-shaped body along the bottom, blowing jets of water into the sand to stir up a morsel of food. Sergeant majors, fairy basslets and banded butterflies, parrot fish and angels, drums and triggerfish, all moved easily among one another, concerned only for the moment that presented a meal, a mate, or an immediate threat.

Here, Washington seemed as distant in time as it was in miles and almost forgotten. Day after day he would glide above the coral forests, observing with indifferent curiosity the simplicity of life uninfected with ego and the plots and schemes that ego fostered. In the eight months since he had come to this island, Michael's memories of Washington had become more selective and his retrospective observations of the city's curious bent toward petty meanness had become more a cause for amusement than anger. Even his minor tributes to the local customs and immigration official had become less an irritant than a welcomed reaffirmation of the calm he had found.

Suddenly, and from a distance, there came the muffled sound of an outboard motor. Michael looked up and lifted the mask from his face to see Maynard Hemsley's johnboat plowing the water toward him. The Hemsleys were one of the older and more prominent families on the island. Until the last two decades, when it had begun to reap the rewards of its overhauled and very strict bank-secrecy laws, the island's population had been represented by barely more than a score of family names descended directly and in equal parts from eighteenth-century pirates, deserters from the British navy, and slaves escaped from the sugarcane fields of the islands to the north. However primal their education or dulled by generations of inbreeding, some of the families—the Hemsleys being one—had been savvy enough to lease rather than sell their land to the developers and to keep an active hand in the governance of their island. Several banks, two small hotels, and a half dozen shops sat on land owned by Maynard and his wife, Alma, an Albury of the West End Alburys and sister of the minister of tourism. The house on the bluff where Michael's hammock hung also belonged to Maynard, who each month collected a modest rent while waiting for his son, Cyril, to come to his senses and return from the States to settle into the house and into the life for which he was intended. Until then, Maynard was content with a tenant who never complained and on occasion shared an evening of conversation and a bottle of Mount Gay. What had brought Michael Holden to this island was of no concern to Maynard, or for that matter to Maynard's brother, Byron, the chief of police.

Maynard raised his hand in a slow wave as the low, pug-nosed boat approached Michael, who had settled his flippered feet on the top of a brain coral and stood waist-deep in the water.

"Michael, meh son," Maynard called. "Listen up. Byron called from town. He say dere's a mon announcin' himself as a detective askin' questions 'bout you at de Banco Popular."

Michael's smile of greeting hardened into a question that he did not need to voice.

"Fo tru, mon," Maynard responded, "Byron say de mon doan mek no accusation but is askin' plenty a questions 'bout you."

"Did he say who it was?"

"No, he doan tell me a name. Jus dat de mon say he's a Homicide detective from Washington and is now sittin' in de jail for violatin' de bank laws."

There was a hint of a smile as Michael asked, "Are you serious?"

"Dass right."

The outboard's soft sputter and the light slap of water against the flat rise of the bow exaggerated the silence until Michael asked, "How 'bout a lift back to the beach?"

"Hop in," Maynard shrugged. He asked no questions.

Indeed, he said nothing until Michael stepped out of the boat and asked, "Would you mind going into town with me to see what this is all about?"

"No problem," Maynard said, and nothing more.

≫ ≪

"Detective James Legget," Jimmy had announced, "from Washington, D.C. I'm with the Metropolitan Police Homicide Squad." That, and the flashing of his badge as he was escorted out of the Banco Popular, had only assured Jimmy's incarceration. Now, two hours later, he stood alone in a cell behind the post office, staring out a small, barred window to an alley, which, from his perspective, led nowhere. It was cool inside the stone-walled structure and Jimmy had removed neither his blue suit jacket nor his tie, although that at least had been loosened.

"Did you bring a bathing suit?" Michael asked the detective's back, and Jimmy turned, looking startled and unsure of himself. His eyes telegraphed nothing but confusion, and he did not answer. "Well, no matter," Michael said. "I guess you won't have time, anyway."

Jimmy remained silent, staring, as if he were trying to identify the former prosecutor. Michael was thinner, his paunch gone, and darker, except for his hair, which had lost a shade or two to the sun and salt water. His expression was relaxed. He wasn't the same man.

"You're gonna be uncomfortable in that suit," Michael said. "Did you bring any casual clothes?"

Jimmy nodded and released a brief sigh. "At the hotel," he answered. Then, with a hint of nervousness, he asked, "Where are we going?"

"Well, I'm afraid we don't have a great deal of time since you've got to be on the first stage out of town. But I thought I'd at least buy you lunch, have a few drinks, maybe show you where you could pick up some souvenirs for the family and all that."

Jimmy looked skeptical. "Am I still under arrest? I mean, what's happened here?"

"You committed a felony, Jimmy. That's what happened. You should have checked with somebody before you came. There must be someone up there who could have warned you about trying to investigate overseas bank accounts. These islands take their secrecy laws very seriously. That's why the banks are so popular. You just can't walk in and start asking questions about depositors or their accounts, particularly if you're an agent of some other government. If you had said you were just curious they might have only thrown you out on your ear. But pulling the badge and all, you're lucky they're not charging you." Jimmy shook his head but kept a suspicious eye. "And just in case you're wondering, the only favors being done here are getting you out of jail, not putting you in. I'm responsible for you and the deal is you'll be on the first flight out this afternoon. That's at four-thirty. In the meantime, let's get some lunch and have a drink. If you want, we can talk. If not, that's okay, too. You want to change? You're gonna be awful hot in that suit."

"Yeah, I guess so. I'm staying at the Grand."

The Grand was the oldest hotel on the island and one of the few not located on a beach. It was of a different era, a large, four-story wooden structure whose wide veranda encircled all but the back of the hotel. Its former elegance now masked by a patina of age and neglect, it was left to play host to the occasional tourist on a limited budget and to the island's patriarchs, who each evening wandered down from Government Hill to exchange gossip and be cooled by the breezes that swept across Victoria Park from the harbor.

Maynard Hemsley had rejoined Michael on the veranda, where they waited while Jimmy showered and changed in his room.

" 'Tis a curiosity fo tru," Maynard offered as they watched Ainsley Bodden run the palm of his hand over the flame of a Zippo lighter, the only one of Ainsley's teenaged talents, apparently, that could capture and hold the attention of an otherwise indifferent Dory Spurgeon. "Dat boy doan never hatch a ting outta his head."

Michael nodded without expression and after a moment turned to the old man, whose clear blue eyes were fixed on the curious courtship ritual. "Is this going to cause you or Byron any problem?" he asked.

Maynard's weathered brown skin cracked with a slow smile. "No, no problem. Goan be plenty a people dippin' dey mout in ever'ting dey doan know. Dat's sartin'." He chuckled, then turned toward Michael. "Byron say you act to de mon lak you two fishes outta de same watta."

"We worked together. I was a prosecutor back in the States."

Maynard nodded. "I'm tinkin' mebbe you and your friend need som time for tarkin' alone. Maybe I goan take care a som business in town."

Michael started to respond when Jimmy appeared, dressed in a powder blue embroidered *guayabera,* dark blue slacks, and a pair of hard leather loafers. "Whaddaya think, Maynard?" Michael laughed. "This man gonna make it doing undercover work on the island?"

Maynard grinned and shook his head. "Mebbe wid dem udder folk wat is always tarkin' wid dem lawyers."

Jimmy self-consciously touched his hands to his shirt.

"We're a long way from San Juan," Michael said. "Local knowledge, Jimmy. The first rule—you can't make it without local knowledge." He introduced

Jimmy to Maynard Hemsley and said, "This is the man that saved your butt."

Jimmy shook Maynard's hand. "I'm sorry for the trouble. I just didn't understand the law here."

Maynard nodded gently and turned to Michael. "I'm goan see to my business." He studied Jimmy for a moment before offering, "Safe journey, Detective."

"Thanks, I appreciate this," Michael said, and Jimmy reached out his hand again. "Thank you, Mr. Hemsley."

≫ ≪

The two men said little during their walk to The Hawksbill, a small waterfront restaurant at the end of the commercial wharf where each day the fishing boats brought their catch to market. It was not yet noon and they had their pick of tables. They settled at one in the open air, shaded by a thatched roof and cooled by a light wind that kept the ripeness of the fish market from interfering with their appetite. They ordered a round of drinks and the day's special, fresh yellowtail with vegetables and fungi, a concoction of spiced and fried cornmeal. The drinks came and they spent some time in idle chatter and catching up on the news from Washington. Michael was polite but indifferent until he asked about Eddie Nickles.

"Somehow Eddie hasn't been able to find the time to put in his retirement papers." Jimmy smiled. "Says he's got a few cases he wants to finish up first. He doesn't talk much about what he's up to and never puts anything in writing. But no one hassles him and the captain's been giving him a wide berth. It's almost as if Ursay's just waiting for the other shoe to drop. But Eddie's not hanging around Chaney's anymore, and every once in a while someone catches him smiling."

Michael raised his glass in toast. "To Eddie," he offered, and Jimmy returned the gesture.

"To Eddie."

An uneasy silence followed until Michael asked, "You want to talk about why you're here?"

Jimmy looked away, toward the harbor and beyond to a town colored in soft pastels and backed by low, verdant hills. "I would never have pictured you in a place like this," he said idly. "It's beautiful but, I don't know, you just never seemed the type." Michael waited silently, patiently, while Jimmy struggled. "Do you ever miss the seasons? The change?"

"No," Michael said simply.

Jimmy took a deep breath and let it out in an embarrassed puff. "All right, I'm sorry, Mike. I really am. I should have come to you first. I just had to know, that's all."

"Is this visit official?"

"Hell, you know better than that. The department wouldn't authorize a cab ride to Alexandria. No, I'm here on my own."

Michael's voice gave no hint to his thoughts and he spoke lazily. "And what is it that you have to know?"

"Did you do it?"

"Do what? Tell me what you're talking about."

"Henning's money. The missing nine hundred thirty-seven thousand, two hundred and twelve dollars and thirty-eight cents. Did you take it?"

Michael exploded in loud laugh. "Thirty-eight cents?" He laughed again, and Jimmy looked wounded. Michael eased back in his chair, letting his laughter, but not quite all of his smile, subside. "What do you mean, it's missing?"

"It's gone. It can't be traced. And Henning doesn't have it. I'm certain of that. I mean, I figure she ended up with about twenty thousand and change, but that's all."

"Is that what she says?"

"She's missing, too. I thought you knew that."

Michael shook his head and asked, "What about her son?"

"The same. Someone claiming to be his uncle took him out of school at the end of the semester. No one's seen or heard from either of them since."

"What makes you think I took this money?" Michael asked impassively.

Jimmy flashed his irritation as he sat forward and planted his hands on the table. "Do you really want to know?"

"I'm curious, sure. But if you don't want to—" The waiter interrupted with their meals and Jimmy sat back, staring at the mounds of food. "It's like eating at your mother's," Michael explained.

Jimmy took a hesitant bit of the fungi and then of the fish and the tomato and squash and onions and salad and johnny bread and then, with a nod of approval, signaled for another round of drinks. When the drinks came he fortified himself with a long swallow and started a motion as if to speak. But he did not, his expression pinched and uneasy.

"Look, Jimmy," Michael said, "if you don't want to talk about it, that's okay."

Jimmy shook his head quickly. "No, that's why I came here. It's just that I don't know where else to start except to say, yeah, I think you did it." And after a pause: "It was McKeethen's death—actually, the fallout from it—that led me to you."

Michael sat up slowly, his voice suddenly hard. "Are you telling me that you think I had something to do with McKeethen's death?"

"No," Jimmy answered quickly. "Not at all. I think it was the one possibility that never occurred to you. It was the one glitch in an otherwise perfect plan. Everything had been neatly covered. Every aspect wrapped tight except for that."

Michael sat back and said nothing.

"I never had a clue, man. Not a hint," Jimmy said. "And I suppose at the time I didn't really care, except for trying to trace Henning's money. But I was stymied. With all the press the case was getting, the banks wouldn't give up any information without new subpoenas. And since we had promised Henning she wouldn't be named as a source or forced to testify, we couldn't tell anyone about her in order to justify those subpoenas. But like Eddie said, 'Who cares?' Even Dennis Curran had figured out that Henning had to be our main snitch and said to let it go. She had paid her dues and all that. Like I said, I didn't have a clue, and I don't think I ever would have, except for McKeethen." Jimmy leaned forward with his story, "Y'know, when they found his body and it looked like a suicide, everyone sorta backed off. I mean, we had the same agreement with Yozkowitz that he'd never be named as a source or have to testify, so there was no way to let the world know officially that McKeethen was the mole. And even Eddie didn't have the heart to try and trace payoffs to Dan. Y'know, we didn't need it since the case against Higgs was solid, and he felt like we oughta leave McKeethen's family alone.

"But I was bothered by what you had said just before you left. Remember? The day you turned in your resignation and Eddie kept trying to talk you out of it? He kept saying—"

Michael raised a hand to stop him. "I remember."

"Yeah, well, anyway, you said that McKeethen hadn't committed suicide. That he would never have had the balls to do the honorable thing and kill himself. At first I thought you might've been stretching things a bit, hoping at least his family'd collect on his life insurance if it wasn't a suicide. So I decided to check it out. Got the gun retested and checked the results of the swabs of his hands from the autopsy, and it turned out you were right. There was no gunpowder residue on the hands, and the test fires showed there should have been some blowback. The man was murdered. That opened everything up. By this time everyone had figured out that there must have been some connection between McKeethen and Higgs, but no one seemed all that excited about digging up more dirt. The DAs just gave me a bunch of blank subpoenas and told me to let them know if I came up with anything.

"So the first thing I did was to get into McKeethen's bank records, and guess what I found."

Michael shrugged. "Some payoffs, I presume."

"Yeah, but not the kind you'd expect. There were a bunch of odd cash deposits going back over the years. A few thousand here and there, but nothing major. And none of them matched anything out of Henning's accounts. That made sense. The payoffs would probably have come from Higgs's business accounts, anyway, and given the volume of cash out of those, we'd never have been able to match them. But there was one big payment. Almost seventy thousand dollars directly into McKeethen's mortgage account. All but paid off his house. And it came out of one of Henning's accounts just a few days before the raid. That didn't make any sense at all. I mean, there was no relationship between Henning and McKeethen, right? If she had known Dan was the mole, she would have told us if only to protect herself, right?"

Jimmy paused, but Michael offered no response. "So now I go back to Henning's accounts and start tracing them with the new subpoenas. And I find out that her money was gone. That didn't surprise me, but what did surprise me was the way it was moved, and when. First, all but about twenty grand, almost a million three, was moved out of her accounts the day *before* the raid. Right after we got the word that it was going down. But the twenty grand? That was transferred the night *after* the raid, and that made no sense at all. I mean, why would Henning leave twenty grand or so in those accounts just to move it a couple of days later? And then, the way it was moved didn't make sense. The million three is all moved into four new accounts we hadn't seen before, brand-new accounts in different banks in New York and Philly and Houston. Almost immediately, the money was moved again, but this time all of it went to a bank in Miami. We'd never seen that account, either. From there, it got wired to a bank in the Bahamas, and that's the last we see of it. We can't get those records. Okay, that fit. We knew Henning had family in the Bahamas. It was a logical place for her to go. But the twenty thousand? That ended up going to an account we had traced, a bank in Georgia, and from there it was taken out in cash by a woman fitting Henning's description. That's what doesn't make sense. Why would she have done it that way?"

Jimmy waited until Michael asked with a chuckle, "Why do I get the feeling that you're about to answer your own question?"

Jimmy raised his finger to his temple and said with an air of triumph, "Because she didn't take the big stash. She got taken by someone else. She was had."

Michael's expression turned inquisitive. "Really?"

"For sure," Jimmy nodded. "It took me a long time but I found it. The big money? The stash funneled through the four new accounts to Miami and then to the Bahamas? That money first came out of the accounts of Henning's that we had already traced. But I couldn't figure out why we wouldn't have seen those new accounts in New York and Philly and Houston until I went back to the banks and found that for some reason all of Henning's consolidation accounts, the ones where all the money was being funneled, had been changed. Someone—and not Henning—had gone around to each bank and added the new bank accounts to the bill-payer lists on the old accounts, and all the addresses where the statements were to be sent were changed. All new post office boxes. There was no reason for Henning to do that. It didn't hide anything. But it did make sense if someone was about to raid those accounts. If they changed the addresses, any verification notices about new payees or account statements went somewhere else. Henning wouldn't see them, wouldn't catch on until she started wondering why her statements were late. I mean, whoever did it had a real small window of opportunity. A few weeks, at most. And then it hit me." He stopped, nodding slowly, his eyes fixed on Michael, and he repeated, "And then it hit me. All those changes to the accounts, every one of them, were made *after* you got back from the islands, *after* Katy was nearly killed. And suddenly it all made sense."

Michael squinted curiously. "Jimmy, I'm not sure I'm following you. What the hell has all this got to do with McKeethen's death?"

"Not his death, friend—McKeethen himself. See, after what had happened to Katy, I think you wanted to be sure McKeethen couldn't walk away from all this. But the only real evidence we had on him would have had to come from Yozkowitz or maybe Henning. But since our agreements prevented us from ever getting them to testify, there was a good chance Dan would walk unless we could turn someone like Higgs. And you knew that wasn't gonna happen. No one was about to cut a deal with Higgs just to get McKeethen. And even if they did, you knew the chances at trial wouldn't be all that good. Juries never like the idea of the boss turning on the worker, even if the worker is a dirty DA. No, you couldn't take that chance. You had to be sure and so you set him up.

"It was the payoff that went to his mortgage account. That would've been something McKeethen couldn't have explained. He was weak and you knew it. He couldn't have stood the pressure and more than likely would have bellied up. You're the one man who knew him well enough to be able to count on that, and the one man who would've had a strong enough motive. So you rigged Henning's accounts and made a payoff to McKeethen. Then you cleaned out Henning and left her just enough to get out of town." Jimmy sat back and for a moment looked satisfied. But the expression quickly dissolved in embarrassment and he looked away, saying, "I'm sorry, I really am. But, yeah, I think you did it."

He finished his drink with a gulp and signaled the waiter for another round. He avoided Michael's stare and spoke in a low, almost whispered voice.

"God, it was beautiful. You're good, man, I mean real good . . . if it was you. You nail McKeethen, and for whatever reason take down Henning at the same time. And she can't holler about someone taking the money she stole from Higgs. Forget the police. Even in jail, if Higgs ever got word that she had scammed him, she knew he'd sell his soul to see her dead. She had no choice but to take her little piece of change and disappear. And best of all, no one questioned that Henning split with the money. Not even the Bureau. And no one gave a shit. Just like Eddie, everyone figured she had paid her dues and was only stealing from Higgs. Who cares?"

Michael nodded in thought for a moment and then said, "It's an interesting theory. What does everyone think now?"

Jimmy frowned. "I haven't asked, except Eddie. When I laid it all out to him he just grinned. The sonofabitch just grinned and never said a word except to tell me to stop wasting my time on things I'd never prove." He looked away. "Maybe he's right. Maybe I'll never be able to prove it was you flying to New York and Miami and Philly and wherever to set up those accounts or ordering the changes to Henning's accounts." He then cocked his head quizzically. "You know, except for everyone saying that whoever was doing all that was a white male, the descriptions are all over the place. I mean, one day we're talking about a guy with straight black hair. The next time he's got gray, curly hair or he's half bald. Sometimes he's clean-shaven with a scar over his eye or he's got a beard with no scar or a mustache with no beard. I mean, either Henning had a lot of white friends or this guy was damn good at camouflaging himself. Not one of these bankers thought this guy might have been wearing a disguise, and not one of them described him the same way."

"You sound like you're not so sure—"

"Except!" Jimmy blurted out. "Except for one thing."

Michael let go a chuckle and shook his head. "Ah, Jimmy, running those old games, are we? Saving the punch line for last? Looking for a telltale reaction? A nervous twitch?"

Jimmy did not move as he said, "Except for the hands—the one thing that seemed to be common with two or three people. It's not much, nothing anyone'll swear to. Just impressions. You know, the little signs no one pays any attention to until someone like you or me keeps bugging them over and over about any strange traits or habits, and suddenly they remember?"

Michael nodded.

"It was something about the hands. The banker in Miami—Trezza, I think his name was. He remembered that the guy who called himself DiPrete seemed real awkward putting cream in his coffee. Like he only used one hand, and it wasn't the hand he was used to. You know, like a right-handed guy trying to use his left, or vice versa. And Maureen Lambe, the lady from First National up on Sixteenth. Remember her?"

Michael shook his head. "Sorry, can't say that I do."

"Well, she remembers you, or at least your name. Remembers trying like hell to get ahold of you while this guy claiming to be Jervis Banyon was in the bank asking to see the files and ordering changes to the account. But you weren't around. She even remembers leaving the account file on her desk while she was out trying to call you. Anyway, she said there was something strange about the way this guy Banyon shook her hand, almost like he didn't want to, like there might've been something wrong with his hand. People were all over the place on descriptions, but I thought it was interesting that these two both remembered the hands." Jimmy looked down at Michael's right hand, cupped around his glass, and said nothing.

Michael turned his palm up and offered it to him. Two lines of faded, pink scars met to form a lopsided V. "Is that what you're looking for?"

Jimmy eased back in his chair. "I don't know. It just seemed odd, that's all."

"Jesus, Jimmy, that's it? That's what made you think I walked off with . . . how much did you say? Nine hundred thousand or whatever?"

Jimmy winced a bit and shrugged his shoulders. "Man, we could spend hours doing this. There's a hundred little bits and pieces, but I know it's not going anywhere." His face suddenly broke into a grin, unable to resist more of his story. "There's even a signature card with McKeethen's name on it that mysteriously showed up in the bank file Lambe showed me. It's dated before you went to the islands. Makes it kinda hard for me to convince anyone you were setting him up even before you knew he was the mole. But I can't prove it was switched for the original, and Handwriting says that they can't make it one way or the other. If it's a forgery, it's a damn good one. Anyway, I guess I've got nothing except the possibility of finding the money. And if it's here, there's no way I'm gonna find it. Right?"

"If it's here, I guess not."

"Which reminds me of one other thing. A little over three hundred thousand was left in the account in Miami. That's on top of the nine hundred thousand plus that went off to the Bahamas. Why? I can't figure it. There's got to be a reason for leaving that behind, but I just can't figure it out."

"You're asking me?"

"Yes, I'm asking you," Jimmy said angrily, but Michael offered not a word, not a gesture. Jimmy let the silence go on, seeming to swell with frustration until finally, like a man who had held his breath too long, he deflated in a long, slow sigh. "Yeah, well, anyway, so here I am, just where Eddie said I'd be. Wasting time on something I'll never prove. I can't tell you why, but I just had to know."

They sat for a while, Jimmy's head bowed, the fingers of both hands moving back and forth, rotating his glass between them as beads of condensation slid from the sides and puddled on the table.

When he finally looked up, his eyes were pleading. "Man, just tell me you didn't do it. Tell me anything."

Michael took a moment before he answered. "It won't help, my friend. It's like the old riddle about the two Indian tribes—the Black Feet, who always lie, and the White Feet, who always tell the truth. You're asking me which I am. Okay, so what if I tell you that I'm a White Foot, that I didn't do it? Does that help? Does that satisfy you? Does that make me a truthful White Foot, or just a lying Black Foot posing as a truthful White Foot?"

Jimmy stared without answering.

"And what if I ask you the same question? What if I ask you to prove to me that you didn't take the money yourself? You knew as much about those accounts as I did. Prove to me that you didn't steal it. How are you going to do it? Black Foot or White Foot, Jimmy? Which are you?"

"Man, don't run that game on me. You act like none of this matters."

Michael leaned forward. "Matters? To whom? A few minutes ago you said no one gave a damn about the money. No one blinked an eye over Henning walking off with a million or whatever of Higgs's dope money. What was it you said—she'd paid her dues? Do you think she paid her dues?"

"I don't know if she did or not. It doesn't matter. We made a deal with her."

"Curious. Your priorities, I mean. You just shrug it all off. It doesn't matter to you if Henning walks away. It doesn't matter to you if just to protect the money she's stolen she runs a game which ends up getting an FBI agent killed and damn near killing Katy. Hell, it doesn't even sound like you'd be all that upset if Ishmael Dubard—the man who probably ordered the car run off the road—slips the noose. I mean, the last I heard, he had escaped and was somewhere off in Europe. Did they ever find him?"

Jimmy shook his head.

"Is anyone even looking?"

Jimmy offered no response.

"Not even you? I mean, I haven't heard you mention any plans to chase around Europe looking for Dubard. Yet you fly down here on your own dime because you *think* I might have scammed Henning out of the money she stole from Higgs, who made it dealing dope by the boatload and corrupting every cop and government official he could lay his hands on. Curious."

"Man, you know what this is about. It's not the money."

"No, I don't know. Tell me what this is all about."

Jimmy turned his eyes to the harbor and studied the boats bobbing erratically in the freshening wind, straining at their moorings. "You were one of us," he said finally.

"Us? Who's us? I'm not sure I ever *did* figure out who was on whose side. It was getting pretty hard to tell the difference."

"You knew the difference. You know what I'm talking about."

"Hell!" Michael said. "What difference does it make? Us or them. You're either a winner or a loser. Isn't that what the game was all about?"

"Game? Are you telling me it was all just a fucking game? That you didn't give a damn for the difference between the lying Black Feet and the truthful White Feet? Am I supposed to believe that in the end it doesn't really matter? That it's only who's best at playing the game?"

Michael's attention seemed to wander. "I don't know," he said quietly. "I can't tell you what matters 'in the end,' as you put it. At least not what matters to you."

Jimmy reached over and put his hand on Michael's forearm, drawing his attention back. "Man, what happened to you?"

Michael looked up, expressionless. "Not much," he said. "Maybe I just got tired of playing a game where everyone made up his own rules." He drained his glass and looked back toward town. "Shall we take a walk? Find some souvenirs for your family?"

Jimmy nodded slowly. "I just had to know. It was important."

"I'm sorry, Jimmy, I don't have what you're looking for. I only know what's important to me. And that's right here on this island in the middle of nowhere. And in the end, that's all that matters."

> <

Michael returned to the house on the bluff and found her sitting in a wicker rocker on the porch, feet propped on a padded stool. She was fresh from a shower, her short, wet hair only beginning to show bits of its true color in the drying breeze. She took a sip from a tall rum and tonic and looked up from the book in her hand. "The wind's coming around to the west," she offered as Michael looked out across the Bight and nodded. "Is everything all right?"

"Everything's fine."

"Has he gone?"

He looked at his watch. "In a few minutes."

A puff of air lifted the soft cotton skirt from her legs and revealed the still-thick veins of surgical scars.

He leaned over and kissed her. "I think I'll get myself a drink. Need anything?"

"No, I'm fine."

He got his drink and returned to the porch where they sat together, facing a garden of hibiscus and bougainvillea and aloe and several small palms standing sentinel at the edge of the bluff where the vegetation stopped and the ground sloped down to the beach. In the distance he heard the echoed roar of airplane engines and saw the DC-3 rising slowly, diminishing to a speck as it climbed and banked into the sun, moving north and disappearing with its lawyers and their empty briefcases.

ABOUT THE AUTHOR

For fifteen years an Assistant U.S. Attorney in Washington, D.C., WILLIAM D. PEASE is now a partner in the Washington law firm of Eastland, Hardy & Pease, specializing in federal white-collar crime defense litigation. Mr. Pease is working on his second novel.